CHINA'S FOREIGN

China Today Series

Michael Keane, *Creative Industries in China*

Pitman Potter, *China's Legal System*

Xuefei Ren, *Urban China*

Judith Shapiro, *China's Environmental Challenges*

CHINA'S FOREIGN POLICY

Stuart Harris

polity

First published in 2014 by Polity Press

Polity Press
65 Bridge Street
Cambridge CB2 1UR, UK

Polity Press
350 Main Street
Malden, MA 02148, USA

ISBN-13: 978-0-7456-6246-6
ISBN-13: 978-0-7456-6247-3(pb)

A catalogue record for this book is available from the British Library.

Typeset in 11.5 on 15 pt Adobe Jenson Pro
by Toppan Best-set Premedia Limited
Printed and bound in Great Britain by Clays Ltd, St Ives PLC

The publisher has used its best endeavours to ensure that the URLs for external websites referred to in this book are correct and active at the time of going to press. However, the publisher has no responsibility for the websites and can make no guarantee that a site will remain live or that the content is or will remain appropriate.

Every effort has been made to trace all copyright holders, but if any have been inadvertently overlooked the publisher will be pleased to include any necessary credits in any subsequent reprint or edition.

For further information on Polity, visit our website: www.politybooks.com

To Pamela

Contents

Chronology

1839–42	First Opium War
1857–60	Second Opium War
1894–5	First Sino-Japanese War
1900–1	Boxer Uprising
1911	Chinese Republican Revolution and the fall of the Qing dynasty
1912	Republic of China established under Sun Yat-sen
1927	Split between Nationalists (KMT) and Communists (CCP); civil war begins
1931	Japan invades Manchuria
1937–45	Second Sino-Japanese War: Japan invades China
1937	Nanjing massacre
1945–9	Chinese Civil War between the Nationalists (KMT) and Communists (CCP)
1949	Mao Zedong founds People's Republic of China (PRC), KMT retreats to Taiwan
1950–53	Korean War: North Korea invades South Korea
1953–7	First Five-Year Plan: PRC adopts Soviet-style economic planning
1954	First constitution of the PRC; first meeting of the National People's Congress
1955	Afro-Asian (Bandung) Conference
1957	Hundred Flowers Movement: Brief period of political debate followed by repressive Anti-Rightist Movement

1958–60	Great Leap Forward: Chinese Communist Party aims to transform agrarian economy through rapid industrialization and collectivization
1959	China invades Tibet; Dalai Lama flees to India
1959–61	Three Years of Natural Disasters, widespread famine with millions of deaths
1960	Sino-Soviet split
1962	Sino-Indian War
1964	First PRC atomic bomb detonation
1966–76	Great Proletarian Cultural Revolution and its Effects
1971	PRC regains UN seat and Security Council membership
1972	President Richard Nixon visits China; 'Shanghai Communiqué' pledges to normalize US–China relations
1976	The Great Tangshan Earthquake: Largest earthquake of the twentieth century by death toll
1976	Death of Mao Zedong
1976	Ultra-leftist Gang of Four arrested and sentenced
1978–89	Democracy Wall Movement
1978	Introduction of one-child policy restricting married, urban couples to one child
1978	Deng Xiaoping assumes power; launches Four Modernizations and economic reforms
1979	US and China establish formal diplomatic ties
1979	PRC invades Vietnam
1980	China joins International Monetary Fund, World Bank
1980	Chins joins Conference on Disarmament
1984	Sino-British Joint Declaration agreeing return of Hong Kong to China in 1997

1989	Tiananmen Square protests culminate in 4 June military crackdown
1989	Fall of the Berlin Wall
1991	Dissolution of the Soviet Union
1992	Deng Xiaoping's Southern Tour re-energizes economic reforms
1992	China accedes to Nuclear Non-Proliferation Treaty
1993–2002	Jiang Zemin President of PRC
1996	China signs the Comprehensive Nuclear Test Ban Treaty
1996	Missile 'crisis' across the Taiwan Strait
1999	China initiates its 'going out' overseas investment policy
1999	US missile hits Chinese embassy in Belgrade
1999	Falungong demonstrations in Beijing
2001	Collision of US EP3 surveillance plane and Chinese fighter plane
2001	China accedes to membership of World Trade Organization
2002–12	Hu Jintao President of PRC
2003	SARS outbreak
2006	First Forum on China–Africa Cooperation
2007	China overtakes the US as world's biggest emitter of CO_2
2008	Sichuan earthquake
2008	Summer Olympic Games in Beijing
2010	Shanghai World Expo
2010	Google closes its self-censored mainland China search engine service
2013	Xi Jinping President of PRC

Preface

This is a book about China's foreign policy. It is not about China as a whole. The distinction is important. To implement foreign policy, states need to deal bilaterally and multilaterally with a wide range of countries. With some they will be comfortable; with others there may be elements of moral distaste or a lack of trust. States need to be able to co-habit with both, even where warmth and mutual trust are lacking, if they are to pursue effectively their interests and maintain peace. Mao Zedong and Richard Nixon were prepared to deal with each other despite the fact that China had long seen Nixon as a 'warmonger' and Americans did not trust Mao. Commonly, foreign policy involves dealing with people who think differently from us. Yet having been involved in international dealings with other countries over much of my career, I was often surprised by assumptions of colleagues that there is a similarity in how problems are seen and approached; or, at times, that others ought to think like us. Knowing not just where your counterparts differ, but understanding why they differ, facilitates handling of differences and makes cooperation possible.

One of Britain's most distinguished historians, Michael Howard, in his 1988 E.H. Carr memorial lecture, said that '[t]he first duty both of the theorist and of the practitioner of international relations . . . is *empathy*: the capacity to enter into other minds and understand ideologies which have been formed by environment, history and education in a very different mould from our own.'[1] This book is sensitive, however imperfectly, to that requirement, and seeks to place foreign policy decisions in the context of the challenges and vulnerabilities that Chinese leaders believe they face in their international environment. It is less sensitive, for space reasons, in the use of the term 'China' despite acknowledging that in reality there are many Chinas; even more problematic is the use, lacking an alternative, of the ambiguous term, the 'West', often meaning the developed world and, for China, usually now the US and its allies in the developed world.

Looking at China, it is not hard to find examples of the good, but also the bad and the ugly. I have tried to avoid judgements about China and its policies, although clearly there are policies that reflect values that conflict sharply with our own. While there are many reasons for criticizing the Chinese Communist Party's often abused monopoly of political power, its claims to have maintained social and political stability in China, at least since 1989, improved the material wellbeing of its citizens, and increased China's standing and status in the world are not without substance. I have also been inclined to assess China's foreign policy responses not against absolute criteria, but relative to the general practice of other countries. While not done systematically, it is useful to remind ourselves from time to time that, where interests are involved, few, if any, countries are totally trustworthy or compliant with international rules and norms. The following study reflects a view that the international discussion on the rise of China underestimates its governing regime's perceptions, valid or not, of international and domestic challenges and vulnerabilities. It also draws out some of the implications of Western foreign policy that is looking for regime change.

When I first became interested in China, as a government official in the 1960s, most around me were sceptical that it could progress or were fearful of it – a yellow peril or a communist threat. I first visited China in 1973, during a period commonly seen as the latter part of the Cultural Revolution, and have returned on numerous occasions since. I come to this subject not as a Chinese linguist, but as one who has dealt extensively with China in the foreign policy field and studied China on and off for over four decades, both as a government official and an academic. I have negotiated with Chinese officials on a diverse range of subjects, including various bilateral issues (from export contracts to human rights), broad regional, political and economic cooperation issues, and specific issues related to Cambodia, Taiwan and Japan. Over the years, and on innumerable occasions, I have discussed many of the issues in this book with officials and scholars in China. I have also discussed and debated China extensively, at the official and scholarly level, with colleagues in the West, notably in the US and in Australia.

I wish to acknowledge the considerable support and encouragement I received in undertaking this study from the Department of International Relations at the Australian National University, under the headship of Professor Bill Tow. I have also been greatly assisted in writing this book by colleagues who have been good enough to read drafts. Special thanks are due to Kathy Morton who read a full draft and to Pete Van Ness who read almost every chapter. Both made many valuable suggestions. Others who read and commented helpfully on chapters or significant parts are Shiro Armstrong, Greg Austin, Paul Dibb, Frank Frost, Ian Hall, Michael Harris, Ron Huisken, Kirill Nourzhanov, John Ravenhill, David Shambaugh, Brendan Taylor, Ramesh Thakur and You Ji. Their input was substantial and is gratefully acknowledged here. Helpful comments were also received from two anonymous reviewers. I have benefited substantially from discussions on the ChinaPol listserv as I did from the earlier ChinSec listserv. Numerous translation sites, especially China Wire and BBC Monitoring, were very helpful.

Particular thanks are due to two special people. Mary-Louise Hickey, the Publications Editor of the Department of International Relations, was a continuing help throughout the development of the study and brought the manuscript into its final shape. My wife Pamela not only read each chapter and greatly improved the logic and consistency of the argument, but also provided sustained support and understanding of the demands of the book at the expense of time we would otherwise have spent together.

Abbreviations

APEC	Asia-Pacific Economic Cooperation
ARF	ASEAN Regional Forum
ASAT	anti-satellite
ASEAN	Association of Southeast Asian Nations
ASEM	Asia–Europe meeting
BRICS	Brazil, Russia, India, China and South Africa
CAFTA	China–ASEAN Free Trade Agreement
CCP	Chinese Communist Party
CD	Conference on Disarmament
CMC	Central Military Commission
CMI	Chiang Mai Initiative
CMIM	CMI Multilateral
DDA	Doha Development Agenda
DoC	Declaration on the Conduct of Parties in the South China Sea
EAEC	East Asia Economic Caucus
EAS	East Asia Summit
EEZ	exclusive economic zone
EU	European Union
FALSG	Foreign Affairs Leading Small Group
FOCAC	Forum on China–Africa Cooperation
G2	Group of Two
G7/8	Group of Seven/Eight
G20	Group of Twenty
GATT	General Agreement on Tariffs and Trade

GDP	gross domestic product
IAEA	International Atomic Energy Agency
ICCPR	International Convention on Civil and Political Rights
IMF	International Monetary Fund
LSG	leading small group
MFA	Ministry of Foreign Affairs
MOFCOM	Ministry of Commerce
MTCR	Missile Technology Control Regime
NATO	North Atlantic Treaty Organization
NDRC	National Development and Reform Commission
NOCs	national oil companies
NPC	National People's Congress
NPT	Nuclear Non-Proliferation Treaty
NSA	National Security Agency
ODA	official development assistance
ODI	outward direct investment
OECD	Organisation for Economic Co-operation and Development
PBSC	Politburo Standing Committee
PLA	People's Liberation Army
PRC	People's Republic of China
R2P	responsibility to protect
RCEP	Regional Comprehensive Economic Partnership
RMB	renminbi
SARS	severe acute respiratory syndrome
SCO	Shanghai Cooperation Organisation
SOE	state-owned enterprise
TND	New Tang Dynasty television station
TPP	Trans-Pacific Partnership
UN	United Nations
UNSC	United Nations Security Council
WTO	World Trade Organization

1 | Continuity and Change in China's Foreign Policies

China is no longer just an emerging power; it is already a regional great power with major global significance. Although not yet a superpower, it is still rising, even if with some potential fragility. For the more than 60 years since the establishment of the People's Republic of China (PRC) in 1949, its foreign policies have been of particular international interest. Over that period, those policies have reflected both ideology and pragmatism, and have undergone considerable change and development as China has developed and global circumstances have changed. China is now more active in the international arena and there is considerable interest in whether its future foreign policies will follow peaceful lines or will become aggressive and eventually seek to dominate.

Inevitably, much of the international discussion of China's foreign policy has focused on the concerns of the international community. Among security analysts and media commentators, the focus is on China's military modernization/expansion and the future of China–US relations; among policy officials and academics, the spotlight is on whether China will support or challenge the existing international system of rules, norms and institutions. In the early 2000s, there appeared a widely held view that China was demonstrating broad acceptance of the status quo, accommodating to, and integrating with, the existing international system, with no strongly articulated views about changing that system (Johnston 2003; Kang 2007). In recent years, however, there has been heightened media attention on an apparent increase in China's self-confidence and assertiveness, even to the point, it is argued, of arrogance in its international dealings.

Examples of this apparent assertiveness include its responses to US 'spying' on China's military developments when, in 2009, Chinese ships harassed an American surveillance ship, the *Impeccable*, in China's exclusive economic zone; and abrasive responses of some Chinese officials to statements by US officials about the South China Sea. In the economic field, examples include China's strong response to criticisms of China's trade surpluses and to pressures to revalue its currency; China's criticism of US mismanagement of its economy and weakening of the dollar, threatening China's large investment in dollar-denominated securities; and its strongly stated views in Group of Twenty (G20) meetings and particularly at the United Nations (UN) Climate Change Conference in Copenhagen in November 2009.

To what extent do these examples portray China as a confident, assertive power, demonstrating hubris and increased nationalism, unwilling to accept the international system as it is and wanting, as is often argued, to push its own ideas on norms and policies, indeed wanting to remake the global rules? How much substance is there, as well, in the argument that China sees a faltering and weakened US and a failing Western capitalist model, whereas now there is a successful Chinese model that enables it to challenge the American leadership of the global system? These are important questions with major implications for the future.

China's greater self-confidence and pride in its achievements no doubt contribute to what can be termed 'assertiveness'. Whether this is arrogance is unclear. Is it, as Swaine (2011b) has observed, that China is less willing to accept US positions, notably US arms sales to Taiwan, political leaders' meetings with the Dalai Lama, US coastal surveillance of China, and Western lectures on human rights?

Despite the priority given to domestic issues, China's elites generally aspire for China to be accepted as a global great power. The implications of this for China and its foreign policies are part of our more general consideration of which domestic and international factors will influence the formulation of China's future foreign policies. For this purpose, we start by noting on the one hand the substantial changes in China's foreign policies since 1949 and, on the other, various continuities that have framed the context in which these changes have taken place and that have influenced China's policies from 1949 to the present. The purpose is to identify, as far as possible, continuities that may remain significant in China's future foreign policies.

In practice, even today, China's foreign policies are unlikely to be fully consistent over time, for several reasons. These include: the idea that past experiences probably still affect decision makers, although not uniformly; China's integration in the international system continues to make its foreign policy increasingly complex; because of globalization, few domestic interests are now unaffected by international developments, and those people representing those interests have risen to influential positions in the foreign policy decision-making process; and debate within China about foreign policy objectives and the methods to be employed has become more active and widespread, with public opinion playing an important role. In China, as elsewhere, moreover, foreign policy is contingent, often simply responsive to events and based on incomplete information.

Finally, the influence of strong leaders on foreign policies can often be decisive. Although China's top leaders today have less personal power, the judgements that they will make in the future, and the decisions that will emanate from this more diffuse decision-making process, with less powerful leaders, are fundamentally important to the international community. We cannot expect to know what the decisions of China's leaders will be in the coming decades: China's leaders today would themselves not know. The intellectual challenge, however, is that we inevitably project our vision of what China's future decisions will be in discussions of China's foreign policies, and we need to examine why we have a particular vision.

In this book, we look at what were understood to have been China's foreign policy objectives since 1949, and the methods that China has used to pursue those objectives. China's ability to pursue those objectives has been shaped by international and domestic developments. Major international developments that have impacted on foreign policies include the Cold War, already underway in 1949 when the PRC was established, the war on terror that began in the early 2000s, and the global financial crisis of 2007–8. Critical events include China's rapprochement with the US in the 1970s, and three major developments outside China's control – the international response to the 1989 Tiananmen Square tragedy, the fall of the Berlin Wall in the same year, and the dissolution of the Soviet Union and, effectively, the fall of international communism in 1991.

In this introductory chapter, we do two things. First, we look briefly at how history and culture have influenced and may influence China's approach to foreign policy. Second, we look at the main elements of the PRC's foreign policies under Mao Zedong and the first decade of Deng Xiaoping's leadership. We do this both to illustrate the major changes that took place over that 40-year period, and to provide a perspective from which to consider changes and continuities in China's foreign policies in the decades since. Subsequent chapters are concerned with China's current foreign policy starting with developments since the beginning of the 1990s.

THE ROLE OF HISTORY AND CULTURE

This is a book about contemporary foreign policies, not about China's history or culture. We cannot, however, totally ignore the likely historical and cultural influences on the views of China's political leaders, on their perceptions of national interests, and on their foreign policies.

Each state develops its own foreign relations culture, including not only strategic and military considerations, but also how peaceful intercourse with other states should be conducted (Stuart-Fox 2004: 119).

China's foreign policies since 1949 have reflected how China's leaders perceived world developments from within their worldviews that were themselves changing. Those worldviews reflected their beliefs and ideological conceptions of the way the world should work. The priorities given at any time to domestic needs versus its international objectives also influenced foreign policy judgements; this became clear over the past three decades with examples of China's reform pro-gramme and its related economic priorities and imperatives.

We can be confident that in some form, China's foreign policies will be a reflection of China's past and its culture, although there is consid-erable debate about what and how much influence each has had. If we examined US foreign policy without recognizing US self-perceptions of exceptionalism, we would fall short of a reasoned understanding of US foreign policy. Similarly, from discussions with Chinese scholars and officials over the years, it is clear that the Chinese people believe in China's exceptionalism, based on its different history and culture that is perhaps seen as superior to that of the West.

China's history, cultures and related traditions play important roles in its literature, public discourse, academic discussion and, indeed, in domestic political contestation; however, when looking at how these traditions have influenced foreign policy, problems emerge, as its history reflects many such traditions and many changes in cultures (Hunt 1996: 8). In the case of history, for example, these reflect the politically salient 'humiliation' in the second half of the nineteenth and the first half of the twentieth centuries, the patriarchal Middle Kingdom sinocentric worldview of much of the last millennium, the cosmopolitanism of much of the previous millennium, the cautionary lessons of the 'warring states' periods (whether in distant history or during the years of the Republic in the early twentieth century), and the quasi-imperialism that the Qing dynasty pursued to try to protect its core cultural areas from the potentially vulnerable peripheral areas such as Tibet, Xinjiang, Mongolia, Hong Kong and Taiwan. As Spence (2005) has noted, China's contemporary concerns about Tibet, Xinjiang and Taiwan stem from China's conquests in the seventeenth and eighteenth centuries and now constitute complex domestic grievances.

While today China's concerns for security have diminished in some respects – notably with the dissolution of the Soviet Union, the altered if still prickly relationship with the US, and the return of the territories of Hong Kong and Macau – it maintains its historic sensitivity to threats to its territorial integrity in its peripheral areas. Particular security concerns about its periphery and its unity have not diminished. Hong Kong and Macau have been reunited, but Taiwan has not. Periodic international developments, some seen as assisted by the West, particularly the US – such as 'colour revolutions', redolent in China's leaders' eyes, of the US's Cold War 'peaceful evolution' strategy,[1] and the Arab Spring – and some not, such as Islamic militancy and Buddhist activism, are considered potential threats to that periphery, notably to Tibet, Xinjiang and, to a lesser extent, Inner Mongolia.

China sees the world in a different way than countries in the West, for various reasons, but most notably because of the Confucian belief in hierarchy. Moreover, while Western analyses commonly assume that the characteristics of the global system are best understood as anarchic, for China this is not necessarily the case. Van Ness (2002: 132–3) argues that for China, it is hegemonic rather than anarchic. China (and Japan), he argues, 'perceive a hierarchical world environment, structured in terms of a combination of US military-strategic hegemony and a globalized economic interdependence. They devise strategies based on the perceived benefits/costs of participation in that system, as compared with opting out of it'.

For China's elites, global politics is concerned with the rise and fall of hegemonic powers. In this view, great powers rise to where they seek global domination and expansion, followed ultimately by the overextension of that great power and decline into passivity (Harding 1984; Shi 2012). This was reflected in China's recent close examination of the history of the various empires of the past, as China has sought to learn lessons as it rises to great power status. It is why China's leaders see that broader security in global terms, but also why they expect the US ultimately to decline, although with uncertainty about when.

Another dimension, however, comes from the different internal views about China's domestic relationship with the world. In the nineteenth century, views about how China should relate to the world were divided, in very broad terms, between a form of nativism (or nationalism) wanting autonomy, little global involvement and avoidance of contacts with foreigners who would contaminate China's culture and polity; and a cosmopolitanism or modernism that saw global involvement with importing technology, values and institutions as essential for China's development, which would provide means to counter imperialist depredations. Within Mao's PRC, nativism remained a favoured view among the more radical segments of the leadership, and Mao held both views at different times.

This division of views created tensions and sustained debates among the Chinese Communist Party leadership, as it had in China long before Mao, and as it does today.[2] Under Hu Jintao, the domestic problems arising from China's rapid economic growth led to concerns with a 'harmonious society' drawing on Confucian thinking; it also led to divisions between those favouring continued acceptance of globalization, implied by the linked 'harmonious world' construct that Hu put forward in 2005 at the UN General Assembly, and those critical of globalization and its influence on society in China (Zheng and Tok 2007). This division accounts for some of the frequent shifts in China's foreign policies, as the influence of one or other interest groups varies.

A further perspective is a moral one in the sense of China's view of how the international order ought to operate over time. The PRC has sought different changes to the international order, being variously critical of capitalism, imperialism and, more recently and currently, hegemonism; it now seeks a harmonious world. Shih (1993: 201) argues that the changes to China's worldview are frequent, but that China is less interested in changing the world order than in establishing a position of moral superiority. In addition, while Mao saw a world of imperialist powers threatening China, he also viewed China's status as one of leadership, whether as a revolutionary state or in terms of the Third World. This reflected a carryover of Chinese history's concern with status and a conviction that China constitutes an exemplar.

While it is often convenient to talk about whether China is a 'status quo' power or not, that term lacks clarity. Johnston (2003) has argued that China wants the increased status and respect that acceptance as a great power and recognition of its increased material power will provide, including a bigger role in international institutions, but that it is difficult to see it as a status quo power, even if only 'revisionist-lite'. At a broader level, its leadership has long held views as to how the international order ought to change, which is effectively a moral judgement. This is not surprising; the US is not a status quo power either, given its interests in the spread of democracy, human rights and market capitalism. As Van Ness has stated, the two states are the civilizing states (quoted in Shih 1993: 126).

As observed earlier, China aspires to be accepted as a global great power and to receive the status and respect that accompanies such recognition. On the other hand, to be acknowledged by others as having great power status is generally understood to mean that one should accept a responsibility to contribute to the preservation of the international order (Bull 1977: 199–222). A Maoist view would be that China had no responsibility, in the sense of obligation, to an international system that was run by two imperialist powers that had in the past humiliated China and continued to exclude it. Since gaining its permanent UN Security Council seat with the explicit special responsibilities of that position, and following Deng Xiaoping's economic reform and opening up programme that began in 1978, however, China has increasingly participated in the global system and benefited substantially from that participation. Moreover, since the 1990s, with its growing concern about its national image, China has increasingly argued that it acts responsibly in its international activities. Consequently, another aim of this study is to consider what constitutes 'international responsibility', and to what extent China is responsible in its foreign policies. This is not a simple matter as it is not always clear what is meant by 'responsibility', how it can be addressed and assessed, and what it implies for China (Chan 2001).

A related interest here is the extent to which history is relevant to China's future decisions on foreign policies and, if so, which particular history? Considerable attention is commonly given, both in discussions with Chinese officials and scholars and in Western analyses, to the influence of 'victimhood' which arose from the century of humiliation; it is also important in official Chinese rhetoric. Although this notion of victimhood is perhaps declining in importance among elites, it remains one amongst a number of influential factors. China's related sense of insecurity and vulnerability has led to a historically conditioned emphasis on sovereignty and the development of comprehensive strength which are now key elements of China's foreign policy.

Besides the 'victimhood' period, there are various experiences that one could draw upon to illustrate the present. There are many cultural traditions in China that provide other precedents for 'after-the-event' explanations of almost any conceivable line of foreign policy. Notably, there is a different imperial history which could ultimately become more important in shaping Chinese views – whether thought of in terms of the Middle Kingdom or, in a regional context, as the hierarchical tributary system. More recent elements of history have also imprinted memories. For example, not only was China subject to sustained hostility from both superpowers in the 1950s and 1960s, but both the US and the Soviet Union implicitly and explicitly threatened China with nuclear weapons in the same period.

A further continuity, which is a legacy of the 'victimhood' period of the nineteenth and early twentieth centuries, was the 'traitor' syndrome which stemmed from the need to blame someone for China's weakness in the nineteenth century. Whilst many Chinese officials negotiated from a weak position versus the foreigners' strengths, many others collaborated with the foreigners for practical or self-serving reasons, as happened under Japanese occupation. It remains a sensitive process to avoid blame for betraying national interests in dealing with international developments, notably over Taiwan. Lampton (2001: 15) reports a Chinese academic's comment to the effect that a hard approach to a problem, even if it fails, is understood, but a leader who has a soft approach that fails is seen as guilty in the eyes of future generations.

Culture is a problematic concept for foreign policy analysts. It generally refers to the norms and values of a society and the rules and standards, as set by law or custom, to reflect these norms and values. Culture matters and contributes, perhaps substantially, to differences in understandings and approaches among different countries. The question, however, of how it matters and how one can get a grip on something that is a mix of ideas is difficult to answer (Bobrow et al. 1979: 23). Under normal conditions, the issue of culture is not seen as relevant, because Westernization and modernization have been so successful in penetrating other parts of the world, that Westernization is assumed to equate to 'civilization'. The distinguished historian Wang Gungwu noted that in international relations today, norms of behaviour and discourse have been established by the West. These are assumed to be accepted by people in all responsible countries and this is often taken for granted. When this happens, it is ignored that these norms have come from a distinct culture, and actually represent a large expansive political culture that has developed since the post-Enlightenment world of European nation states. Moreover, when we talk about international order, 'what China sees today is not an inter-national order at all, least of all *the* international order, but merely the product of the struggles among the Great Powers of half a century ago' (Wang Gungwu 2008: 24). China now argues the importance of the UN and international law which, however, it believes is under chal-lenge by the West.[3] As we see in chapter 3, China has largely adapted to this international system, but with a degree of ambivalence, despite Western pressure to be more fully involved. China's integration within the international system is largely true in material and institutional terms; integration, however, is an ambiguous concept and is more limited in respect of China's values and identities, which relate to its participation as part of a changing international community.

At the general level, world cultures impact not only on values and the way a country pursues its international objectives, but also on what it sees as effective approaches to problems. In the strategic field, the idea that China's way of thinking is different from that of the US received some serious discussion when a US congressional report noted that 'Chinese strategic thinking and military planning differ markedly from our own' (US–China Security Review Commission 2002: 15). Henry Kissinger revived the idea that China's way of war and diplomacy is shaped by attitudes developed from the game of *weiqi* (or *go* in Japan), commonly linked to the writings of Sun Tzu, while in the West (or perhaps just in the Anglo-Saxon countries), the way of war and diplomacy is seen as more linearly oriented (Sun Tzu 1963; Lai 2004; Kissinger 2011). A strong case was made for the *weiqi* basis of Maoist strategy, both in the insurgency period to 1949 and in China's revolutionary strategy towards the developing countries after 1949. Kissinger emphasized that China's defensive concerns and its quest for territorial security of its long borders encompassing 14 coun-tries could be linked to the relational non-linear approach of *weiqi*.

While some features of post-Mao foreign policy, such as the development of strategic partnerships in the 1990s and the political links associated with the 'going out' process of the early 2000s may seem consistent with such thinking, the connection is not clearly established. Indeed, given the interactive process of strategic interrelationships and changes over time in strategic structures, China may have simply absorbed lessons from others. Sisci (2011) has argued that the difference between the US and the Chinese traditions of dealing with problems can be likened to the difference between a scalpel – reflecting the US inclination to solve a problem, often by militarily eliminating its cause – and a needle, reflecting the Chinese medical tradition of preventing a problem through the practice of acupuncture.[4]

Strategic culture reflects, among other things, the circumstances in which coercion may be judged appropriate. Some analysts see the Chinese approach as a realpolitik one (Christensen 1996), but today it lacks a realpolitik response such as balancing or alliance building as Van Ness (2002) has argued. Periods of Chinese history, however, such as that of the 'warring states', lend support to the realpolitik argument. Nevertheless, cultures are changeable. Although ideology has not completely declined in importance, as evidenced by the 'upholding socialism' mantra, a greater Chinese aim is likely to be one of achieving increased national power through its foreign policy. China's realpolitik is more likely to be time and circumstance-related, rather than an inherent collective personality of the Chinese people. After an examination of China's response to its membership of multilateral institutions, Johnston (2008: xviii–xxvii) concludes that certain parts of China's decision-making processes have been weaned off realpolitik calculations. Moreover, as noted earlier, a moral component can also be found in China's traditional approach that continued in Mao's foreign policy, and indeed that of Hu Jintao's with his 'harmonious world'. Whether China's leaders will seek to present themselves again as 'the supreme moral rectifiers of the world order', as Shih (1993: 243) implies, is an open question.

We will return to these issues in later chapters when we look at how history, culture, values and China's political and strategic views, as distinct from its interests, influence China's foreign policies. Our purpose is ultimately to see what will influence China's future foreign policies and what changes to the status quo we might expect.

THE LEADERSHIP CHALLENGE

Turning to the second purpose of this chapter, we noted that, regardless of institutional arrangements, strong leaders can have an important impact on foreign policies. This is true of both Mao and Deng. In the Mao period, Mao made or greatly influenced most major foreign policy decisions until his death in 1976. He was driven by ideological and traditional influences. As Lu Ning (2000: 190) argues, he was heavily influenced by China's history and traditions, unlike the more pragmatic Deng. Mao's ideological belief about the world was concerned with international proletarian solidarity and world revolution, but his pragmatic belief was that war-torn China needed the international community's aid. Even when he was close to gaining power in 1949 and spoke of 'leaning to the left' (towards the Soviet Union), he foresaw the possibility of also developing relations with the West, including the US. That became impossible as a consequence of the Cold War. The major powers saw the Nationalists, who had fled to Taiwan, as anti-communists fighting communist China. In 1950, China's support of the North Koreans in the Korean War meant that Chinese troops were fighting troops allied under the UN flag. The PRC was denied UN membership, and the Security Council seat remained with the Nationalists until 1971. For the PRC government's first two decades of existence, few countries recognized it as the legitimate government of China.

In the early 1950s, dependence on the Soviet Union, and China's membership of the socialist bloc, was deemed by China's leaders as essential to ensure its security. Within a few years, however, that relationship soured and led to Chinese feelings of neo-colonialism that rubbed up against its idea of foreign policy that desired equality and was strongly opposed to both imperialism and great power hegemony. This triggered a shift back to self-reliance, tapping popular energies through the disastrous 1958 Great Leap Forward.

Although comfortable, therefore, in the early 1950s as part of the socialist bloc, by the 1960s, Mao saw the socialist bloc as equally imperialistic and threatening to China as the US. The situation between China and the Soviet Union became serious. The Soviet troop build-up on China's border continued, and although China increased its own troop numbers, China was so fearful it would be attacked that, starting in 1964, Mao created a military industrial complex far inland, secure from foreign attack (*People's Daily Online* 2003). By 1969, China's relations with the Soviet Union had deteriorated to the point of open conflict across the Ussuri River, on the China–Soviet border. Reflecting both China's rejection of the Soviet Union and Mao's continuing siege mentality, feelers were sent out to the US that eventually led to Richard Nixon's visit to China in 1972 and provided a 'US card' to play against the Soviets.

China's domestic politics became more radical in the late 1950s and 1960s. This radicalization and Mao's fear of reactionary subversion was ultimately reflected in the Cultural Revolution. Radical domestic politics also reflected a revisionist international agenda. Chinese revolutionary rhetoric argued that the Chinese revolution constituted one part of a world revolution; China launched fierce verbal attacks on the existing international order presided over by the two superpowers. At the peak of the Cultural Revolution in the late 1960s, China broke off relations with the Soviet Union, which led to an economic policy of self-sufficiency, or no dependence on major powers (Loehr and Van Ness 1989), and to working towards the 1972 Nixon visit.

In the 1960s, China argued that it portrayed an example of a revolution to the Third World that the post-colonial countries could emulate in order to become a revolutionary force to overturn the existing world order. Later in the 1960s, China viewed the Third World as a third force apart from the Western and the socialist camps, and in the early 1970s, Deng and Mao articulated the Three Worlds theory. Yet China did not join the institutionalized forum of the Third World, the Group of 77.

Views differ about the importance of ideology for Mao's foreign policy. Many Western commentators saw Maoist ideology as the most important factor behind Mao's foreign policies and his alliance with the Soviet Union, which helps explain the West's antagonism towards China in the early years of the PRC. Chinese analysts, however, tend to view the Cold War and anti-communism as critically determining China's 'leaning to the left' and its subsequent attempts at autonomy and self-sufficiency. Certainly, most of China's big foreign policy issues – supporting North Korea in the 1950–53 Korean war, the 1950s Taiwan Strait crises, the 1962 clash with India, involvement in Vietnam in the 1960s, and the 1969 Soviet border dispute – can just as easily be explained by traditional security concerns as by ideology (Hunt 1996: 28).

This is not to deny the importance of Mao's ideological belief, especially in domestic affairs, in communism (or socialism) as an important basis of China's identity, and in the Leninist theory of the inevitability of war. This was illustrated in the Sino-Soviet split, where China claimed to be the legitimate defender of Marxism–Leninism. An ideological basis may have existed, perhaps, for the concept of the Third World that, from the 1960s onwards, was intermittently given important attention by China depending on its need, as a united-front response to the domination of the global order by the two superpowers. In practice, however, that attention can also be seen as coalition building or as part of a competition with Taiwan for diplomatic recognition and international legitimacy.

Mao's PRC is commonly seen as isolationist and inward-looking, whereas Deng is commonly viewed as the architect of change, including of the outward-looking policies that followed Mao's death in 1976 and that continue today. Both views need some qualification. For decades, the PRC faced not only US non-recognition, hostility, and encouragement from the US to its allies to isolate the PRC, but it was also denied the UN seat held by Taiwan. As Zhang Yongjin (1998: 156) argues, alienation may be a more appropriate term than isolation. Moreover, Mao's adoption of Marxism–Leninism can be seen as a form of the cosmopolitan or 'self-strengthening' movement. Again, for part of the period, Mao looked to the Soviet Union for support, committed to an alliance, and argued for world revolution and international proletarian solidarity.

Moreover, although China gradually turned inwards in the 1960s, in the 1950s China was involved in several international conferences including the great power deliberations on Korea and Indo-China in Geneva in 1954, and the Afro-Asian Conference held in Bandung, Indonesia in 1955. Bandung was important for China's foreign policy for two reasons. First, along with India, China had earlier formulated the Five Principles of Peaceful Coexistence. These principles constituted part of the final statement of the Bandung conference, which gave them wider significance. With their emphasis on state sovereignty, non-interference in the internal affairs of other countries, and mutual interest, those five principles have remained major principles of China's foreign policy. Second, the Bandung conference also helped China develop external links with African and Asian countries which led to providing increased, if limited, foreign aid programmes to those countries. Those links have remained important.

During the late Mao period and into the Deng period, even with the major shift towards opening up, China's foreign policy was clearly not consistent. Rather, it responded both to domestic changes and to signals and threats from Washington and Moscow, with China trying to balance between the two superpowers. Following the end of the Cultural Revolution, however, the influence of ideology gradually declined, and issues of sovereignty, national unity and economic growth became major concerns.

Generally, China was cautious in its foreign policy approach, although in the 1950s and 1960s its ideological fervour at times outweighed its caution. Urged on initially by the Soviets, radical politics, however, were important for China's support for communist insurgencies in many of its Asian neighbours and in Africa; China also sought to exercise some control over ethnic Chinese communities in Asia. These activities caused conflict both with the US, which had developed an alliance network system largely to contain China, and with the Soviet Union, which was competing with China for regional support and, in response to these activities, built up large forces on China's border.

China's growing support among non-Western and Third World countries had become sufficient by 1971 to outvote the West in the UN, and China regained the UN Security Council seat previously held by Taiwan. This took away a major US weapon against China's involvement in the international system. Once that logjam was broken, many countries were quick to establish diplomatic relations with China. Overall, this was the end of China as a revolutionary state, as China started to develop normal state-to-state relations, gradually disentangling its support for communist insurgencies. The Nixon/Kissinger visits marked the beginning of developing relations between the US and China, both to press the China card against the Soviets, but also to enlist assistance to end the Vietnam War.

The 'lean to one side' policy under Mao had involved not just security support from the Soviet Union, but integration into the socialist economic camp which strongly influenced the direction of

China's economic links. After the split with the Soviet Union, however, China's economy was, to a large extent, self-reliant and slow-growing until the gradual opening up after 1972. The development of the reform policy that led to China's rise and the story of the opening up are also subject to considerable debate. China's economic reform and its opening up to the outside world is usually ascribed largely to Deng's initiatives (in part because he said so). But it is widely held that there was a sense of political and economic crisis before the reforms. The reforms were based on the Four Modernizations first articulated, not to much effect, by Zhou Enlai in 1963, but presumably with Mao's approval.[5] With Deng's support, Zhou tried again in 1975 shortly before Mao's death.

Hua Guofeng, Mao's successor, supported economic reform and put forward his own Four Modernizations. These proposed reforms for imports of Soviet-style, capital-intensive heavy industrial plants, whereas Deng argued for the need to partner with foreign investment firms for the imported technology to be effective.

Although trade started to expand rapidly under Deng, it had expanded earlier under Mao during the first years of the Soviet alliance: and then again from 1972 to 1978 before Deng was fully in charge. Nevertheless, since then it has grown spectacularly and sustainably, making China the second largest economy in the world and ensuring that China has changed the regional and global international order.

Yet although there was some continuity, including between Hua and Deng, Deng's critical contribution was to ensure political support for the reforms and opening up, and to break with Mao's economic constraints, something that Hua would not do. Moreover, although reform and opening up dates from 1978, domestic opposition was maintained, and it was not until 1981–2 that Deng's programme was really assured. Even then, vigorous internal debate on economic issues continued through much of the 1980s, as the author's discussions in China in the 1980s indicated.[6]

The Nixon visit helped the US–China relationship move forward to formal diplomatic relations, although normalization was slowed by continued radical protests in China, and US congressional opposition over constraints on arms sales to Taiwan, which led ultimately to the Taiwan Relations Act. Diplomatic relations were finally established in 1979. Meanwhile, China had been opening up significantly; it joined a wide range of international organizations including, in 1980, the Conference on Disarmament, the World Bank and the International Monetary Fund. Membership of the latter two involved some concession of China's sovereignty through the conditions they applied.

Internationally, China's need for a friendly and stable environment was deemed essential. However, China–US relations in the early 1980s cooled, with the strategic alignment with the US viewed less favourably as the Soviet threat diminished, and with the election of US President Ronald Reagan, who was unsympathetic to China. Secretary General Hu Yaobang announced an 'independence and autonomy' line for China's foreign policy at the 12th Party Congress in 1982 (Lu Ning 2000: 169). After a few years of an independent foreign policy, however, China's bilateral balancing stance returned as it moved to restore relations with the Soviet Union. Nevertheless, with the change in the international situation, in 1985 Deng officially stated that Mao's belief that a world war was inevitable no longer held, and that 'peace and development' were the two main global trends.

China's economic growth seemed unstoppable; however, various factors, including inflation, corruption and domestic discontent, led to the tragedy around Tiananmen Square in 1989. This had a major impact on China's foreign policy due to the hostility of the West, which imposed economic sanctions on China, and the flight of Western capital. Many reforms were put on hold until Deng, whose reforms faced strong opposition in Beijing from those who blamed international influences for the 1989 events, went on his 1992 'southern tour' to argue for his reforms and, in practice, to resume leadership in the reform movement. This period also saw the fall of the Berlin Wall, and the dissolution of the Soviet Union. All of these events sent shock-waves through the Chinese leadership.

In recovering from the aftermath of Tiananmen Square, and despite strong US criticism over China's claims on Taiwan in the early 1990s, Deng laid out continuing guidelines for China's foreign policies known as the '24 character' strategy. They are often translated as: 'bide our time, take a low profile and do not lead', and have since provided a general guide to China's foreign policy. Whilst China hoped for an end to US unipolarity, in the meantime it developed many bilateral strategic partnerships to strengthen its international position.

AN OUTLINE OF THE CHAPTERS

The following chapters discuss these issues in more detail. Chapter 2 deals with who makes the foreign policy decisions in China, and what role the military plays. As we have already noted, the process has become more diffused. The end of the Maoist period and the onset of the reform period saw a gradual institutionalization of the decision-making process, which was an important development. This institutionalization was never complete, however, and more recently, the range of influences on foreign policy making has increased. We ask how this more diffuse decision-making process is likely to affect future foreign policies.

Chapter 3 examines China's perception of the world in relation to its international goals. With that worldview in mind, we then consider how it frames its overall foreign policy. This consists of a broad overview of foreign policy before looking at more specific foreign policy issues in subsequent chapters. It sets the scene for looking at the extent to which China is coming to terms with the world system of norms, rules and multilateral institutions when in pursuit of a global role reflecting its values and interests. In that context, we consider in broad terms the extent to which China is contributing responsibly to that international system and to global governance, a theme we carry through in subsequent chapters.

While China's growth raises concerns in other countries about the insecurity its rise provides, less attention has been given to China's insecurities that arise from the world's perception of China. In chapter 4, we ask why do many Chinese analysts emphasize China's entrenched mentality about insecurity and vulnerability? We discuss these and their foreign policy implications at four levels: first, the vulnerability of the PRC's political regime; second, a historical sense of vulnerability about the unity of the state; third, a geographic sense of insecurity in China's neighbourhood (its maritime borders in particular reflect China's traditional vulnerability to attack from the seas, and its land borders relate largely to insecure regions); and fourth, the specific vulnerability to US dominance of the international system, but including China's concern about Taiwan.

We discuss in chapter 5 how China views the international community's capacity to coerce or to inflict harm on China by military means. In addressing these vulnerabilities, China wants to increase its hard and soft power. Interesting questions include: how do these vulnerabilities influence China's foreign policy? How far do the apparent responses to these vulnerabilities indicate a desire to achieve superiority, parity, or just a sufficient level of deterrence, including by asymmetric means? The four areas we explore in this context are China's nuclear, space, cyber and conventional weaponry policies.

In chapter 6, we look at China's economic foreign policies. China's economic growth has provided the basis for its increased comprehensive power and international status. It also provides China with considerable leverage with which to exert influence; we consider the extent to which economic coercion is used by China. In the economic field, the corollary of the peace and development mantra was China's acceptance of global interdependence with its major benefits. While the economic benefits of China's continuing rise have been welcomed internationally, China's economic rise has created problems for China, including its growing need for energy and raw material sources. China's 'going out' policy in the late 1990s and its substantial overseas investment in resource-rich countries, has led to international political and media criticism. It also impinges on China's continuing tension as an aspirant great power with a developing country self-image.

Chapter 7 looks at the regional aspects of China's foreign policies, bearing in mind that within this region, its relations with Japan, Northeast Asia, Southeast Asia and India are part of the power transition process around which its relative rise is underway. Many observers believe the South and East China Seas have become a critical part of that transition process, given the rivalry and disputes that have arisen between China and the major powers, notably the US and Japan. In this chapter, we also look at China's relationship with Europe.

In the final chapter, we look at domestic factors influencing China's foreign policy and ask what domestic issues might be likely influences on China's foreign policies in the future? As well as international developments, two principal factors will influence China's future foreign policy: how fast China's material wealth and power will grow, and how much domestic developments will constrain China's leaders. In particular, we note the various domestic problems facing China's development and, although their influence on China's foreign policy is mainly indirect, and the continued rapid development and influence may be open to question, conclude that the effects on foreign policies could be substantial. We ask whether, given the leaders' preoccupation with domestic issues, China will remain a 'revisionist-lite' state. We then look at other patterns in China's foreign policies that may suggest how future polices might develop. Since China accepts the need for a constructive and stable relationship with the US, we discuss the possible consequences for US–China relations, where there are differences not just of interests, but of values.

Finally, we ask how China will interpret its role in the international community, as distinct from the international system, given that the community is commonly assumed to be made up of states that share values as well as interests.

2 | Foreign Policy Decision Making

When China launched its first aircraft carrier in 2012, which was rebuilt from the stripped hulk of the Soviet *Varyag*, Chinese media commentators saw this as indicating changed relations between an ascendant China, returning to its historical role as a global power, and a US that wanted to retain its military supremacy in Asia. This could have been its purpose, although it is doubtful whether China's leaders believe that aircraft carriers would be effective tools for such a purpose. We do not know, however, the motivation of China's decision makers in this instance. It could have been a bargaining chip offered to a navy faction amidst hard bargaining among different interest groups; in the past, outcomes not particularly desired by the leadership have been conceded in order to gain support for other objectives. It could also have been a sop to nationalist emotions in a public aroused by navy propagandists who might have seen it as a symbol of China's great power. Our knowledge of China's foreign policy motivations and indeed its decision-making processes in general is limited. This is despite valuable research about the workings of China's foreign policy decision-making processes that has expanded our knowledge considerably, and on which this chapter draws substantially.[1]

In this chapter, we bring together what we know about Chinese foreign policy decision-making processes, which include various aspects of security policy, and the principal actors involved in those processes. Our main interest lies in what impact specific organizational processes may have on foreign policies themselves. We then look in some detail at the role and potential implications of the military in the foreign policy decision-making processes.

We noted in chapter 1 that in the first 30 years of the People's Republic of China (PRC), China's foreign policies were influenced significantly and often determined by strong leaders. After 1949, Mao Zedong and a small group of close colleagues, notably Zhou Enlai, made and influenced foreign policy decisions. That foreign policy decision making was highly centralized remains true of major foreign policy decisions and is an important continuity. The period after Deng Xiaoping's accession to power in 1978 saw an institutionalization of decision-making processes, with the tight central control characteristic of Mao's era gradually being relaxed. Following Deng's reforms, China's decision making has become less based on radical ideology, the personality of the leader has been less dominant, and a more collegial, institutionalized and professionalized process has occurred.

The range of issues involved, however, increased as China's integration with the international system proceeded. China's growing involvement with globalization has meant that decision making has become more diffused. It is difficult to discern easily who actually makes the decisions about foreign policy, or at least who influences foreign policy decisions. As in earlier decades, however, the supreme leader and a small group of senior colleagues have ultimate authority on setting the foreign policy framework, the objectives of foreign policy and the management of crises. This study suggests that apart from crises and some key foreign policy issues, mostly those surrounding Taiwan, the US, Japan, the United Nations (UN) and perhaps the BRICS (Brazil, Russia, India, China and South Africa), the extensive range of other foreign policy issues do not rank highly on the leaders' agenda.

In most countries, when we ask who initiated a foreign policy process leading to a decision on a major issue, the answer is often unclear. Given its lack of transparency, and the Chinese Communist

Party's (CCP's) need to retain a perception of unanimity, this is more so in China than elsewhere. China's government operates through more informal than formal processes compared to the Western world (although we often underestimate the importance of informal processes in the West). In China, unlike in democracies, political competition is waged through the vertically organized Leninist system – within the CCP and government departments – rather than being open to the public. Political competition also reflects the importance of personal power and the critical nature of relationships (*guanxi*), notably with a patron (Dittmer 1995). Despite the formal prohibition of the open formation of blocs or factions, this lends itself to the formation of patron–client factions within the leadership. The so-called Shanghai faction under Jiang Zemin is often cited as an example. Such faction formation appears to have been less evident under Hu Jintao, who focused more attention on major institutional constituencies, such as the Party apparatus, state authorities and the provinces (Miller 2013). Horizontally structured interest groups have become more widespread, despite the contested view that the 2012 leadership outcome was a win for the Shanghai faction (Li Cheng 2013).

More generally, Chinese politics consists of an endless web of bureaucratic and political constituencies that compete and bargain for power and resources (Shirk 1993: 37; Shambaugh 2002: 36). How decisions are interpreted is also frequently a matter of bureaucratic or other interests. Power and policy, however, are fused in Chinese politics. In pursuing power and resources, and, in particular, leadership positions – whether for top leadership positions or for positions in particular committees or commissions – policies, including foreign policies, are important instruments of competition.

To understand how decisions about China's foreign policy are made, we need to look at the formal organizational structures that are designed to deal with foreign political policy and the relationships between them. There is less informality in much foreign policy decision making than in other elements of governmental decision making. 'Informality' is more important, however, in economic foreign policy decision making, including in questions of economic reform (see chapter 6). We then look at the interactions between the formal organizations, before considering the informal processes involved and the various other influences on foreign policy decision making.

CHINA'S GOVERNMENT

China's government consists of three principal, hierarchical systems: the CCP (the Party), the government (the state) and the military (the People's Liberation Army or PLA). At the top of the Party pyramid sits the National People's Congress (NPC). Under the NPC is the Central Committee, with over 200 members (and a considerable number of alternate members). The Central Committee is not normally an important decision-making body, but it elects members of the Politburo (Political Bureau) and has many important Party departments under it. The Politburo, made up of up to 25 Party members (as at present), is more significant, but most important in the foreign policy field is the Politburo Standing Committee (PBSC), historically made up of between five and nine members (since 2012, there have been seven members). Most major foreign policy decisions are made by the PBSC or by a few of its senior members and the supreme leader, usually the General Secretary of the Party. Important issues, however, are referred for approval to the full Politburo.

Several Party departments also have influence in foreign policy decisions. Formerly known as the International Liaison Department that was linked with foreign fraternal parties, and now limited to a few countries such as Vietnam, North Korea and Cuba, the International Department is responsible for the Party's relations with foreign political parties. Although today not as central as in the past, it remains important enough for its head, Wang Jiarui, to have been appointed a member of the Foreign Affairs Leading Small Group (FALSG) from 2008 (see below). Another important foreign affairs bureaucracy is the Xinhua News Agency. It plays an important role providing information on foreign policy to the Party and to the government, and, along with the State Council Information Office, it also publicizes internationally China's foreign policy.

The State Council, and the State Councillor for foreign affairs, are important foreign policy players. As the prime governmental body, the State Council is headed by the premier, and consists of vice-premiers, state councillors and heads of government ministries, including the two most directly involved in foreign policy, the Ministry of Foreign Affairs (MFA) and the Ministry of Commerce (MOFCOM). The MFA is responsible for implementing foreign policy and day-to-day decisions. With China's growth and increased international involvement, the foreign affairs bureaucracy has also grown – it now has diplomatic relations with over 160 countries. As Jakobson and Knox (2010: 1) note, however, it 'is today merely one actor in the realm of foreign policy and not necessarily the most important one'. Neither the State Councillor, Yang Jiechi, nor the foreign minister, Wang Yi, are members of the PBSC nor of the Politburo. In part this reflects a widening of the range and complexity of foreign policies and the involvement in international issues of a wide range of previously domestically oriented bureaucracies and agencies. In practice, all central ministries and agencies now have international units. As international economic issues burgeoned, MOFCOM rose in importance. The foreign minister's relative position and that of the MOFCOM minister have since declined, however, as other players, such as the Finance Department, Ministry of State Security, and the National Development and Reform Commission (NDRC) have grown in importance. The State Council has an Executive Committee which the State Councillor for foreign affairs attends, but the ministers for foreign political or economic affairs, who are junior in rank to the State Councillor, do not.

The military, unlike most modern militaries, is a core pillar of the Chinese power structure. It has foreign policy interests in various areas of military activities, and important departments in this regard are the General Staff Department and its Second Department. Subordinate units, such as the Second Artillery, concerned with nuclear weapons and arms control, and the PLA Navy, are also influential at times. The main institutional node is the Central Military Commission (CMC) which is chaired by the CCP General Secretary. The 11-member commission consists of senior military officials, and as a change in the Party's leadership approaches, the intended successor becomes Vice-Chair. Given its responsibility for defence policy and the difficulty of separating foreign, economic and security policy, the military has important interests in foreign policies and, on particular issues such as Taiwan, relations with the US and in times of crisis, can exercise considerable influence.

Coordinating inputs into policy decision making and overseeing the implementation of decisions is largely undertaken in China through the establishment of leading small groups (LSGs), which reflects particular characteristics of China's system. These groups coordinate policy advice, communication, monitoring and implementation functions of the linked Party, state and military organizations, sit within the Central Committee, and report directly to the Politburo and its Standing Committee. The main groups, which include the Foreign Affairs LSG, now headed by Xi Jinping, are normally headed by a Standing Committee member. Xi is expected to take over Hu Jintao's (and earlier Jiang Zemin's) role on the National Security LSG and now chairs the Taiwan affairs LSG. The Party, state and military systems are all represented in these groups. Wen Jiabao chaired the Finance and Economic LSG, and Li Keqiang is the presumed head under the changed leadership. With China's growing involvement in the international economy, and a shift in priorities from security to economic development, the Central Financial and Economic Affairs

LSG has also become more important in relation to economic foreign policy.

As with many other LSGs, the FALSG has no formal bureaucratic structure and no permanent staff. The State Councillor (previously Dai Bingguo under Hu Jintao, and now Yang Jiechi) is director of the State Council Office of Foreign Affairs that serves as the general office of the FALSG, the primary foreign affairs organ of the Party. The State Councillor is also director of a comparable general office of the National Security LSG. The latter provides the State Councillor with an influential role, effectively as a national security adviser to the supreme leader.[2]

Effective coordination has become more desirable, particularly given the increasing overlap of foreign, economic and defence policy. On the one hand, the role of a strong individual leader has passed and no single leader can be an unquestioned authority in each of the Party, state and military areas of responsibility; the need for consensus decisions is now more critical, but at times more difficult to achieve. On the other hand, issues of foreign policy have become more complex. As globalization has proceeded, a growing number of functional government interests have been affected by international developments. Consequently, those functional interests have sought a greater say in foreign policy decision making. Further, greater expertise in various areas is now required in order to participate in a rapidly globalizing world, thereby enhancing the importance of the technically expert functional departments at the expense of both the MFA and MOFCOM. MOFCOM (previously called the Ministry of Trade and Economic Cooperation) rose in importance relative to the MFA, but it too was affected when, as part of the decentralization that occurred during the reform process, some of its decision-making authority was shifted to provincial authorities, state-owned enterprises and state trading corporations.

There have been frequent changes over time in the institutional arrangements for foreign policy decision making. In the shift in influence among the Party, government and military, bureaucratic rivalries have been in play at each level. Party organizations wished to hold or extend their control, the state institutions wanted more influence, and the military in particular sought greater autonomy. Associated personalities have played a role in the change in institutional arrangements for decision making. Deng Xiaoping wanted to reduce the overlap between Party and government organizations, and to bring about a greater degree of separation between Party and government than had existed under Mao. Although some steps were taken in the 1980s to achieve greater separation, it was thought that too much freedom was being given to General Secretary Hu Yaobang, and further moves along these lines were deferred. The Tiananmen crisis of 1989 led largely to their abandonment.

Factional politics were important under Mao and Deng, but apparently are now less so. In the past, there were broad and often bitter factional differences based on ideology, as during the Cultural Revolution, and also over other interests. For example, the petroleum faction in the 1970s and 1980s wanted support for its efforts and argued for the use of oil revenue for major capital imports from the West (the energy faction of today is discussed in chapter 6). Lam (2011) argues that factions are usually linked with geography or *guanxi*. This is often true as in the case of the Shanghai and Shandong (Navy) factions, the *tuanpai* faction based on the Communist Youth League, and even the so-called 'Princelings' faction (consisting of the children of past leaders), to which Xi Jinping reportedly belongs. It is not clear what influence factions have; they do not appear to constitute a firm voting bloc. Now it is argued that there is a more collective leadership; Hu Jintao was less a paramount leader and more a first among equals. To the extent this remains the case, Xi Jinping and other PBSC leaders will need to build coalitions, bargain and seek compromises with other Standing Committee and Politburo members. Although competition and rivalry remain intense, it appears to be less of a zero-sum competition than previously (Li Cheng 2005). In addition, rather than fighting over ideology, there seems to be a complex interplay of bureaucratic and business interests over policies, which may reflect a more norms-based approach to factional differences in order to avoid leadership differences (such as that which occurred during the Tiananmen crisis), given that the legitimacy of the Party requires an appearance of consensus. Decisions, however, may be more difficult to achieve.

Both Jiang Zemin and Hu Jintao viewed summit and head of state diplomacy as important functions; Xi Jinping is following their example. They made a large number of bilateral overseas visits and attended international meetings, including the Asia-Pacific Economic Cooperation (APEC) forum, the Shanghai Cooperation Organisation (SCO), and the Association of Southeast Nations (ASEAN)+3 (China, Japan and South Korea) meetings. Hu Jintao also attended meetings of the Group of Twenty (G20) and BRICS. The Chinese constitution was amended in 2008 to give the president a constitutional basis for conducting a more active international diplomacy (Zhang Qingmin 2008: 155).

During Hu Jintao's leadership, Wen Jiabao was premier and head of the administrative branch, and he played an important diplomatic role as had many of his predecessors – from Zhou Enlai under Mao to Zhu Rongji under Jiang Zemin. Wen Jiabao led Chinese delegations to international meetings such as on SARS (severe acute respiratory syndrome) or the UN Conference on Climate Change at Copenhagen. One could argue that this enhanced the role of the existing administrative agencies (such as the MFA) and the State Council Taiwan Affairs Office (Lai Hongyi 2010: 150). Yet it did not always provide the MFA with the leading influence; Wen wanted to support a moderate MFA line at the 2009 Climate Change Conference in Copenhagen to support the establishment of targets, but was successfully opposed in this by the Head of the NDRC

(Jakobson and Knox 2010). At the December 2011 Durban meeting of the UN Conference, the NDRC representative led China's delegation.

Where the MFA sits in the bureaucratic pecking order is significant in terms of its influence on foreign policies. The MFA is expected to offer more moderate advice than that from a single interest source since its responsibility is to look at the broader and longer term context that takes account of the full range of China's international relations interests. At times, this has led to criticism of the MFA by the military or other bureaucracies for being too soft in its approach. Examples of this include the MFA's agreement in 1993 to allow a joint Saudi-US team to inspect the Chinese container ship, *Yinhe*,[3] and its soft response at times to US policies towards Taiwan and, initially, to the 1999 bombing of the Chinese embassy in Yugoslavia.

THE MILITARY

Periodically, concerns emerge over whether the military remains under the Party's control. This is of critical international interest (see Hille 2011). Particular concern has arisen with respect to the role of the PLA Navy, given that much of the assertive public rhetoric by senior PLA officials has been from naval officers. Extensive literature (Swaine 1998, 2012a, 2012b) exists about the contested issue of relations between the Party and the military. Our interest here, however, is limited to how far the military is involved in China's foreign policy decision making. There have been many changes in the Party–military relationship during the reform process, and they have also involved the military's relations with the state. Whilst the military has gradually pushed for greater autonomy from the Party, the government has pursued greater management control of the military,[4] and the Party has wanted greater political control of the military. Surprisingly, perhaps, all three have achieved some of their aims.

The military has achieved greater autonomy in its relations with the Party. This has enabled the military to pursue effectively its goal of greater professionalism. By the mid-1990s, the military had moved towards 'a more corporate, professional, autonomous and accountable military' (Shambaugh 2002: 31). This has been further helped by the development of the People's Armed Police, thereby reducing the PLA's responsibility for internal security that it had undertaken during the Cultural Revolution and in the Tiananmen Square crisis in 1989.

The diminished military involvement in political issues was reflected in the reduced military representation in the important Party institutions that were concerned with security and foreign policy – the PBSC and the CMC. Military officers sit on the CCP institutions that formally elect China's leaders, including the NPC, Party congresses, the Central Committee, and the Politburo (Kiselycznyk and Saunders 2010: 3), and at the time of leadership change that role becomes more important. Although the military is represented in the Politburo, there is now no military representative on the PBSC and has not been since 1997. The military's influence on foreign and security policy is thus more indirect than in the past. The main avenue through which the PLA can convey its views to China's leaders is through the CMC and the relevant LSGs.

Links between the military and the Party are commonly referred to as symbiotic; the early PRC political leaders were members of the military or were commonly linked as political commissars in the Party–army that had successfully implemented the revolution. This remained a central feature of the Mao and Deng periods, but changed with Deng's successors, Jiang Zemin and Hu Jintao. Unlike earlier leaders, they had no military background or experience, and lacked the shared experiences and connections with the military leaders of earlier generations, while the military leaders had little of the political experiences of their predecessors. This reduction in symbiosis also led to an increased concern about the loyalty of the military to the Party, a concern that was enhanced by the somewhat equivocal response of elements in the military to restoring national security in 1989. Frequent injunctions are published that either counter arguments that the military should be a national army (to protect the nation) rather than a Party army (to protect the Party), or strongly uphold the principle of the absolute leadership of the Party.[5]

For its part, the military wanted to be less tied to political involvement with the Party. The involvement of political commissars and the time spent on ideology and political indoctrination was a time-consuming process that appears to have greatly diminished since its post-Tiananmen peak. PLA leaders wanted the PLA to become more professional with technical criteria, rather than political reliability, being the major criteria for recruitment and promotion. The military still acknowledges that its main function is to protect the Party, not the nation, as it did when maintaining social order during the Cultural Revolution and at the time of the Tiananmen tragedy. The latter, however, which raised questions for the Party about the military's loyalty, also raised questions in the military about its role in maintaining social stability. The problem of other communist states in the period 1990–1 reinforced the Party's interest in 'commanding the gun'.

Although the military is no longer strongly represented on the main decision-making bodies, there is continued Western concern that the PLA is having more indirect influence on foreign policy making. Military influence can be exercised in a number of ways. A principal method is through the CMC. This meets frequently and gives members the opportunity to make their views known to the supreme leader (and at times his deputy). The recent establishment of a strategic planning department in the PLA is arguably to strengthen the CMC's leadership and management of China's army building (Zhou 2011).

As noted earlier, Jiang Zemin was sensitive to the military's interests over national security and foreign policy issues concerning Taiwan, the US, Japan and theatre missile defence. Shambaugh (2002: 37) notes that this sensitivity was a key element in Jiang Zemin's ability to gain the support of the military, despite his lack of experience and limited military connections. Reportedly on occasion, the PLA sent messages to the leadership expressing concerns about policies concerning particularly Taiwan, the US, Japan and India. The military has reportedly asserted itself over issues such as the US granting of a visa to Taiwan's president Lee Teng Hui in 1995, for which Jiang Zemin and foreign minister, Qian Qichen, reportedly made self-criticisms in the CMC. While some situations seem to have stimulated this process, whether over the *Yinhe* incident or the Lee Teng Hui visa issue, there are questions about how often this has happened in the post-Deng period, and whether messages were sent from serving or from retired officers.

The PLA Navy's increased maritime patrolling, its successful anti-satellite exercises, or its demonstration of new military equipment such as an anti-ship missile has raised fears that the PLA is becoming more active in China's foreign policy. Swaine argues that 'there is little if any evidence that it dictates *basic* strategy or policy outcomes, including those relating to national security' (Swaine 2012a: 5, emphasis in original). He notes, however, that while China's civilian leaders exercise ultimate authority over all major aspects of foreign policy, they mostly do not exert clear and decisive control over two types of activities with significant implications for foreign policy: military tests and other action regardless of location, and military operations undertaken outside of China's territorial borders. China's leaders do not have the structures and processes to ensure coordination with foreign policy and diplomatic structures. At times of crisis, this lack of coordination structures is even more evident (Swaine 2012b).

In the last decade or so, the PLA has been actively engaged in military exchanges and cooperation with militaries of other countries, and has an extensive range of military attachés in China's embassies. Serving PLA officers now appear to have greater freedom to publicly discuss foreign policy and to influence Chinese public opinion on foreign policy issues. Military publications contain articles about foreign policy issues and military officers write articles for newspapers and comment on foreign policy issues on radio and television. This has been startlingly evident on nuclear issues, but more sustainably on a broad range of sensitive nationalist issues, as for example, to gain public support for the need for a blue water navy, including a Chinese aircraft carrier. Ross (2009: 65) concluded that 'Chinese military publications directed at a popular readership exaggerate the maritime capabilities of countries that rival China for great power status or of countries that possess less claim than China . . . including . . . not only of Britain, France, and Russia, but also of Brazil, India, Japan, South Korea, and Thailand'.

GLOBAL DIPLOMACY

China's integration into the global system has signalled a major change in China's foreign policies, notably, but not only, in the economic field. Not only are China's leaders involved in foreign policy matters that have arisen from its increased integration, such as those arising in the G20 and the bilateral issues of China's US dollar investments, but more central and regional bureaucratic interests have also become involved. Most central ministries and agencies have direct dealings with overseas agencies and national and international instrumentalities. For example, the Peoples' Bank of China, the State Administration of Foreign Exchange, and the Finance Ministry are involved with China's currency issues, as well as with the International Monetary Fund and World Bank, and the Ministry of Public Security supplies police for UN peacekeeping missions.

China's international activities have meant an increase in consular assistance and protection for the approximately five million Chinese citizens that make annual overseas trips, and the more than one million Chinese citizens working overseas. Hu Jintao's work report to the 18th Party Congress emphasized the need to protect Chinese nationals abroad. As well as bringing Chinese citizens home from the conflict in Egypt and the nuclear accident in Japan, this became a major challenge when rescuing some 35,000 Chinese citizens trapped in Libya when hostilities broke out in 2011. The successful operation involved not just the MFA but considerable inter-agency cooperation, including the PLA Navy and Air Force, MOFCOM, and the Ministry of Public Security working closely with China's Civil Aviation Authority, and the Chinese oil and other companies located in Libya (Collins and Erickson 2011).

Although often falling outside the official system, Chinese corporations, including military agencies, are active participants in China's international processes, as are many Chinese provincial governments. These various instrumentalities seek to have a voice in foreign policy decision making when it directly affects their interests. China's reform processes sought to decentralize much of China's economic decision making and this has led to an increased international role for provincial and local governments. Provincial governments have broad international interests – they are recipients of inward foreign investment, support local companies with their own outward foreign investment, and export contract labour and contractors in overseas infrastructure and engineering projects which provide revenue and employment. This involvement has been encouraged by the central government and is commonly supported with concessional loans. Lobbying by local leaders has become simpler with increased representation now provided to provincial and city leaders in the Politburo and the PBSC. Given this development of local and international economic and trading ties, provincial governments tend to favour open trading systems and China's international economic integration.

Within China's business sector, many groups exercise considerable influence on the formulation of government policies, including foreign policies. Notable among them are the telecommunications, mineral resource, energy and banking industries. Many state-owned and private companies in these industries have become more autonomous, although they are ultimately still subject to Party–state control. The energy industry in particular, has exhibited a strong influence in the past and this seems to be growing. The extensive overseas interests of the national oil companies (NOCs) in particular, and their subsidiary companies (notably PetroChina, Sinopec and China National Offshore Oil Corporation), means that they are strategically important to China because of their oil and gas activities, their financial contribution to Beijing's revenue receipts, and the broader economic links that these companies facilitate in China's diplomacy. Moreover, given that their subsidiaries are listed on foreign stock exchanges, there are some constraints on how far the Party–state can regulate the NOCs. As discussed in chapter 6, the activities of the NOCs, who are major overseas investors, have at times created diplomatic problems for China.

Many, indeed perhaps most, of China's senior leaders have business enterprise experience. The strategic state-owned enterprises in particular provide recruits for the top leadership jobs at the political, bureaucratic and provincial levels. For example, Zhu Rongji, premier under Jiang Zemin, had oil industry experience, and Jiang Jiemin, head of the China National Petroleum Corporation (the parent company of PetroChina) and previously a provincial vice-governor, was appointed in 2013 to a ministerial-level position heading the State Assets Supervision and Administration Commission.[6] While those so appointed do not necessarily pursue the interests of the industries with which they were associated, 'personnel movements certainly create a tremendous amount of flexibility and informal connections between oil companies and the country's leadership at various levels' (Kong 2010: 22).

Although a traditional interest group, the energy industry does not always act in a united manner. Whilst they share some common interests, there can also be competitive and divergent elements to these interests. Moreover, the Chinese government has found it difficult to

exercise authority over the energy sector. An energy LSG was established in 1995, but was subsequently collapsed into the National
Energy Administration along with various other energy agencies.
Under Wen Jiabao, a National Energy Commission was set up, designed
to be a high-level supervisory and coordination body. However, it was
unable to formulate a national energy policy that could integrate
domestic and overseas interests because of divergent bureaucratic and
state-owned enterprise concerns. The newly formed National Energy
Administration comes under the NDRC.

INFORMATION SOURCES

In formulating foreign policies, the information base is a critical deter-
minant of the quality of the ultimate policy; specific sources of information significantly influence the quality and effectiveness of decisions.
In the case of foreign policy, the sources of information are more specialized than, for example, domestic policy, and are more susceptible to
limitations of incompleteness and to the interpretations of the information providers and the decision makers, who are often selective in
their readings, according to preconceived understandings.

Institutionally, China's foreign policy processes are dependent upon
a few major information sources. As noted earlier, the Xinhua News
Agency is a principal source. It systematically provides information and
advice to foreign policy decision makers based on material sourced
from its extensive overseas representation covering most countries.
Although it provides daily summaries of overseas information, it also
provides foreign relations analyses relating to the countries in which it
is represented. This material supplements reports from Chinese embassies and consulates.

In addition, various advisory and research groups and think-tanks
also provide important sources of information and analyses which at
times is sent to the top leadership. Among the more important ones

are the Central Party School, the China Institutes of Contemporary International Relations, and the Chinese Academy of Social Sciences. The FALSG maintains a list of experienced researchers and senior academics with expertise in foreign policy who are based at leading universities such as Beijing University, or at institutes such as the Shanghai Institute of International Affairs. At times, they are invited to present analyses to the participants in the decision-making processes or to participate in discussions that sometimes involve the top leaders.

Chinese officials and academics now argue that Chinese foreign policy decision makers must take Chinese public opinion into account in their decisions. The question of how far public opinion in China is affecting China's foreign policies is a contested one. According to a report of the China Internet Network Information Center, the number of Internet users had reached 564 million by the end of 2012 (cited in Osborne 2013). It is true that the Internet and social media, particularly Weibo, China's version of Twitter, allows greater public discussion of policy issues. It is also true that China's leaders have taken steps to limit the use of such technologies and, as some judge, 'to control and regulate the Internet in any way it wants' (Chung Jongpil 2011).

Although much of the Internet use would be for other purposes, such as online shopping, it has enabled wide access to information that is relevant to policy thinking. In the foreign policy field, however, it is more complex than in the domestic field. Relatively few Chinese get their international news directly, but those that do, follow it intensely. Most receive their international news from the domestic media, which is tightly controlled by the state. Nevertheless, the Internet, together with widespread and competitive media coverage, has raised the level of public interest in, and discussion of, foreign policy. These outlets, however, are closely monitored by the authorities; the information that comes through the official or popular press or on Chinese websites 'comes through Chinese lenses' (Shirk 2007: 98). Certainly, the Chinese commercialized mass media – radio, television, newspapers and magazines – compete aggressively for audiences by meeting the desire for news; in that competition, as in the West, wars, conflicts and areas of international tension are of particular interest and attract audiences. In China, nationalism, and nationalist concern for China's international image, often provides an element of particular interest. When issues arise that appear to reflect on that image, the nationalist response, and popular support for their arguments, is likely to be vigorous – as in the case of the accidental bombing of China's embassy in Belgrade in 1999, or Japanese active reassertion of their claim to the Diaoyu/Senkaku Islands.

Whether China's nationalism is a self-generated mass movement or a government-stimulated nationalism is open to question (Gries 2004: 117–18). The government at times encourages nationalism or allows it to develop; at other times it seeks to suppress nationalist urges since much of the associated implicit or explicit criticism equates to criticism of the government, which can turn sharply against leaders who might be seen as failing to meet nationalists' goals. Nationalist urges are often encouraged by the media – again with or without government influence. The media also provides opportunities for retired military officials, academics and think-tank personnel to participate in radio talk shows and television debates, and to write opinion pieces for news media (Hao 2005; Jakobson and Knox 2010). Many of these contributors tend to promote a more nationalist line. Rapid and large popular responses to incidents that relate to Taiwan, Japan and the US in particular, but also to a range of other issues, such as Tibet, Xinjiang and the South China Sea, can turn negative if the government underplays the desired response. Issues that affect these relationships in particular become domestic issues that need to be carefully managed by China's leaders. To some extent, the difficulty of their management and the need for the government to respond strongly – even though they may not want to do so – arises in part from the strength of the state's own propaganda on the issues.

How far general public opinion influences foreign policy decisions is not easy to determine. Just as Western leaders and diplomats commonly use the pressure of domestic public opinion as a defence against providing concessions on an international issue, Chinese officials often use claims of public opinion as a way to resist pressures from the outside world, strengthening apparent negotiating positions. Others include actual or constructed legal constraints. The Anti-Secession Act (dealing with Taiwan) was once described to the author by a senior Chinese official as in part a counterfoil to the US Taiwan Relations Act which has been used so effectively by US officials in discussions with Chinese counterparts to indicate that their hands are tied. Nevertheless, while public opinion can at times be helpful in negotiations, as for example when explaining to Japan why China could not support Japan's bid for the UN Security Council, it can also be unhelpful. While border disputes with neighbours have been mostly settled without public knowledge of the details, such deals would now likely be challenged, as happened with the most recent settlement in 2008 of the disputed border with Russia.

China's leaders receive daily reports about what the websites, blogs and bulletin boards are publishing, including on foreign policy issues. Former foreign minister Li Zhaoxing was one of the first ministers to go online and accept interchanges with the public. The MFA has an interactive and heavily patronized website. Hu Jintao and Wen Jiabao reportedly went online to see what was being said on the Internet. That what is being said is likely to be representative only of the more extreme nationalist views is, in one sense, a problem. Yet, as Shirk (2007: 103) suggests, for China's leaders, extremists are more worrisome as potential leaders of street demonstrations and organizers of mass protests, and therefore are of more importance to them.

Debate continues as to how successful the government's response to the new technology has been. Some argue that it has only been partially successful, and that China's leaders and decision makers need to be more sensitive to public opinion as expressed via the Internet and social media. Against this are arguments that the government's control is quite effective, and that the Internet and the media are used effectively by the Party–state to shape public opinion.

Although public opinion has become more important in foreign policy decision making, it is difficult to assess its importance. Fewsmith and Rosen (2001: 174–5) suggest that its importance varies over time according to the cohesion of the leadership, the state of China–US relations and popular mobilization. Thus, various issues in the 1990s, such as the 1993 *Yinhe* incident, Zhu Rongji's humiliation in the failed World Trade Organization (WTO) negotiations in April 1999, the 1999 missile strike on China's Belgrade embassy, the 2001 EP3 surveillance plane collision with a Chinese fighter plane, and continuing tensions with Taiwan and Japan, mobilized popular opinion, indicating that public responses can be important domestic political influences on how China's leaders respond in foreign policy terms.

Our main interest in this chapter has been what continuities and changes may be observed in foreign policy decision making, and what impact the changes in foreign policy organizational processes may have on foreign policies. The increased professionalism of the foreign policy process was a continuation of Zhou Enlai's initiative, whereby MFA officials were sent to Mexico and later to Britain for Spanish and English language training in the 1960s. It is evident that Chinese diplomats have become more skilled in international diplomatic practice, as their approach in the UN and the WTO illustrates. On the other hand, changes in the processes have been substantial as China has responded to the pressures of globalization. Institutionalization has continued, but so has the growth of informal influences. Continuities remain in that decision making about important issues – conflicts, crises and policies towards Taiwan, Japan and the United States – remain in the hands of a small group of top leaders, even if the role of the supreme leader has diminished since the time of Deng Xiaoping.

Transparency on these issues has not changed much – but then cabinet discussions on foreign policy issues in Western countries are commonly not made public until many years later.

The diffusion of decision making and the increased influence of vested interests pose considerable problems in coordination and policy formulation. The WTO negotiations involved at least ten ministries or agencies; implementation of the outcomes of the first Sino-African Forum in 2000 brought together some 22 ministerial-level organizations (Zhang Qingmin 2008: 168). This places enormous pressure on the leadership to manage foreign policy coordination, and to reconcile the often competitive interests to ensure not just implementation but to try to ensure, not always successfully, that China speaks with one voice. That reconciling the various interests involved appears more difficult in China than in most major states, greatly complicates China's international negotiating position. While China is making more effective use of traditional diplomatic practices, how far it also follows traditional diplomatic norms will be discussed in the next chapter, as will issues affecting the future direction of China's foreign diplomacy and foreign policy. It seems probable, however, that with the more diffused processes we have discussed, less foreign policy predictability, and possibly less consistency, is to be expected.

3 | China, the World and the International System

When Chinese, American and European leaders look out at the world, the perceptions that each has of that world are very different. China's perceptions of the world, filtered as they are through Chinese history, culture and self-images as both a developing country and a great power, are critical influences on its foreign policy. So too is the need for the Chinese Communist Party (CCP or the Party) to survive. The top priority for the Party leaders is that the Party survives in the face of what it perceives to be an unstable and largely hostile international environment. How China, in its foreign policy, responds to that view of the world is the subject of this and subsequent chapters. Various goals are commonly attributed to China's foreign policy – for example, international status, respect, equality and a peaceful environment. Like other countries, however, its broader goals are to ensure that the international environment is stable, to pursue a global role that reflects its values and interests, to be secure, and to prosper. We examine the latter goals in more detail in subsequent chapters.

In this chapter we are interested, first, in what China's perceptions of the world are in relation to these goals – in effect its worldview. We then look at that worldview to see how it frames China's foreign policy. Finally, we examine how China views the existing international order and the extent to which, in broad terms, it can be said to be contributing responsibly to the international system and to global governance. These latter aspects will emerge more specifically in chapters 4–7, and will be brought together again in chapter 8.

CHINA'S WORLDVIEW

Chinese elites do not hold uniform worldviews; some see the world from a Chinese history perspective, others take a more cosmopolitan view; some want to change the world, some do not, and various gradations exist among these different views. Debate continues among them about, for example, how much China's integration in the world economy remains beneficial. Nor are worldviews immutable; as noted earlier, China's worldview changed from one of thinking that the main theme in the international system was war and revolution (the Marxist–Leninist approach of Mao Zedong) to the peace and development theme (identified by Deng Xiaoping) which remains the underlying trend according to the 2013 white paper on China's armed forces (State Council Information Office 2013). Contrary to earlier views, Deng argued that war could be avoided, and that war would not break out because of the nuclear deterrent and the stabilizing impact of social developments in Western societies (Zhu Liqun 2008: 111–12). This was a fundamental change in China's worldview, which led to major changes in China's foreign policy – the introduction of its 'opening up' and reform, and later its 'going out' policies.

The elements of today's world that are important to China's foreign policy are: first, the distribution of global power, wealth and prosperity; second, the outside world's intentions towards China; third, the management of international relationships among global actors through the norms, rules, practices and customs of the international system; fourth, how far these norms, rules, practices and customs cohere with China's own values and interests; and fifth, the benefits and costs for China of globalization and economic interdependence. We look briefly at each of these before looking broadly at China's response.

First, we have already observed that in the early 1990s, following the dissolution of the Soviet Union and the end of communism in Europe, China viewed with considerable unease the emergence of a unipolar US superpower whose behaviour towards China had been, and would continue to be, a mixture of cooperation and confrontation. During that period, China had hoped, with little result, for a multi-polar world to emerge to offset US strength. Although China now sees increasing multipolarity emerging with countries such as the BRICS (Brazil, Russia, India, China and South Africa), it still perceives a global system largely dominated by US power. Despite China's quali-fications about the US and global economies, China accepts that the US is still strong in many dimensions, and that its own comprehensive national power still lags behind the US and several European powers.

Second, not only was there a unipolar world in the early 1990s, but China also faced a largely hostile West because of the killings around Tiananmen Square in 1989. Although China–US relations seemed to have eased by the mid-1990s, various tensions resurfaced in the latter part of the decade, particularly after a missile struck China's Belgrade embassy. Despite China's rapid economic growth and considerable military modernization that has led to its enhanced international standing, it looked at a world in which it believes that its role as a great power has long been denied. China recognizes the benefits of economic cooperation with the US, which has contributed substantially to its rapid growth and development. It is also aware, however, that Western approaches to cooperation with China are widely viewed in the West as having particular motivations – political reform and democratic processes are regarded as beneficial in Western eyes, but as meaning deleterious regime change in China's eyes, part of the peaceful evolu-tion discussed in chapter 1.

Third, nevertheless, China has adhered extensively to the West's international norms and rules, and claims to be a responsible power. Later in the chapter, we look at the issue of responsibility. Since norms and rules constitute part of the body of international law, we also examine China's attitude to international law, including the principles set down in the UN Charter.

Fourth, China's interests and values do not align closely, however, with Western interests and values, and the definition of 'responsibility' is not shared. How much China responds to the idea of international responsibility, including why it accepts some norms and rules but not others, is a complex question. Ultimately, the question is to what extent does China want to change existing global norms and rules so that they accord more closely with its own interests and values? To some degree, this process is illustrated in its approach to human rights, as discussed later.

Fifth, the final element important to China's foreign policy is its view that globalization is the dominant global influence that facilitates a rapid diffusion of ideas, and that there is increasing economic interdependence in an economic system that is in difficulties, if not in crisis. It sees continued complex interdependence not just with the US and Europe but with other countries in Asia, Africa and Latin America. This interdependence involves a growing Chinese political, social and economic involvement in order to meet its growing need for resources and markets. It is concerned at the global nature and impact of such forces and their impact leading to divisions among China's elite over whether the benefits still outweigh the costs. Given their concerns for the Party's survival, China's leaders remain wary of the impacts of globalization in the political and social arenas, such as those underpinning the Arab Spring. These global pressures also challenge China in fields such as AIDS, arms smuggling, cybernetics, drugs, pandemics and terrorism.

CHINA'S BROAD FOREIGN POLICY RESPONSE

How has China shaped its foreign policy framework, given its understanding of the world? In its foreign policy, China's leaders employ the same methods that most countries do. They use coercion (force or economic pressure), inducement (most commonly trade, aid and investment), or persuasion (including reputation, ideology and soft power more generally) to pursue their international objectives. China's ability to employ one or other of these methods depends not just on its own capabilities, but on the international environment – the continued impact of globalization, the gradual shift towards multipolarity, and developments in its relative military and economic power – as well as on international pressures that emanate from the US, Japan, Russia or elsewhere, and on domestic pressure from particular organized interests or rising nationalism. China's willingness to use such methods also reflects how far China does or does not adhere to the norms, rules and practices of the international community.

China's approaches to coercion and inducements are discussed more specifically in the following chapters. Broadly, however, China needs a peaceful regional and global environment that will make those objectives feasible, prevent situations emerging that might stir domestic nationalist activism, and avoid any adverse reactions to China's rise from regional neighbours, others outside the region, and the US. As an aspiring great power, it might be expected that China would have a long-term foreign policy vision, or a grand strategy by which to achieve its objectives. Wang Jisi (2011: 68) argues that it is debatable whether China has such a strategy. Some argue that Deng's '24 character' guideline is China's grand strategy.[1] Others see 'peace and development' or 'China's peaceful rise' as grand strategies (this can be seen in Ye Zicheng 2011 and Zheng Bijian 2005). Although they do not offer much detail about how to achieve their strategic objectives, what all these suggest is that to the extent that China has a grand strategy, it is defensive in nature.

We noted in chapter 1 that China's sense of being a 'victim' remains an important, if variable, influence on China's perception of itself, and the lens through which it sees the world. This does not immediately translate into a foreign policy influence, except as an underlying reason for building comprehensive national strength on which the overall policy of peace, economic development and integration with the international economy depends. It does, however, often lead to domestic responses to events that seem to resonate with history; as one senior Chinese official put it to me – 'knocking the scab off an old and deep sore'. The strike on the Chinese embassy in Belgrade clearly knocked the scab off, but an insensitive remark from a Western or Japanese politician can do the same, hence China's concern for international respect. Victimhood has often been used expediently, however, in negotiations to claim special entitlements, even when the scab may have been unaffected.

Following the embassy missile strike in particular, the question of how China should respond and the appropriateness of Deng's injunction to maintain a low profile were seriously discussed among China's leaders in Beijing. Whilst some argued for a more active foreign policy response, the overall conclusion was that Deng's guidelines remained relevant, with some necessary qualifications involving a somewhat higher international profile. Despite increased diplomatic activism by China from the mid-2000s onwards, however, and given China's continued need for economic cooperation with the US in particular, direct confrontation with the US has been limited.

As occurred in the late 1990s, there has again been much debate in China and the West about the precise meaning and underlying purpose of Deng's guidelines. Often translated as 'don't lead, hide brightness, cherish obscurity', was it an expedient guideline for a particularly difficult period of China's international relations and internal discord? Did it imply biding time until China was strong enough to promote a hidden agenda, as many Western commentators believe? Or did it reflect a position that was beneficial for China in the long term, calling on China's moral principles of dealing with foreigners, which still has some support among Chinese analysts? Zhao Suisheng (2010: 364) argues that 'Deng's low-profile policy was never simply meant as a passive posture. It was a dynamic process to hide China's ambition and bide for time'. Deng's policy guideline has been challenged further by China's post-2010 maritime border disputes, but not yet discarded, although Wang Jisi (2011) argued that a low profile cannot cope effectively with the multifaceted challenges facing the country. Moreover, if China responded substantially to Western demands to be a responsible international power and act constructively in international affairs, China would need to go beyond a strict interpretation of the guideline. Hu Jintao's instruction that 'proactively' be added to getting 'some things done' in Deng's guideline was taken to be an important addition, implying the need for greater international activity in China's foreign policy (Chen Zhimin 2009).

Some of that activity had been directed earlier to establishing strategic partnerships. Following the Tiananmen Square episode, and when unipolarity was at its height in the post-Cold War period, China needed friends. It turned first to Russia, and in December 1992 announced a strategic partnership. While this partnership is now more important, it had little substance initially. It was, however, regarded by China as a new kind of bilateral relationship (although not uncommon in the West); not an alliance, but a non-confrontational link that did not target a third country. China's use of the term 'strategic' is not limited to a military or security dimension, but reflects the overall framework of China's relationship with a country where economic, political and other factors are important. Similar to commercial strategic partnerships designed to counter a competitor's moves, China's strategic partnerships were, and remain, a means of countering US primacy. In the years since, China has signed partnerships, described variously as strategic, constructive and cooperative, with a wide range of partners: Argentina, the Association of Southeast Asian Nations (ASEAN), Brazil, Britain, the European Union (EU), France and South Korea, for example (Harris 2008: 212–15). With the passage of time, partnerships have largely developed into normal and stable relationships between China and other countries, with their importance varying according to the ups and downs of China's global position. Under Bill Clinton's administration, there were moves towards a strategic partnership between China and the US, but these fell away under the George W. Bush administration.

Despite its success in developing partnerships, China's diplomacy has had mixed results. The extent of China's growth and its military modernization led, in the late 1990s and early 2000s in particular, to arguments about a 'China threat'. Although echoed among China's neighbours in Asia, it arose most notably in the US where there were concerns about a possible challenge from a rising power to the dominance of the hegemon. In response to those 'China threat' fears, China sought to develop a vision around the concept of 'peaceful rise'. The word 'rise', however, became domestically and internationally problematic, and was replaced with the new concept of 'peaceful development', but that had limited significance in foreign policy terms. Chen Zhimin (2009: 17) viewed Hu Jintao's harmonious world as 'poised to become China's new foreign policy strategy'. That, however, was more of a narrative than a grand strategy, with no indication of what operational measures would lead to this end, although China's oft-stated views of international equality of states, reform of an unequal economic system, and a greater role for the developing countries point in that direction. Its assertive responses in the South China Sea disputes, in particular, appear to have undercut some at least of the progress it was making, notably in Southeast Asia, in its efforts to demonstrate a peaceful process of China's rise. How far this assertiveness was a conscious implementation of a central government decision is discussed in chapter 4.

Besides partnerships, China has also substantially expanded its contacts with countries across the globe, especially by encouraging its companies to invest overseas, particularly through its 'going out' or 'going global' policy. Although earlier efforts had been made basically to improve the efficiency and productivity of its state-owned enterprises, the 'going out' policy was initiated in 1999, and is now viewed internationally, and often exaggeratedly, as designed to provide China access to resources and raw materials. The process has required a broader foreign policy, however, including leadership diplomacy which, on balance, has probably helped increase Chinese international influence. There is little evidence, on the other hand, that this process is seen by China's leaders as a means for developing hegemonic influence or control, a subject we return to in later chapters.

CHINA'S VIEW OF THE GLOBAL ORDER

As already observed, China's choice of foreign policy methods depends, in part, on its approach to the existing global order and how it judges the impact of the current order on its national interests. A central question of this study is how far does China accept the rules and norms of the existing world order, rather than aiming to influence and change them? In general terms, China appears substantially committed to the existing international order in the economic field through its economic interdependence and policy coordination (see chapter 6), but there is continuing debate over how far China has become part of the world's wider system of rules and norms.[2] China strongly endorses the external norms of sovereignty and non-intervention that are commonly associated with the Westphalian system.[3] China's emphasis on Westphalian sovereignty[4] and non-intervention was one of the byproducts of the 'century of humiliation', which saw the end of the Chinese empire and the adoption of the state-system culture which now extends globally.

The established nation states, comfortable in this state-system culture, are keen to see other states, particularly China, fully commit to this system; however, the traditional understanding in the West of sovereignty now includes other features, such as property rights, democracy and the right to intervene to protect human rights. It is often argued that China's apparent unwillingness to accept this Western view of sovereignty, including humanitarian intervention, shows that China is not being a responsible member of the international system. China is firmly opposed to intervention as a constitutional principle; indeed, it has been argued that because of its strong support for the sovereignty principle in its traditional form, China is the last of the Westphalian states (Etzioni 2011).

China's strict adherence to the external sovereignty and non-intervention principles needs some qualification. China's approach is, at times, pragmatic. Historically, during the time of China's support for communist insurgencies in Asia and Africa, these revolutions in sovereignty conflicted with the non-intervention norm (Zhang Yongjin 2008: 136). Furthermore, since 1978, China has joined a number of international organizations, many of which have intrusive membership conditions, notably the International Monetary Fund (IMF), the World Bank, the World Trade Organization (WTO) and the International Atomic Energy Agency (IAEA). In addition, some bilateral agreements involve conditions, such as its agreement that permits US officials to inspect Chinese factories that manufacture CDs.

In the political field, the 'one country, two systems' approach to Hong Kong and Macau qualifies the absolute sovereignty principle. As well, China's intervention in foreign countries has increased, most notably via peacekeeping activities. Although China was originally opposed to the UN's notion of peacekeeping, since the mid-1980s, it has become acceptable to China, provided it has UN approval, obtains the consent of the relevant country, maintains neutrality and does not use offensive force (Chu Shulong 2001). It has also accepted that 'responsibility to protect' (R2P) situations will arise where intervention, under strict UN conditions, may be justified.[5] Despite its strategic partnership with Russia, however, China opposed the Russian 2008 invasion of Georgia on the grounds of international legal principles (see chapter 7).

THE UN AND INTERNATIONAL LAW

The UN underpins the global order. Even after 1971 and the admission of the People's Republic of China to the UN, which provided it with legitimacy and, through its Security Council seat, nominal recognition as a great power, for some years the PRC government remained equivocal about the UN. After 1978, with economic reform under way, China slowly began to participate in a wide range of UN activities, joined practically all the important UN-related instrumentalities including the IMF and the World Bank, as mentioned earlier, and became more interested in the potential gains from participating more actively.[6]

For China, the UN is now an important organization that buttresses the principle of state sovereignty which protects China legally from outside intervention whether by the US or the North Atlantic Treaty Organization (NATO) member states (and earlier the Soviet Union), and China accepts the UN Charter as the basis of international law. Yet Mao's China saw international law as rules that allowed it to be excluded and isolated at the dictate of the leading powers, and that largely reflected its exclusion from the UN. China at that time was dismissive of the role of international law as an instrument of power, rather than as a set of universal norms and rules to guide international relationships. It accepted that some of the principles were valuable, notably the principle of sovereignty, and it advocated norms that were closely related to traditional international law principles, notably the Five Principles of Peaceful Co-existence.[7] These principles are similar to those of the UN Charter. Later, as China increasingly participated in international organizations and treaty making, it became more comfortable with the idea of international law, and the guides and rules that it provides, and with being more active in rule making. It gradually accepted international law not just as an instrument of power, but as a set of norms and rules that provide the foundation of international order. Apart from the critical issue of human rights, China's contributions to international law have subsequently been relatively constructive and sympathetic to existing norms and principles (Kent 2008: 70–1).

China's membership of the United Nations Security Council (UNSC) and the right to veto that goes with it is important for China's status and for providing some limitations on Western, notably US, power. China's performance in the Security Council has been the focus of international attention, much of it often critical on the infrequent occasions that it exercises its veto. Since resuming its UN seat in 1971, the PRC has applied its veto eight times, which is fewer than the other UNSC members. Since the beginning of the twenty-first century, China has used its veto four times, which is less than the number of times that the US and Russia have used their vetoes. China's vetoes have generally been in support of its allies – Pakistan, Burma and Zimbabwe – or against the deployment of UN peacekeeping troops in countries that maintained diplomatic links with Taiwan, such as Guatemala and Macedonia. It tends to abstain when it cannot support a UNSC resolution, as with the intervention in Iraq in 2003, usually to avoid a confrontation with the US. China's decision to veto the February 2012 Security Council draft resolution that demanded that the Syrian President step down in the face of continued violence was seen as a surprising move by a UNSC member that had less than one year earlier abstained on UNSC Resolution 1973 on Libya.

Various explanations have been given for China taking this path. The logic of China's policies illustrates again some of the principles that dictate its foreign policy approach. Unsurprisingly, China is against international intervention that seeks to change a regime; it is also suspicious of Western unwillingness to be limited by the terms of UN resolutions. It remains sensitive to the June 1999 UNSC Resolution 1244 on Kosovo, which it had supported.[8] Great powers argue that there is a need at times to act inconsistently with existing rules and norms in order to maintain international order, as for example when mass slaughter is underway. Humanitarian motives were effectively the reason for the US-led NATO air strikes on Kosovo. China opposed the attacks, but it also argued its international responsibility to protect international law.

China was also unhappy with what it saw as an over-interpretation of the UN decisions relevant to the invasion of Iraq, and uncomfortable that the Europeans, with US support, went beyond the UN mandate in Libya. It also viewed US action against Iran, where China had supported UN sanctions, and then the US had unilaterally enlarged the mandated sanctions regime, as another example of exceeding authorized action. Whether or not regime change is against the UN Charter, as one Chinese commentary claimed (*China Daily* 2012), China argues that the UNSC should not be an instrument for regime change. With respect to Syria, China had argued earlier that regime change was unlikely to reduce bloodshed since the Syrian polity is complex, has many political and religious interests competing for influence, and whose interactions with surrounding countries would lead to considerable regional instability.[9] Russia had its own reasons for exercising a veto (including its need to access its naval base at Tartus in Syria), and seemed to lead the opposition to the draft resolution. China's willingness to use its veto most likely reflected a willingness to support Russia in something that China was unhappy about in any case. The costs that China incurred were substantial: the Arab countries in general supported the resolution; members of the BRICS on the UNSC voted for it; and China's soft power campaign more generally suffered a setback.

China values its veto power by using it infrequently. As far as UN reform is concerned, China is conservative, and political. Not surprisingly, it would not welcome an enlargement of the UNSC because that might dilute its influence. Panda (2011: 25) has argued that China is less favourable to the idea of the creation of new permanent members than to the idea of including new semi-permanent members. The candidates that are collectively pressing for an expansion of the UNSC (the G4 – Germany, Japan, India and Brazil) would swing the Council's balance in favour of the US.[10] China has argued that there is a need for more developing country representatives, particularly from Africa; however, while India is a developing country, it is not favoured by China given its closeness to the US, and its support for the Dalai Lama. Overall, while China favours UN reform, it remains unclear exactly what that means.

CHINA AS A RESPONSIBLE POWER?

China's veto of the Syrian draft resolution raised questions about China's role as a responsible power. This added to concerns about China's use of its increased material and, to a lesser extent, military power. A common question is whether China is, or will become, a responsible power. A question less frequently asked is what do we mean by a 'responsible' power? What would generally be held to constitute responsibility in the West was famously specified by US Deputy Secretary of State, Robert Zoellick (2005), in an address where he argued that China should be encouraged to become a 'responsible stakeholder' in the international system.

Despite initial questions about what 'stakeholder' meant, the Chinese response was favourable. The speech came after a difficult period in US–China relations and reflected a broader political engagement by the US with China. It gradually came to be seen, however, as implying that China should be a stakeholder in a US-managed system. This view was reinforced in China by the apparent frequency with which US leaders visiting China used Zoellick's list of what was involved as a laundry list of complaints and demands seeking Chinese responses (Wang Jianwei 2009). This was not a solid basis for the stable relationship that Zoellick wanted, although the Zoellick approach did lead to various helpful bilateral strategic dialogue mechanisms between the US and China. Nevertheless, it also raised more basic questions about what responsibility means.

First, what constitutes responsibility? We are concerned here with responsibility as obligation or duty, rather than as accountability. Other members of the international system look to 'great powers' to manage the system in ways that maintain peace, advance material progress and improve equity (Bull 1977). This, however, is largely a moral obligation – what great powers ought to do, thereby involving values. How far China will absorb Western perceptions of universal values is important when looking at responsibility, which we discuss later. Great powers also have a greater stake in the existing international order.

One problem is that as China was beginning to join the international system, the international view of what constitutes responsibility was changing, and the 'bar' of membership of the international system was being raised. Foot (2001: 2) noted that the international system moved from acceptance of an ethic of difference to a notion of common values and a global common good, with political heterogeneity now less tolerated. Soon after Beijing decided to integrate fully into the international system, it found that it did not share the dominant new directions of responsible statehood – the domestic issues of good governance, human rights and humanitarian intervention. Now it is widely accepted that responsibility includes how states' domestic governance mechanisms shape their attitudes towards power and responsibility, and their perceptions of the responsibility that goes with it. Yet given different cultures, different values are likely to become more important.

Second, as Chan (2001) asked, what is China's responsibility? We noted in chapter 1 that during the Mao period, when China was not acknowledged as part of the international system, it had little obligation to contribute to the management of the international system. The question then becomes, how has China responded since the 1970s, when it was accepted as part of the system?

Third, how and by whom should this responsibility be assessed? As Foot (2001: 12) noted, 'international consensus on what constitutes responsible behaviour is, and always has been, a highly political act'. In practice, it has been, and is, defined by the dominant powers. There are no objective criteria for judging how compliant any country is in meeting its international responsibilities, nor what such responsibilities are. Nor, in China's case, are there many comparisons with the performance of other states. In China, the level of an obligation of responsibility traditionally depends upon the position in a hierarchy of power. So China's leaders would expect to be accorded responsibilities related to their growing power, but presumably since their material power is well short of that of the US, they have fewer responsibilities, an argument consistent with their constrained response to pressures to do more internationally.

Foot (2001) argued that there were three phases in developing the idea of international responsibility: the first was a passive acceptance of the rules of diplomacy and the basic principles of international law; the second was contributing to various multilateral regimes in a rapidly integrating world; and the third was a new phase of protecting human rights and fostering legitimate forms of popular representation. She concluded that China was widely considered to have been quite responsible on the first two, but that under its authoritarian regime, China would face difficulties in relating to the standards of responsibility in the newly evolving system.

China basically meets the first criterion: acceptance of the rules of diplomacy and the basic principles of international law. This legal order, an immense framework of legal mechanism built up over the years, indeed centuries, provides the essential underpinning of the international order. With some exceptions – in the initial years of the PRC, during the Cultural Revolution, and in recent examples of its failure, despite mutual consular agreements with Australia and the US, to observe the norm of consular assistance to foreign citizens subject to legal action in China – China has generally met the requirements of this criterion.

Foot's second criterion – China's involvement in multilateral regimes – is now commonly seen as evidence of its integration with the international community. Kent (2007: 4–5) had earlier set out criteria for judging China's compliance that distinguish between formal, procedural and substantial compliance through accession to treaties and regimes. Her conclusions were that, in general, China complies with the rules and norms of international organizations and treaties and its compliance has usually improved over time. Compliance has also reflected domestic and international pressures, however, and hence has not been consistent over time or across regimes. Foot's conclusion on the third criterion was similar to that of Kent in that China had reached the outer limits of the effective impact of socialization, especially when China saw compliance as threatening critical domestic interests and the effectiveness of domestic governance.

MULTILATERALISM

Big powers tend to prefer dealing with other countries on a bilateral basis, as it enables them to apply their greater bargaining weight. This remains true of China, but until 1971, it had little opportunity to participate in the major international organizations because its exclusion from the UN meant exclusion from the various related organizations as well. It has since moved towards accepting multilateral approaches to many, although not all, problems.

In the South China Seas boundary disputes, for example, there is considerable internal Chinese opposition to multilateral approaches to the problem that would include non-claimants. These views have been expressed particularly by uniformed military officials who do not want outside countries, notably the US, involved. Premier Wen Jiabao was reported as saying that 'territorial disputes and disputes over maritime rights and interests should be resolved between the countries concerned . . . We disapprove of referring bilateral disputes to multilateral forums' (cited in National Institute for Defense Studies 2012: 41). Multilateralism was the basis for the 2002 ASEAN–China Declaration on the Conduct of Parties in the South China Sea (DoC), and the Chinese minister for defence stated at the 2011 Shangri-La dialogue in Singapore that China would comply with the 2002 DoC. In practice, that seemed to involve restraint but not much more.

China is, however, often an active participant in multilateral meetings, such as the 2009 UN Climate Change Conference in Copenhagen. The expectations for the conference were excessive, many participants or commentators were unfamiliar with such conferences, and when its results were disappointing, fingers were pointed in various directions, including at the conference organizers, the US and India. China's performance, however, was widely criticized by the Western media for allegedly being hard-line, obstructive and insulting. Swaine (2011b) reported that, according to his discussions with some knowledgeable US officials, the Western media's characterization of Chinese behaviour was entirely inaccurate, based on misunderstandings of those events. China's claims that the conference showed China as a constructive and responsible power were also excessive; there were lapses in its decision-making processes, and a difficult to defend opposition to the inclusion of European emissions reduction targets in the final statement. It has been more constructive in subsequent meetings on climate change, perhaps learning from the criticisms, but fundamental differences with the West over responsibility for carbon dioxide emissions remain.

China's approach to participation in international organizations, as with most countries, was often instrumental, rather than reflecting agreement with the norms that the institution represented. While China was eager to join the UN in 1971, this was not evidently an acceptance of multilateralism as a principled means for obtaining its foreign policy objectives, but a legitimizing process for Mao's China. Initially it was cautious in its participation in UN activities and functions. It used the opportunities that the UN provided to support 'Third World' objectives and to criticize Soviet, and to a lesser degree, US, hegemonies. For some years it was not otherwise active in the UN until the reform and opening up of the post-1978 period. It mainly stood to one side to learn how the UN and its specialized agencies worked. It gradually understood better the benefits that came with membership of the UN agencies and the Bretton Woods institutions, including the diplomatic victory that such membership gave China over Taiwan.

Despite invitations to join these institutions, domestic political circumstances limited how far China could go in the 1970s towards participation in them. China faced financial problems, however, which in the late 1970s led to decisions to seek membership of the IMF and World Bank. This move was significant. Despite Western concerns that China might not adhere to the conditions of membership, by the end of the first decade it became clear that this was not the case,[11] making evident the nature of the change in China. Moreover, in doing so, China accepted the domestic legal and institutional consequences of membership as specified by the institutions, thereby qualifying its absolute sovereignty. Participation in international organizations was, however, also seen by China as strengthening China's sovereignty through its legitimizing effect.

It has since become more comfortable with multilateral organizations; it is a member of many international intergovernmental organizations and subscribes to a large number of the associated regimes. It also belongs to many non-governmental organizations. It was more comfortable with the economic institutions where the advantages for

China were more readily apparent and less challenging to core concerns. It has, however, joined various arms control regimes, such as the Conference on Disarmament, in part due to pressure from developing countries to do so. China remained hesitant about regional multilateralism well into the 1980s, but it participated in several second track economic meetings such as the Pacific Economic Cooperation Council from which the Asia-Pacific Economic Cooperation forum emerged. Such meetings offered useful lessons for China, but its caution remained, and continued, particularly over Taiwan's actual or potential memberships.

After the Tiananmen crackdown and the Soviet dissolution, the early 1990s saw greater interest in regional multilateralism, notably with ASEAN (see chapter 7). The meetings with the newly independent Central Asian republics and Russia over borders and military movements, which later developed into the Shanghai Cooperation Organisation, provided important lessons in the dynamics of multilateralism and its efficacy as a foreign policy instrument. Officials closely involved in the early meetings said they had expected the Central Asian countries to coalesce with Russia against China, but this did not eventuate. China's overall experience was positive and encouraged further interest – or less resistance – in participating in other regional groupings.

Although China's acceptance of multilateralism remains qualified, participation in multilateral processes socializes those participating not only in terms of willingness simply to comply with international norms and rules, but also to cooperate in related activities more readily. Socializing has also been influential at times in reforming participants' perceptions of their interests and values. These effects have been observed for China (Johnston 2008). The socialization process, however, affects only a small proportion of those involved in China's foreign policy decision making and is criticized, notably among conservatives and the Chinese military.

CHINA AND HUMAN RIGHTS

In this preliminary survey of China's response to global governance, while China appears to have integrated within the international system and pursued a reasonably compliant and cooperative approach to abiding by the norms and rules of that system, in the field of human rights there remains considerable international concern about China's policies. There are, however, two aspects to this concern. The first is the question of the universality of Western views of human rights which are based on the autonomy of the individual; as Shambaugh (1991: 276) noted, '[a]s long as China remains a socialist state, this clash of values will persist'. The second is the unjust, repressive and often brutal treatment of Chinese citizens and sustained legal injustices. Both remain major, but arguably distinct, issues in Western–China relations. While both are important, different time frames are relevant to advocacy of change since much of the arbitrariness and brutality is not linked to any principle; indeed, it is against principles which inform China's arguments that, contrary to Western ideas of human fulfilment, they see humans finding fulfilment, not in isolation but in the context of their social environment.

China appears not to accept Western human rights principles for three, linked reasons. The first is that countries generally have different views on what constitutes justice; in those circumstances there is a danger that international order will be undermined if one state tries to impose its views of justice on another (Linklater 2001, drawing on Hedley Bull). China sees order, through state sovereignty, as a prior requirement of justice.

The second is the existence of a social structure based on China's cultural distinctiveness that favours the community over the autonomy of the individual and emphasizes the primary leadership of the state. For China, this complies with its interpretation of the Westphalian system and the related non-interference principle which it carried over into the harmonious society and harmonious world concepts. This, as we have seen, did not create major problems in relations with the West in the early stages of China's engagement with the international system. The international community, as defined at the time, accepted that international order benefited from co-habiting with states with distinct and different cultures, and many Western analysts still do. It has since become an area of conflict, however, as the US and much of the West have now included human rights, along with individual freedom and democracy, as desired international values, a move ascribed by Chan et al. (2012: 37) to the US neoconservative mission in search of world peace. China's leaders often claim to accept the universality of human rights, but they do not mean the same thing as the West's ideas. Rather, they define rights as part of a reciprocal process, with individual rights increasing the individual's capacity to contribute to society.

China argues that in China's circumstances, social and economic rights, notably the right to subsistence, are more important, and that China's performance in raising much of the Chinese population from hunger and poverty should be internationally recognized as a major human rights achievement;[12] since 100 million Chinese people reportedly still live under the poverty line, still more needs to be achieved. When President Barack Obama stated in his 2011 speech to the Australian parliament that prosperity without freedom is another form of poverty, implicitly addressing China, he not only went against China's beliefs, but he may have overlooked the priority given to freedom from want by President Franklin D. Roosevelt during the Depression of the 1930s. Despite general progress in Chinese living standards and increased personal freedoms, since the 'colour revolutions' and some Internet discussion of a possible 'jasmine' revolution in China, there has been greater uncertainty among the leadership and some tightening of political constraints in China.

The third linked reason, not restricted to China, is the question of expediency, of principles versus interests. In China's case, this is reflected especially in its foreign policy towards the UN standards and rules on human rights. China, a member of the UN human rights institutions since 1982, has since acceded to most major human rights instruments. It has signed and ratified the International Convention on Economic, Social and Civil Rights and signed but not ratified the International Convention on Civil and Political Rights (ICCPR). While Chinese leaders have often said that they will ratify the ICCPR, they remain cautious, given fears about the effects that implementation would have on domestic social and political problems that could threaten their control and the Party's survival. International interest in China's human rights practices and increased UN institutional criticism of China became intense following the killings around Tiananmen Square and elsewhere in 1989, and has remained strong, particularly over China's repressions in Tibet and Xinjiang. When changes occurred in the UN human rights institutions, China sought greater representation for developing countries, arguing that the West applied double standards in targeting principally developing countries, including China, for criticism. When the UN Commission on Human Rights was replaced by the UN Human Rights Council in 2006, China's permanent membership of the Security Council helped it influence the institutional outcomes, opposing some provisions that could have increased criticism of its human rights performance, or could have protected international human rights more generally.

Increased representation and the influence of developing countries could be expected on balance, but not always, to help China counter criticism. Nevertheless, changes for the better in China's human rights practices have taken place, due perhaps less to direct outside pressures than to the spread of the Internet and social media in China.[13] In moving more flexibly towards sponsoring R2P intervention in third countries, albeit in limited circumstances where sustained instability could threaten regional peace (such as in Darfur), or threaten China's international reputation, China also influenced the ground rules for

R2P interventions – sanctioned by the UN, acceptance by the host nation, and peacekeeping forces desirably coming directly from the region.

The overview presented in this chapter suggests there remain major gaps in how far China's leaders accept the values of the Western system, notably in the fields not just of human rights, but also of Western democracy, censorship and business practices. Having examined the broad principles of China's foreign policy at the global level, when we consider China's foreign policy in more detail in chapters 4–7, one element for examination will be China's specific participation in the international system. In chapter 8, we return to this issue, and to the question of China's integration with the norms and values of the international community as well.

4 | Insecurity and Vulnerability _____

In chapter 3, we argued that China's view of the world and the international system broadly underpins its foreign policy. When discussing China's growth, it is commonplace to be concerned about the regional insecurity that China's rise provokes. Less attention, however, has been given to China's insecurities. In this chapter, we ask why do many Chinese analysts emphasize China's insecurity, or its 'deeply entrenched mentality about insecurity and vulnerability' (Zhang Yongjin 2008: 134)? Whilst China faces no imminent threat from any source, it feels vulnerable in terms of international (particularly US) intentions towards China, and the capabilities of the international system. In this chapter, we examine the principal vulnerabilities and uncertainties that China perceives and what this means for its foreign policy. We also consider how it views international intentions towards China. In chapter 5, we consider China's perspectives on the associated international capabilities.

China's perceptions of vulnerabilities range widely from those reflecting the general international environment to those affecting particular territories or territorial claims. We discuss these at four levels: first, the vulnerability of the People's Republic of China (PRC)'s political system under the leadership of the Chinese Communist Party (CCP); second, a historical sense of vulnerability concerned with the unity of the state; third, a geographic sense of insecurity in China's neighbourhood – its maritime borders in particular reflect China's traditional vulnerability to attack from the seas, and its land borders relate largely to insecure regions; and fourth, the specific vulnerability to US dominance of the international system, but also including China's concerns about the region and the return of Taiwan. The four broad areas of vulnerability provide a useful framework for a discussion of China's national security concerns. Here, we examine China's 'core interests'. In 2009, Dai Bingguo, then State Councillor with responsibility for foreign affairs, defined China's 'core interests' as: to maintain China's fundamental system and state security; to protect state sovereignty and territorial integrity; and to maintain the contin-ued stable development of the economy and society (*China Digital Times* 2009). Although Chinese commentators and US officials claim from time to time that China's core interests extend more widely, this is the extent of China's official position.

VULNERABILITY OF THE POLITICAL REGIME

The domestic legitimacy of the Party depends on its ability to maintain stability, foster economic development and raise China's international status. International integration has, on balance, greatly helped China's economic development and has thereby contributed to greater domes-tic stability and legitimacy, but it has also led to greater domestic sensitivity to international events that adversely affect China and that generate nationalist responses. At times, China's international policies reflect China's need to respond to these nationalist outpourings.

Threats to China's basic political system are perceived to emanate from several directions. There is a general sense of a largely hostile international environment. The international interest in humanitarian intervention and in its links with regime change, whether through the concept of the responsibility to protect, or by action to effect change in Iraq or Libya, is a major concern to China's elites. Hence UN resolu-tions that seek leadership change, as in Syria, strike an unpleasant chord among China's leaders. China's leaders also express concern at the flow of ideas from the West into China, particularly about reforms in domestic governance processes that involve human rights and democracy. While welcoming the benefits that result from economic globalization, the Chinese government has tried, with limited success, to limit the inflow of political ideas that go hand in hand with greater integration into the international system.

We noted earlier China's concern with the process of peaceful evolution that the West saw as being influential in bringing about change in the Chinese governmental system. Hu Jintao recognized the impact that Western culture has on China's culture, and argued for a need to counter it. His statement in an article published in a Party magazine that 'hostile foreign powers are intensifying strategies and plots to Westernize and divide our country' attracted media and intellectual attention in the West (China Copyright and Media 2012). It was not a negligible statement, given the importance of culture to China's identity and concerns about the potential loss of cultural diversity, and no doubt it will resonate in elite thinking. It was, however, a relatively brief reference nestled within a long argument about developing domestic capacity for increased cultural development, including growth abroad of a culture based on China's soft power to counter Western cultural influence. Needless to say, China is not the only country in the world where complaints about the adverse cultural influence of globalization are heard.

Hu's statement was associated with a Central Committee decision to develop China as a cultural great power, an action that is largely due to domestic concerns with regime stability. However, it also reflected a deeper concern that China does not enjoy international soft power commensurate with its international status. To this end, China has been investing substantial effort and resources into a cultural offensive. Most notable have been the more than 300 Confucius Institutes set up around the world, and the expansion of international media outlets, such as, for example, the New Tang Dynasty (TND) television station that broadcasts in the Washington, DC area. Together with China's peaceful rise campaign, the aim is that as China grows, it would be seen as benign in its approach to the world.

Yet countering the possible benefits arising from these efforts have been the intensifying crackdowns on dissent with international ramifications, notably in Tibet and Xinjiang (as discussed later), the harsh diplomatic and economic response to Norway over awarding the Nobel Peace prize to Chinese dissident Liu Xiaobo, assertiveness in the South China Sea, and China's Security Council veto of a draft UN Security Council resolution on Syria.

China's continued successful economic growth because of international integration has been a critical factor in the continued legitimacy and wide popular support of the Party. In a climate of rising expectations, the Party is likely to be vulnerable to any significant slowing of China's growth. China's integration within the global economic system also means it is dependent upon access to energy and other resources, as well as production inputs and technologies. In regard to energy in particular, it considers itself vulnerable to interference in the sea lanes, whether from piracy, terrorism or the US. These issues are dealt with more fully in chapter 6.

A HISTORICAL SENSE OF VULNERABILITY

As noted earlier, China's insecurity also stems from its historical experiences: foreign depredations of traditional Han China in the nineteenth-century 'unequal treaties'; the West's 1900 military intervention against the xenophobic Boxer uprising linked to some suggestions for partitioning China; the Republican and Nationalist periods of the twentieth century; and Japan's invasions in particular; but also disputes over European and US concessional privileges at times involving foreign militaries. These privileges continued to compromise China's sovereignty until China was accepted by the allied powers as one of the 'great powers' during the Second World War. With the emergence of the Cold War, Western hostility resumed after the establishment of the PRC under Mao Zedong and his successors.

Deng Xiaoping's reading of China's history was that modernization of the Chinese economy was the key to national strength, security, international stature and the preservation of the Party. Deng believed that a stable and prosperous China was essential in order to guarantee China's external security against great power pressures, power politics and the undermining of the socialist system and the Party (cited in Gurtov and Hwang 1998: 2). An emphasis on building comprehensive national strength, and stressing non-military dimensions of national power as a prime defence against the hostility of other great powers, remains a major security objective. Deng did not deny the importance of a military build-up, but viewed economic development as a higher priority and a necessary condition for subsequent military modernization.

Contemporary arguments about China's future development continue within China. Despite a substantial modernization of its military, Chinese modernizers believe that comprehensive national power that is essential for national security cannot be achieved only by military means or from domestic resources. They are concerned with an economic development process that encompasses technological advances and scientific developments, much of it available only through continued international integration. That implies cooperation and non-confrontation with the major Western powers.

This has implications for foreign policy decision makers. Modernizers and the institutions associated with cooperative diplomatic approaches, notably the Ministry of Foreign Affairs (MFA) and the Ministry of Commerce (MOFCOM), are often criticized by nationalists (particularly those associated with the military) who are uncomfortable with cooperation and non-confrontation, and who are more inclined to argue for the need for force to meet security problems.

Responsible for some of the stronger Chinese pronouncements, the nationalists' approach to security is more concerned with gaining and developing modern military technologies and with being assertive internationally in the defence of China's national interests. Nationalist groups commonly include interests from the 'left' who are concerned with the destabilizing effects of inequality and continued economic disadvantage, and who are similarly interested in slowing down economic reforms, although for different reasons, and in returning to more state involvement in the economy.

A GEOGRAPHIC SENSE OF INSECURITY AND VULNERABILITY

Issues of state sovereignty and territorial integrity are important to China. The existence of China's many land borders and disputed sea borders and its concern to defend or restore the unity of the Chinese nation influence its national security policies. Taiwan has not yet rejoined the 'homeland' and China's objective remains that it should, in due course, become part of China, peacefully 'if possible'. As we discuss later, the issue of Taiwan has been central to, and effectively determinative of, the China–US relationship for much of the post-Mao period. China also feels vulnerable at several of its continental borders, particularly Tibet and Xinjiang: Tibet because of the international support for the Dalai Lama and Tibetan culture, and Xinjiang because of fears about the effects of radical Islam on the large ethnic minority group of Moslem Uighurs in Xinjiang's population.

Traditionally, China has seen itself as a continental power and, although this notion has been debated at times, according to Ye Zicheng (2011: 259) it should continue to do so. This seems, however, contrary to current opinion. China has substantial maritime borders and there is increasing strategic uncertainty over them. Many claims of increasing Chinese assertiveness arise in the maritime area, and many Chinese analysts see an increase in US assertiveness in these areas. Therefore, while we consider other aspects of China's geographic vulnerability, we are particularly interested in its maritime border issues to see what we can learn about China in these disputes. The recently increased involvement of the US in the South and East China Seas issues has enhanced Chinese belief in its vulnerability.

Chinese scholars often compare China's geographic position with that of the US, which has a limited number of land and ocean borders, which means fewer strategic constraints for the US. Whilst most of the disputes along China's 14 land borders have been settled or operate under arrangements that hold dispute settlement in abeyance, this is not the case in relation to various ocean boundaries, where China is in dispute with a number of Association of Southeast Asian Nations (ASEAN) members in the South China Sea and with Japan in the East China Sea.

Maritime borders

After the issue of Taiwan, China's claims in the South China Sea rank high on China's list of security vulnerabilities. In the South China Sea, China, Taiwan and Vietnam claim sovereignty over the Paracel Islands and the Spratly Islands. In the 1970s, the occupation of islands in the South China Sea proceeded apace, despite China laying claim to them since the 1930s, and again, as the PRC, since 1951. China under Mao, however, did not join the rush to defend and occupy islands because of a lack of capability, and perhaps interest. While China occupies the Paracel Islands completely, it controls only seven reefs in the Spratly Islands, compared to 27 occupied by Vietnam and eight occupied by the Philippines. China's claim is based on history, propinquity and effective occupation and control. Competing interests include South China Sea fishery and energy resources. Similar to other regional states, China also has a vital interest in freedom of the regional seas.

China has become increasingly active in attempting to deter other claimants from seeking to exploit resources in disputed areas. To a large extent this has been in response to other claimants' increased activity in fishing and resource exploration, such as, for example, Vietnam's oil and gas exploration efforts in 2007–8. China's activities increased, however, after 2009, when regional interest rose further as a United Nations Convention on the Law of the Sea deadline approached for lodging claims to South China Sea waters based on continental shelves. The submissions drew public attention to existing but relatively quiescent disputes over respective claims including those of Malaysia, Brunei and Indonesia, but particularly those of China, Vietnam and the Philippines. Added to this was a US claim that Dai Bingguo had referred to the South China Sea as a core Chinese interest. Zhu Feng, an influential Beijing academic, however, reportedly stated that this was a misunderstanding and that the text indicated it was peace in the South China Sea that was a core interest (cited in Hong Nong and Jiang Wenran 2011). There has been no official statement making such claim; nor has there been an official denial.[1]

Despite media claims, Swaine and Fravel (2011) have questioned whether China has become more assertive. Contrary to much media comment, China did not extend its traditional claims in its submission and, in responding to perceived challenges to its long-held claims from neighbouring states, it has relied on non-government actors and five seemingly semi-autonomous civil ocean fishery management and maritime law enforcement agencies rather than the military. Swaine and Fravel did note, however, an increased willingness by all claimants, including China and especially Vietnam, to assert and defend their claims. Assertive rhetoric from a number of serving and retired Chinese officials was evident at the time, but appeared to reflect Beijing's failure to control its naval and maritime officials and related organizations. According to the International Crisis Group (2012: 1), the 'conflicting mandates and lack of coordination among [Chinese] government agencies, many of which strive to increase their budget, have stoked tensions in the South China Sea. China has now, formally at least, brought the five agencies under a revamped state umbrella institution, the State Oceanic Administration with proposals for a State Oceanic Commission as an overall coordinating mechanism.

China's claims and others' counter-claims present China with two dilemmas. China's responses to developments in the South China Sea have long been used as a criterion of China's international responsibility (You Ji 1995). In addition, China has sought to nurture good relations with ASEAN as part of its good neighbour policy, and in order to avoid ASEAN strengthening its ties with the US. The challenge for China, therefore, is either to accept the status quo and adapt to it, or forcefully assert its claims and accept the associated reputational costs. Past experience, however, suggests it is unlikely that China will use force to occupy islands and other features which are currently occupied by weak garrisons of mostly friendly states.

China has an unshakeable belief in the legal basis, according to commonly accepted standards of international law, of its territorial claims. Although it has largely accepted the status quo, it believes that others are being encouraged by the international community to take advantage of China's acceptance in order to strengthen their positions. In this context, Austin (1998: 3) argued that while the international community is quick to point to China's obligations under international law, it has been less quick to accept that China has rights under that law. Pressing and asserting one's claim is a requirement of international law as a basis for establishing a territorial claim. For example, as Beckman (2012a) notes, China's protests against the Philippine actions seeking to explore for hydrocarbons in disputed waters is a legitimate action to protect its rights.

We are not concerned here with the validity or otherwise of China's claims, some of which, such as its claims within the 'nine dashed line' map of the South China Sea, are clearly contestable legally; in any case, the sovereignty issue is unlikely to be determined by questions of legal niceties. We are concerned, however, with China's policies, and what China's actions can tell us about them. Depending on how one interprets the history of China's actions, it is possible to see it as a willingness to be aggressive, or to take some comfort from their past and current policies towards the South China Sea which frequently included negotiation. Lo Chi-Kin (1989: 6) noted that the use of force is but one of many variants of Chinese behaviour in territorial disputes.

It is common for commentators to cite two events as evidence of China's aggressive policies in the South China Sea: the occupation of Fiery Cross Reef (claimed by Vietnam) in 1987–8, and the building of structures on Mischief Reef (claimed by the Philippines) in 1994. From China's point of view, it saw a need to establish a greater position of strategic influence in the area, and thus selected unoccupied reefs in order to avoid the need for force. Vietnam's military response to the occupation of Fiery Cross Reef led to an exchange between naval vessels, which incurred the death of 74 Vietnamese.[2] This was the last violent incident over a boundary dispute involving China in the South China Sea. The Philippine response to the takeover of Mischief Reef was diplomatic rather than violent. In both cases, China had applied what it saw as only limited strength.

Since then, China has had little alternative but to deal with these issues by diplomatic means, as it wishes to pursue its economic development and comprehensive national strength objectives. Since the time of Deng, China has argued for joint development of the marine resources, without prejudice to the sovereignty claims. It has received only limited responses from other claimants.[3] China considers it necessary, however, to reassert its claims in the Spratly Islands. Arguably, along with the international law reasons noted earlier, this is considered essential because of the increasingly vocal nationalist views and added interest from the People's Liberation Army (PLA) Navy for narrow budget resources. As Fravel (2012) notes, China's foreign policies remain largely reactive to challenges from other states. Yet we have argued that the leadership responds from the perspective of the broader international context, and the evidence suggests that China is more likely than not to use its military strength only as a last resort when there are direct threats to its sovereignty or territorial integrity. This was a conclusion drawn two decades ago by Glaser (1993) and more recently by Swaine and Fravel (2011).

China had responded earlier to ASEAN members' concerns about the South China Sea. While no agreement was reached on a proposed code of conduct, they agreed in 2002 to the adoption of a Declaration on the Conduct of Parties in the South China Sea. In practice, however, this provided little effective constraint on any of the interested parties. Following heightened tensions in 2010, ASEAN and China agreed to negotiate a Code of Conduct in 2011, and subsequently established the ASEAN–China Joint Working Group on the Implementation of the Declaration on the Conduct of the Parties in the South China Sea. A number of meetings of the working group and of senior officers have been held to pursue the development of activities under the guidelines. Divisions between ASEAN and China, and within ASEAN, remain, however, and China's foreign minister, Wang Yi, warned against unreal expectations of rapid progress.

The South China Sea, however, holds more than just a regional interest for China, given the importance of the shipping lanes for global shipping. Freedom of navigation is in China's national interest. Most of its oil and gas imports, and its export and import trade, goes through the South China Sea. Japan and other Northeast Asian countries also have import and export requirements that pass through the sea. Yet, as China claims, there is no evidence that China intends to pose a risk to the freedom of the seas in the South China Sea, as elsewhere, under normal conditions; sovereignty disputes 'do not appear to pose any credible threat to the freedom of navigation and overflight' in the South China Sea (Beckman 2012b).

In March 2009, a separate dispute arose which raised sensitivities over different legal interpretations of the rights of military passage through an exclusive economic zone (EEZ). In contrast to the US interpretation, China's interpretation of the UN Law of the Sea was that passage of military vessels through EEZs should be subject to permission of the border state, and that of a number of other states with large coastal zones. While such restrictions have the potential to pose problems for freedom of the seas (as the majority of states, as well as the US, interpret it), Franckx (2011) and Beckman (2012b) note that whilst the Soviet Union initially had a similar interpretation to that of China, as its blue water naval capability developed, that interpretation changed and became aligned with that of the US.

These various tensions led to a sharp but general response from US Secretary of Defense, Robert Gates, in 2010. Subsequently, however, US Secretary of State Hillary Clinton made a statement about the South China Sea at the 2010 ASEAN Regional Forum (ARF) in Hanoi. Given the location in which the statement was made, and Clinton's specification that legitimate claims should be based on land features, one could interpret that statement as the US not only stating its national interest in the South China Sea, but also as reflecting a move away from its long-standing neutrality in the South China Sea dispute.[4]

The response of China and the other claimants was mostly lukewarm to the idea of international arbitration proposed by Clinton at the Hanoi meeting.[5] This was probably due in part to the fact that many of the claims, including some but not all by China,[6] have a weak legal basis. Another concern for ASEAN members, while welcoming a greater US interest in Asia, was the fear of having to choose between the US and China. Importantly, the lack of clarity over sovereignty leaves unresolved the separate issues of who can claim jurisdiction over the waters around the various islands, reefs or features, many of which are, in any case, inadequate as a basis for establishing EEZ or territorial waters claims.

In the future, tensions are likely to remain, with assertive statements from Chinese naval or maritime officials (unless better controlled by the leadership) with real or perceived confrontations arising from invitations to international oil companies to explore that could internationalize the issues; and at times from the more difficult to control (or easy to manipulate) activities of fishing fleets. Consequently, the number of incidents is likely to increase.

Yet perspective is important. While disputes are likely to eventuate which might lead to local violence, they are unlikely to develop into major conflict. There have been considerable efforts on both sides at moderation (Chubb 2013) and the disputes appear to have been carefully managed. Moreover, if China needs to coerce other claimants, it is likely to do so indirectly rather than through military action. Even where there are deeper differences, as in the cases of Vietnam or Japan, past experience shows that care is taken to avoid escalation and for other links to remain stable.[7] Clinton's statement at the ARF was interpreted as implying a greater US involvement in South China Sea issues and may not have helped to moderate the dispute or to encourage all parties to reduce assertive behaviour. Indeed, following the statement, the number of incidents in the South China Sea increased, notably due to further Vietnamese and Filipino activity, to which China in turn initially responded more assertively.[8] Clinton's subsequent support for the Philippines was taken as a further shift from the long-held US policy of neutrality. A US Department of State statement in 2012 was also seen as showing a lack of balance (Paal 2012); however, the US has since emphasized its neutrality on the sovereignty issues. Even moderate Chinese commentators, however, question whether the US has a hidden agenda. More generally, though, US involvement in the South China Sea disputes is seen as part of an American return to Asia and, linked with closer relations with other regional powers, is seen by many Chinese analysts as part of an enhanced 'soft containment' policy (Shen 2011; Li Mingjiang 2012).

In the Senkaku/Diaoyu islets dispute, a number of similarities with the South China Sea issues can be observed. A key difference, however, is that risks that a military clash might occur may be greater; Japan may perceive the US as shifting from a claimed neutral stance by re-affirming an extension to Japan's administration of the islands under the umbrella of the US–Japan defence treaty (*Japan Times* 2010), a position to which China objects.[9] The arguments supporting the re-spective sovereignty claims are complex, in some respects more complex than in the South China Sea. Legal arguments can be made that support the sovereignty claims of China, Taiwan and Japan, but no side has a clear case.

The islets were to be handed back to China after the defeat of Japan in the Pacific War, but under arrangements made by the US in 1972, Japan controls and administers the Senkaku/Diaoyu islets. The 2012–13 stand-off began with an attempt by the mayor of Tokyo to buy the islands from their private owner. The subsequent Japanese government decision to nationalize the islands angered China. The Japanese government claims sovereignty on the historical grounds that they belonged to no-one in 1895 when they occupied them, despite Taiwanese documentary material from Japan's archives that appears to dispute this.[10] China claims they were traditional Chinese fishing grounds and were annexed from China by Japan in 1895. When nego-tiating the resumption of diplomatic relations in 1972, and then the peace agreement between China and Japan in 1978, Zhou Enlai and Deng Xiaoping respectively, according to Chinese records and contem-porary reports, suggested that decisions on sovereignty should be postponed for later generations to settle. Japan interprets these conver-sations differently and indeed continues to deny that there is a disputed claim, making difficult a return to the traditional fishing status quo under a fisheries management regime, which is a potentially feasible compromise. Given that a dispute evidently exists, although still denied by Japan, Japan may eventually have to concede its existence thereby opening up opportunities for compromise.

Even more than in the South China Sea, the direct issues concern resources, notably fish, as much as sovereignty. China continued Deng's approach with Japan (until 1975 by way of Chinese and Japanese civil entities) and had earlier negotiated several fishing agreements; a further agreement in 1997 is still in operation. Although this did not include waters around the Senkaku/Diaoyu islets, based on the exchange of a diplomatic note, both countries adopted the attitude of avoiding conflict at the government level over sovereignty and maritime rights (Gupta 2010). Until 2010, Chinese fishing vessels were commonly fishing around the islands without interruption by Japanese coastguard vessels that were monitoring the area. In 2010, however, a collision between a Chinese fishing boat and a Japanese patrol boat led to the arrest and imprisonment of the Chinese ship's captain, in effect breaching the implicit political understanding. The Japanese action meant that the issue was treated as a sovereignty rather than a fisheries management matter, and bilateral tensions increased. Japan increased its public rhetoric over its claim. China responded with its own heightened rhetoric, various diplomatic measures including, allegedly, blocking rare earth exports to Japan, and an increased presence of its patrol boats. Following high-level talks and the return of the captain, the patrol boats were withdrawn and rare earth exports resumed. Efforts at dispute management, at least, continued (Manicom 2013), but China will find it difficult to pull back unless Japan accepts that a dispute exists.

A further casualty of the dispute over the Chinese fishing boat was a Sino-Japanese arrangement for joint development of the Chunxiao gas field in the East China Sea. While the field apparently does not contain a large gas reserve, this arrangement for joint development in 2008 cooled a dispute about it that had lasted over four years (Manicom 2011). The lack of trust and nationalist opposition in both countries had ensured that only slow progress had been made in defining the specifics of the joint development treaty. Following the arrest and charging of the Chinese fishing boat captain, however, the talks were discontinued.

Land borders: Tibet and Xinjiang

From China's perspective, Tibet and Xinjiang signify national security problems that are vulnerable to foreign influence. Tibet's history has been one of continuing resentment at China's rule, periodic unrest and, earlier, rebellion and international interference in a country that had been seeking independence (now perhaps just full autonomy), and with a government in exile in India. For China, vulnerability in the case of Tibet is not a result of disputed borders, although in the early days of the PRC, its control of Tibet was limited and challenged. After China's 'one country, two systems' approach failed with a Tibetan uprising in 1959 and China's subsequent invasion, China's sense of vulnerability changed. It now refers to subversive influences from external sources. This interference is seen as originating from the US and India, although previously Britain and the Soviet Union had also been involved.

Since China's occupation of Tibet and the Dalai Lama's escape to India, Tibet has been restive with periodic and sometimes violent demonstrations against Chinese rule. Viewing this as a national security problem, the Chinese government has repressed the demonstrations harshly. Vulnerability in Chinese official thought is often stated in standard 'boilerplate' language, such as that 'the periodic unrest is caused by hostile forces abroad and the Dalai Lama clique'. The international community, especially the US Congress, takes a strong line against China's Tibet policy as it understands it, and it may have some influence in raising nationalist sentiment in Tibet. China's main diplomatic effort has been to try and stop overseas political leaders from seeing the Dalai Lama, or to punish them if they do (see chapter 6). Efforts to communicate China's case through China's public diplomacy, however, have been neither skilful nor effective.

As mentioned earlier, Xinjiang has a large population of Turkic Moslem Uighurs. To help maintain control of the province, Han Chinese have been encouraged to settle in the province to the point where they now constitute almost as high a proportion of the population (39 per cent) as the Uighurs (42 per cent). Historically, the Uighurs have sought independence, usually with related ethnic groups in neighbouring states. They have had grievances not uncommon among ethnic minorities elsewhere, such as harsh government control, limited self-rule and meagre returns from the rich resources of the province.

From 1980, and in the 1990s in particular, small groups of radical Uighurs demonstrated against central government control, sometimes embracing violence. Chinese repression led to further unrest until in 2009, the killing of two Uighur workers in Shaoguan in south China led to a large disturbance in Xinjiang which involved nearly 200 Uighur and Han Chinese deaths. On this occasion, blame was attributed to both domestic nationalists and to external influences, notably the East Turkistan Islamic Movement headed by Rabiya Kadeer and designated as a terrorist organization by the UN and the US.

External influence and the need for assistance from neighbouring states in limiting secessionist influences has made China compromise more easily in border negotiations with the newly independent states of Kazakhstan, Kyrgyzstan and Tajikistan (Fravel 2005: 79–80). Those concerns were also a factor in the establishment of what ultimately became the Shanghai Cooperation Organisation, whose agenda we discuss later.

Subsequently, China's leaders have become exercised by the rise of Islamic-based extremism (especially following the attacks on the US homeland on 11 September 2011), and its potential influence on the considerable population of Uighurs and other Turkic ethnic groups in Xinjiang and in bordering countries. China is also sensitive to Islamic sentiment in Iran and Turkey, who were critical of China's handling of the Moslem Uighurs in 2009, and the widespread cautioning international response to the violence. Its diplomatic response is to develop relations with Turkey in particular. It also tries to prevent Ms Kadeer from being received by countries outside of the US where she lives, and to protest diplomatically when she is; often, as with her 2009 visit to Australia, China's heated reactions generate worldwide publicity about the Xinjiang situation that is greatly counterproductive for China.

A SPECIFIC VULNERABILITY TO THE US

Most of the vulnerabilities discussed so far, and the Chinese foreign policy responses to them, reflect China's predominant concerns with the policies and actions of the US. While there is considerable debate about these issues within China's elite circles, there has emerged a seemingly wide belief, probably shared by much of the leadership elite, that the US aims to obstruct China's rise and to keep it weak and divided. Wang Jisi, usually regarded as moderate, has spoken of the lack of strategic trust between China and the US about their long-term intentions. Perhaps exaggerating for his particular US audience, he stated that the US is on the wrong side of history – 'nor is it trustworthy, and its example to the world and admonitions to China should therefore be much discounted' (Wang Jisi 2012: 10).[11] Chase (2011) notes that 'Chinese analysts have harbored deep suspicions about US strategic intentions for many years, but a changing strategic context and a series of recent incidents in the region have intensified their concerns'.

China's distrust of the US started with the establishment of the PRC and has remained. According to China's 2010 defence white paper: '[s]uspicions about China, interference and countering moves against China from outside are on the increase' (State Council Information Office 2011b). Although these suspicions have fluctuated over time, they seem to have intensified again in the light of what Chinese analysts judge to be the response of Barack Obama's administration to the increasing challenge of China's rise.

While no longer fearful of an imminent invasion, and despite the disappearance of some major security issues facing China in recent decades (such as Soviet threats), China continues to feel insecure, with the US remaining as a significant potential threat. Military preparedness for a potential conflict with the US over Taiwan is a major priority. We noted earlier China's belief that the US sees itself as increasingly challenged by China's rise, and is seeking ways to re-assert its dominance. At the same time, the US need for China's help has lessened with the downgrading of the war on terror, and US–China relations are driven more by US concerns about China's challenges to US primacy.

Zha Daojiong (2005) has argued that Taiwan is *the* strategic and security issue between China and the US. For China, Taiwan is not a foreign policy issue, as China considers Taiwan to be part of China; yet the first item on the policy agenda for any bilateral discussion is the 'one China' policy. In particular, it is a significant factor in its foreign policy towards the US and, to a possibly declining extent, in China's global soft power. It continues to have special significance for military relations between the two countries. China's military seeks to be ready and able in due course to deter, and if necessary prevent, any Taiwanese bid for full independence, and the US military is concerned to be able, if necessary, to help Taiwan defend itself in the event of an attack from China. The periodic supply of US arms to Taiwan is a major challenge to China, which it sees as illustrative of US failure to honour previous commitments to China.

US arms sales to Taiwan are driven by strategic, commercial and domestic political interests. Chinese reactions to these sales are driven by domestic nationalist and elite beliefs that they reflect US sustained support for Taiwan and its eventual independence. There is increasing acceptance on both sides that the arms provided cannot match the growth in PLA capabilities across the strait, but that they reflect US symbolic support for Taiwan that disturbs or angers China. China's response to such sales tends to be vigorous, but its robustness tends to vary according to what other factors may be affected – such as conditions of China–US or China–Taiwan relations, or prospective electoral developments in Taiwan or the US.

China faces a difficult balancing exercise in its approach to reunification with Taiwan. Taiwan is so entrenched in the Chinese leader's minds, and in Chinese public opinion, that anything that seems to threaten reunification is regarded as totally unacceptable. There is a similar entrenched view among the majority in Taiwan for, if not independence, then a realistic autonomy. If China emphasizes threats in its policy towards Taiwan, it produces negative Taiwanese public opinion about China; if it takes an accommodating line, it fears it might tempt more provocative actions from Taiwan's leaders, as well as domestic protests.

China still feels vulnerable over Taiwan because of the uncertain role that the US plays, and because of doubts about its capacity to prevail in a contest over Taiwan. It was particularly exercised during the terms of President Chen Shui-bian and his various proposals for moving towards what the Chinese saw as *de jure* independence. Chen's departure eased the tension, and China's acceptance of the status quo was helped by President George W. Bush's statement in 2003 that the US opposed any unilateral decision by either China or Taiwan to change the status quo (Knowlton 2003).

Under Hu Jintao, China was relatively pragmatic, notably since the election of Taiwanese President Ma Ying-jeou, and China has shown greater flexibility in its dealings with Taiwan. This is particularly so in regard to economic relations and the restoration of direct transport, including airline links across the strait. Economic links have been further enhanced with the negotiation of the bilateral Economic Cooperation Framework Agreement and regular economic discussions. These help to tie Taiwan's economy closer to the Chinese economy, and therefore are not hard decisions for China to make. More difficult are decisions about international representation. China has accepted Taiwan's participation in some functional arrangements, normally under the rubric of Chinese Taipei, notably in the Asia-Pacific Economic Cooperation forum, the Asian Development Bank, the World Trade Organization, the Olympics, and the World Health Assembly, but not the World Health Organization or other functional organizations, such as the International Civil Aviation Organization.

China and Taiwan have softened their dollar diplomacy competition over diplomatic recognition that resulted from China denying diplomatic relations with countries that recognized Taiwan, but China's economic clout is likely to eventually reduce the number of Taiwan's diplomatic partners below the two dozen it currently claims. A particular irritant for Taiwan is the existence of short-range missiles on the Chinese mainland opposite Taiwan, the numbers estimated to be between 1,050 and 1,150.

At present, China appears to accept the status quo on the basis of the compromise '1992 consensus' that accepts the concept of one China, but with each side interpreting what that means.[12] Chu Shulong and Guo Yuli (2008) argued that neither side has the ability to alter the status quo at present or in the immediate future. China has curbed its impatience that was evident at times in the past, but it may believe it is making progress towards the objective of unification, desirably peacefully.

By and large, China accepts that currently a mostly stable working relationship, if hardly a trusting one, holds with the US. Although it accepts that the potential remains for a clash with the US over Taiwan, with an apparently stable Taiwan Strait, the re-election of Taiwan's

President Ma, and no direct military threat along its borders, in traditional security terms it is more secure. Yet the apparent intensification of continual monitoring of the Chinese coastline by US observer (or spy) planes, and the presence of US nuclear-armed submarines patrolling the Pacific waters, is a persistent affront and a security vulnerability to China.

At the international level, China's opposition to US hegemony has been well established and remains. We observed previously that in the late 1990s, China developed bilateral strategic partnerships with a large number of countries as a defensive measure against US dominance of the international system, following which China developed its 'new security concept'. First referred to in relation to its relationship with Russia, it was included in China's first defence white paper when it saw economic security as on a par with military security (State Council Information Office 1998). As Xia Liping (2004) noted, it was based on the Five Principles of Peaceful Co-Existence and a belief in a more comprehensive view of national security based on political, economic and military aspects. Designed as an alternative to the US conception of international order, it was implicitly critical of the US alliance system in Asia as a relic of Cold War thinking. As we suggest later, this new security concept influences the shape of a new international order that China would wish to see in place in the future to replace US hegemony.

We saw in chapter 2 that as reform and opening up progressed, decision-making processes became more institutionalized and more open to other influences, including sharply different interests among the influential foreign policy elites. The historical differences between the modernizers and the nationalists have continued in a modified form; the differences are not so much about moving back, but about moving forward more slowly, involving the state more, and being unwilling to take the next reform steps. These differences had a new salience in the consensus-based leadership under Hu Jintao, as demonstrated by developments in Chongqing in 2012.[13] Not all differences were just between those wanting to continue with the economic reform process and those who would like to return to an earlier period, or at least do not want further reform (including the growing numbers representing vested interests). Those, however, are major issues now affecting foreign policy.

The relationship between China and the US that Yan Xuetong (2010) calls a 'superficial friendship' oscillates between cool and warm, either reflecting renewed US pressures, or Chinese disappointed expectations and/or a resurgence of its victimhood sensitivity, leading to Chinese assertiveness. This state of affairs was viewed by some analysts as stimulating President Obama's announcement in November 2011 of a rebalancing towards Asia, commonly termed the 'pivot', and reaffirmed for many Chinese analysts that the US was trying to contain China. Reflecting a strategic realignment of US policy, the 'pivot' includes an expanded military footprint, ostensibly designed to enable the US to play 'a larger and long-term role in shaping this region and its future' (Obama 2011), and taking advantage of China's apparent assertiveness from 2010. The pivot appears, however, to reset a regional balance of power that was increasingly shifting towards China (see also chapter 7). China's official responses to the pivot have been low-key, emphasizing the 'importance of maintaining the stable development of US–China ties' (Chase and Purser 2012).

Although the pivot may have been influenced by the 2012 presidential election process in the US, over the years China has viewed the US as presenting continued challenges to the relationship. As well as its arms sales to Taiwan, US relations with Southeast Asia and South Asia, and the expansion of NATO into Central Asia, also challenge China. Japan is also important for China because of Japan's close alliance, strategic cooperation and economic links with the US. US encouragement of Japan's militarization exacerbates an already difficult China–Japan bilateral relationship. Uncertainty and insecurity about

Japan, however, seems to focus primarily on the possibility of Japan 'joining up' with the US in the event of a conflict, rather than the possibility of Japan taking unilateral action against China.

Despite what China sees as US provocations and assertiveness, as already observed, China's long-standing foreign policies have been based on not challenging the US. China still depends on the US for its development and for building its comprehensive national strength. China's continuing distrust of the US has not led it to challenge the US, it does not in any case feel strong enough to do so; however, there have been exceptions. In 1996, there were a series of missile firings in the waters off Taiwan that were designed to warn the provocative Taiwanese President Lee, and to act as a wake-up call to a Taiwan-leaning US that Lee was going too far in his provocations (Harris 2002). Seemingly caught by surprise, the US sent two carrier groups to the area and a sense of regional crisis developed. After Lee was re-elected, the firings ceased and the crisis ended. Realizing that war could have eventuated, the US became more cautious in its support of Taiwan and President Lee. The Chinese increased their military modernization programme for denying access by the US military to the areas around and near Taiwan. Yet China has also not attempted to balance against the US except in relation to Taiwan.

Shortly after Obama's 'pivot' address, a new strategic guidance from the US Department of Defense was published in January 2012 (see US Department of Defense 2012). This reinforced for China the strong US objective of maintaining global and regional military superiority. Chinese analysts believe, moreover, that US criticism of China and its exchange rate, trade and economic policies, and human rights and authoritarian practices has increased in recent years. These critiques are seen as emanating from those opposed to China's rise as a potential challenger and as a peer competitor. In discussions, the question is often asked why these issues were not important in the 1970s and 1980s, when China and the US were jointly opposing the Soviets.

The question of capabilities as distinct from intentions raises various new issues, predominantly associated with the US. While China is concerned about its vulnerabilities in what is generally termed 'soft power', it is in the 'hard power' arena that China feels most vulnerable and is making most efforts to reduce the gap between itself and the US. It is also where China has made substantial efforts to cooperate with the US. In chapter 5, we consider these hard power issues, including China's response to the US nuclear posture towards China, to the US space programme and the possible militarization of space, to the US build-up of military assets in the region, including the 'pivot', and to US cyber warfare capacity.

<table>
<tr><td>5</td><td>

Military Threats and Responses
</td></tr>
</table>

In chapter 4, we examined some of China's insecurities and vulnerabilities, leaving aside vulnerabilities in the military field. Although China's hard power vulnerabilities relate not only to the US, the US is China's predominant concern; as Gallagher and Steinbruner (2008: 1) observe, 'countries that are assumed by the United States to be threatening are themselves threatened by the implications of that assumption'. Certainly, many of the Chinese elite accept the idea that the US is a major potential threat.

In addressing these vulnerabilities, China looks to strengthen its hard and soft power. Interesting questions, then, are not just how these vulnerabilities influence China's foreign policy, but also how far the apparent responses to these vulnerabilities indicate a desire to achieve superiority, parity or just a sufficient level of deterrence, including by asymmetric means? The four areas we will explore in this context are China's policies in the nuclear, space, cyber and conventional weaponry spheres.

China's leaders argue that its hard power is for defensive purposes (State Council Information Office 2011b). Intended or not, the very components of hard power – conventional or nuclear weapons, strategic missiles, submarines and the like – cannot be limited just to defensive capacities. Consequently, unless China's intentions are clear and transparent – as, for example, if China is a committed member of a cooperative international system such as the international arms control regime – China will be seen by others as capable of offensive activities, which in turn will give rise to international uncertainty about China. For this reason, we start by examining China's policies towards arms control and disarmament in general, and nuclear arms and non-proliferation policies in particular.

China's policies on arms control and disarmament have changed considerably over the last three decades. The explanation behind these major changes in China's arms control and disarmament policies is important in terms of how far the changes are internalized and therefore likely to be sustained. We also ask how compliant China has been in practice.

China became a nuclear power in 1964, partly in response to several credible threats (or 'nuclear blackmail') of a nuclear attack from the US and the Soviet Union (Zhang Yongjin 1998; Foot and Walter 2011). China's foreign policy shift in this area came when China joined the Conference on Disarmament (CD) in 1980. This was a major step forward for China, although initially it gave less than full support to key non-proliferation norms, and continued to support nuclear testing and the right of states to acquire nuclear weapons capabilities.[1]

Given China's need for a peaceful environment, its involvement in the CD meant that China gradually accepted the norms, rules and processes of nuclear non-proliferation and disarmament, including an acceptance of verification procedures that were a limitation on its sovereignty. Eventually, it became an active participant in arms control debates. It joined the International Atomic Energy Agency (IAEA) in 1984, acceded to the Nuclear Non-Proliferation Treaty (NPT) in 1992, signed the Comprehensive Test Ban Treaty and ratified the Chemical Weapons Convention in 1996, and joined the Zangger Committee (that deals with international export controls) in 1997, and the Nuclear Suppliers' Group in 2004. It applied to join the Missile Technology Control Regime (MTCR) in 2004, having agreed to follow its guidelines from 1991; however, the US has so far baulked at China's wish to become a member. Nevertheless, these efforts suggest considerable internalization by China of nuclear non-proliferation as a norm and as in China's national interest.

More generally, China became an active advocate of nuclear non-proliferation. How far it went in practice, however, partly depended on China's other foreign policy priorities, with its relations with Pakistan, North Korea and Iran at times having a negative effect. China's institutional development was also significant. Its involvement in the various arms control discussions and processes led to the emergence of a Chinese arms control community that underpinned development of China's formal institutional capacity.[2]

As Medeiros (2007) has argued, US diplomacy was a major factor in persuading China to accept the nuclear non-proliferation norm. Other factors, however, included China's increased concern for its international reputation as a responsible power, the socialization process through China's participation in related discussions in the CD, IAEA, and the ASEAN Regional Forum contexts, and pressure within these discussions from developing countries who wanted the nuclear weapon states to take meaningful steps to reduce their nuclear weapons arsenals.

Public debate about China's non-proliferation compliance or otherwise is complicated by several factors. Oft-cited examples of China's proliferation refer to activities that occurred before China acceded to the relevant treaties. Much of the international concern had originally focused on China's missile exports, notably CSS-2 missiles to Saudi Arabia in the 1980s, Silkworm surface to ship missiles to Iran in the 1980s and early 1990s, and missile technology to countries such as Pakistan. There have also been concerns about dual-use technology that is capable of being used in nuclear weapon development, about which there are numerous claims, counter-claims and denials.

In the case of missile proliferation, US diplomatic pressure often led to bilateral undertakings negotiated between China and the US, although adherence to those undertakings was less clear-cut given the ambiguity of guidelines such as those of the MTCR. China's attitudes toward missile control in particular were influenced by the US's compliance policies, missile defence policies, arms sales to Taiwan, abandonment of the Anti-Ballistic Missile Treaty and US-declared intentions for space dominance.

Often, as Kent (2007) notes, what the US claims as breaches also refers to breaches of US non-proliferation and arms control policies and related undertakings that go beyond the requirements of international agreements accepted universally, such as those of the NPT. In addition, evidence that claimed breaches have occurred is often not available for independent evaluation. Moreover, in reviewing China's compliance, it is difficult to judge what constitutes an acceptable level of compliance, since other nuclear weapon states have breached some of their arms control and non-proliferation commitments.

Although it is generally accepted that China has mostly adhered to its nuclear non-proliferation and arms control commitments, China still experiences practical difficulties in fully controlling its defence industries and their economic interests in the nuclear trade and missile exports. It seems to remain the case, as Medeiros concluded, that China's compliance with some of its commitments has been mixed and is the subject of ongoing international concern.

China is a signatory to all but two of the major conventional arms control agreements. Although it supports the goals of the Wassenaar Arrangement, which is concerned with transparent conventional weapons sales and dual-use technologies, it is not a member, as it views the Arrangement as an outdated relic of the Cold War.[3] China views some aspects of the Arrangement's approach as based on Western judgements, such as not selling weapons to countries 'whose behaviour is a cause of concern', and inconsistent with international sovereignty and non-interference principles.

The voluntary MTCR guidelines are designed to limit the spread of missile systems for nuclear weapons. China agreed to abide by the original MTCR guidelines but not the subsequent revisions which tightened these controls. China believed that the guidelines were ambiguous and where questions were raised about what complied or did not comply with the guidelines, the US was the sole judge and arbiter. This was particularly the case regarding Chinese sales of M-11 missiles to Pakistan, which China claimed did not fall within the MTCR guidelines. Another problem was that China believes that double standards apply. Since aircraft could equally deliver a nuclear or other weapons of mass destruction payload, the US sale of aircraft capable of delivering nuclear weapons, especially F-16s to Taiwan, ought logically to be limited as well.

China's support for much of the arms control system in place has been significant for China's foreign policy. The argument that China simply responded positively to strategic, material and at times coercive pressures, and therefore might change its mind once the balance of strategic and material strength changes, is unlikely to hold. China now participates more or less fully in the international nuclear non-proliferation regime, viewing nuclear proliferation in the Asian region as particularly threatening. More generally, China has become an active advocate of nuclear non-proliferation, and understands that the non-proliferation norms are consistent with its national interests. To the extent that it has internalized the arguments, the likelihood of a substantial reversion to non-compliant behaviour is much less probable.

IRAN

China is frequently criticized for its attitude to international nuclear non-proliferation norms in regard to Pakistan, North Korea (see chapter 7) and Iran. While China has been opposed over the last decade to Iran's move towards nuclear weapons, it has balanced its energy dependence and other commercial interests with its compliance with international non-proliferation norms. China has reduced its assistance to Iran's 'peaceful' nuclear activities, and introduced tighter export control regulations, although concerns remain over China's inability to control the export of nuclear material that is deemed sensitive by the US. In recent years, it has supported actions by the IAEA and the UN Security Council including UN sanctions. Despite its opposition to Iran's nuclear aims, however, China opposed the additional unilateral sanctions imposed by the US on Iran's oil trade. As well as China's suspicion that the US is seeking regime change in Iran, China also sees US compliance with non-proliferation norms as selective, a notable example being the US 2005–6 civilian nuclear technology arrangement with India, a non-NPT state.

NUCLEAR POLICY

China's nuclear weapon policy emphasizes small numbers of weapons, no first-use of nuclear weapons and a high degree of political control. China states that its nuclear weapons are for strategic deterrence only (or counter-retaliation) and not for tactical or operational warfare. Despite US claims that China is the 'only major nuclear power that is expanding the size of its nuclear arsenal' (US Department of Energy and US Department of Defense 2008: 6), its modernization has proceeded for decades at a glacial pace, although its precise size is still unknown. China claims that its arsenal is smaller than that of Britain, and Britain claims the reverse.[4] Assessments vary, but the Pentagon estimates that China has over 100 nuclear weapons. Experts such as Kristensen (2011) have calculated that China has some 140 nuclear weapons, 180 delivery vehicles (missiles and aircraft), and approximately 240 nuclear warheads. This compares with a US arsenal of 798 strategic delivery vehicles and 2,150 strategic warheads. Under agreements with Russia, the US has been gradually reducing its arsenal, but in 2012 it still had 2,800 warheads in reserve. Despite sometimes much larger estimates and projections of warheads, missiles and launchers, including by some intelligence agencies,[5] China's nuclear arsenal remains small and unlikely to be strategically overwhelming. Modernization continues, but less in quantitative terms than in quality, sophistication and reliability.

In China's case, the relatively small size of its arsenal is deliberate. Its doctrine was originally stated by Marshall Nie Rongzhen as 'a minimum means of reprisal' (cited in Lewis 2007: 1), but is perhaps better described, as Fravel and Medeiros (2010: 86) suggest, as 'assured retaliation'. According to Yuan Jing-dong (2009: 28), China is mainly 'guided by the principle that nuclear weapons will only be used . . . if China is attacked with nuclear weapons by others'. The emphasis is on the ability to survive a first strike and to retain its subsequent ability to retaliate, as is much of the linked People's Liberation Army (PLA) training.

From its first nuclear test, China has stressed a no first-use strike policy to demonstrate the argument that its nuclear arsenal is defensive and reflected 'the Chinese government's political stand against nuclear wars' (Sun 2005: 28). Critics argue that this doctrine can easily be changed and, although it is a long and strongly held policy, there is debate within China as to whether it should be abandoned since the US will not jointly agree with the doctrine. Shen Dingli (2005: 12) argues, however, that China's minimum nuclear deterrence policy, which only requires a credible nuclear retaliation capability, is consistent with its no first-use doctrine for which fewer nuclear weapons are needed than for a first strike; a first strike strategy would need to ensure that no retaliation is possible. It is also reflected in that, reportedly, the overwhelming majority of new missiles have conventional, rather than nuclear, warheads.

Internal political control is one explanation for China's policy of keeping nuclear warheads separate from the delivery mechanisms, unlike the US which has nuclear weapons mated and ready to launch at all times. It has also been speculated that in peacetime, the Chinese government's control concerns may limit the use of nuclear missiles on new versions of nuclear missile capable submarines (Kristensen 2011). While one reason for this development of nuclear-armed submarines may be prestige – China has been the only permanent UN Security Council member without them – the major purpose appears to be to increase the survivability of its minimum nuclear counter-strike capability.

Increased survivability is a critical purpose of China's nuclear modernization process, predominantly a process of deploying new delivery systems rather than developing new warheads, and replacing liquid-fuelled ballistic missiles vulnerable to US attack with solid-fuelled missiles that are mobile and can be hidden when not in use and quickly made ready for deployment. While the US is pursuing ways to counter that survivability, China is attempting to make its minimum retaliatory capacity more secure. China is pursuing its own missile defence system, but while it does not appear as yet to have accepted that US ballistic missile defence is fully effective, it sees that the potential of the US missile defence system as a threat to its retaliatory capability has increased since Japan has been linked to the US theatre missile defence system. China also viewed the 2006 US national space policy as adding to its vulnerability, with its threat to 'deny, if necessary, adversaries the use of space capabilities hostile to US national interests' (US Government 2006: 2), incidentally a policy that apparently breaches the basic principles of the 1967 Outer Space Treaty (as argued in Gallagher and Steinbruner 2008: v).

CHINA AND SPACE

China is concerned about its vulnerability to US intentions to dominate space in two respects: the potential for an arms race in space, and eventually a space war. US space capabilities are greatly superior to

China's, sufficient to substantially reduce China's satellite communication and guidance capabilities. The US use of satellite guidance systems, including for missile defence and attack, would enable the US to prevail in a terrestrial conflict. China, meanwhile, is researching new types of nuclear weapons and ways to overcome missile defence systems to ensure it maintains its minimum deterrent capability. China may be slowly increasing its nuclear weapon capability in response to the US moves on regional missile defence and space activities.[6] Estimates in the 1990s were of around 20 intercontinental ballistic missiles that could reach the US mainland; now the estimate is around 24.

China and Russia have been pursuing an arms control agreement on the peaceful use of space for some years, both concerned at the possibility of a space arms race and, in China's case, the threat to its nuclear second strike capability. The potentially most potent form of ballistic missile defence would involve deploying interceptors on space-based platforms, a prospect that drives much of the Chinese (and Russian) interest in arms control in space. In 2007, however, the PLA launched a sophisticated anti-satellite (ASAT) missile, ostensibly to destroy its own failing weather satellite. This ASAT exercise, the first such strike since the US's in 1985, and itself a breach of the implicit restraint on the part of the major powers, was criticized on a number of grounds, but particularly for the large amount of potentially damaging debris that it created, most of which remains in space. The Chinese government response was that it was a 'not to be repeated experiment'. Discussions with knowledgeable Chinese officials indicated that its launch – the first successful test of a Chinese ASAT missile, research for which started in the mid-1980s – was a surprise to parts of the government, including the Ministry of Foreign Affairs. Shen's (2008: 170) view was that, fearful of the US militarization of space, China needed to balance US space capabilities. Kulacki and Lewis (2008) similarly concluded that China's objective was to match rather than to counter US military capabilities.

It is possible to see China's space weaponry as Shen, and Kulacki and Lewis do, but it can also be seen as a broader asymmetric response to US overall supremacy beyond the space field, as in a conflict over Taiwan (Tellis 2008: 193). Were that the case, however, in this particularly opaque field, China's attitude to a space-related arms control agreement might logically be different; it would be less likely to give up its capabilities in such an agreement. In practice, it could also be seen simply as a hedging strategy in case the important if not complete restraint that had long been maintained against attacks on satellites should break down. The US's arguable response to China's test was a lower space (little debris) ASAT that brought down a failing US satellite in 2008. In 2010, the Chinese launched a second such test, in this case termed a missile defence interception test, emphasizing the absence of debris arising from it.

CYBER WARFARE

The physical destruction of satellites in outer space could make outer space effectively unusable for satellites (Chen 2011). An inability to use outer space orbiting satellites would be critical for various civil and military purposes. In the 2003 Iraq war, 68 per cent of US munitions were satellite-guided (Moore 2011); this, moreover, was effectively before the use of satellite-guided unmanned vehicles. Consequently, an implicit norm may be emerging against the use of kinetic energy (hit-to-kill) ASATs in outer space. There is, in any case, a large battery of counter-space warfighting assets, such as laser, particle beam and microwave weapons, and miniature satellites, in development. Like the US military, China's military, which sees the cyber area as a major power source, is understood to have developed, or is seeking to develop, such weapons as alternatives to direct attack systems such as kinetic energy ASATs.

China has fewer satellites (107) in space than the US (455) as at December 2012,[7] but the number is expanding given its increasing dependence on space for both civilian and military uses. The 2007 ASAT missile test showed that while China is potentially vulnerable to US space dominance, the US and other countries are also potentially vulnerable to China's space activities. Both the US and China 'are becoming more vulnerable to counterspace threats – notably each other's ASAT capabilities . . . [with] which either global power can harm the essential well-being of the other' (Gompert and Saunders 2011: 95).

Although the US has greater redundancy and therefore greater resilience, paradoxically the greater number of US satellites implies that the US is potentially more vulnerable than China. China's perception, however, is that the US is pursuing a space control strategy (Zhang Hui 2008: 32). It believes that official US Air Force documents reflect the views of US security experts and are responding to US perceptions of the vulnerability of its space assets by pressing the need to protect its satellites from all possible threats by building up offensive space weapons.

The 2010 space policy outlined by Barack Obama's administration is much the same as the George W. Bush 2006 policy, although it uses less assertive language. Unlike the 2006 policy, however, that rejected any constraints from proposed arms control agreements, it foreshadows cautious consideration of arms control measures provided they do not adversely affect US security (US Government 2010). The US has been working on a space code of conduct with other nations since January 2012, but has said it will not support the European code of conduct, in place since 2008, as it is too restrictive.

China has ratified the Outer Space Treaty that blocks the use of nuclear weapons and other weapons of mass destruction in outer space, but does not, in China's view, block the use of other weapons. In 2002, China and Russia put forward to the CD a draft of an arms control agreement. The US rejected this draft on the grounds that it was unnecessary, since the Outer Space Treaty provided sufficient guarantees against the weaponization of space. In 2003, however, the US Air Force Space Command issued a Strategic Master Plan that stated that international laws and treaties do not prohibit the use or presence of conventional weapons in space (see Acronym Institute 2002; Air Force Space Command 2003: 35; Gallagher and Steinbruner 2008: chapter 3). Consequently, China does not see that a weaker code of conduct provides adequate protection against a space war or protection against considerable US superiority in space guidance of missiles or other terrestrial weaponry, which China shows limited signs of trying to match. This is one reason for the attention it is giving to the question of cyber weaponry.

Gompert and Saunders (2011: 1) point out that a paradox of growth is that as power grows, so can vulnerabilities. This is especially so in cyberspace. As China has grown, so has its dependence on the Internet and computer networking as it pursued integration with the international system. It is vulnerable to any breaches in the safety or reliability of the cyber system, although, as we will see, the nature of its vulnerabilities differ from those of the US. Cyber issues have become a sore point in the bilateral relationship; both see the other as a problem in the cyber context (see Obama 2013). Both refer publicly to the economic consequences, but for both, cyberspace is not a single domain, but involves the whole fabric of command authority over all areas affecting military and supporting domains (Austin and Gady 2012). While for both, the question of the strategic use of cyber warfare enters into the vocabulary of their militaries, political concerns about vulnerabilities range more widely.

Other countries have also reflected on their vulnerabilities to cyber attack, with the downgrading or destruction of computer systems or parts thereof. Russia was seen as the geographic location from whence many of the early notable hacking experiences in Western countries emanated, but Russia has claimed to have received major attacks, as have a number of Central Asian states (Interfax News Agency 2012).

Nevertheless, the US argues that China is to blame for a major series of attacks in the US. A US report stated that China appeared to be conducting 'a long term, sophisticated, computer network exploitation campaign' (Northrop Grumman Corporation 2009: 7). A later report argued that large-scale cyber attacks on international, particularly US, organizations, came from a PLA source and that the Chinese government was likely aware of them (Mandiant 2013). Similar views of US activities against China were articulated by scholars from the Chinese Academy of Military Sciences, arguing that 'every nation and military ... is making preparations to fight the Internet war' (cited by Lieberthal and Singer 2012: 6). At the same time, China claimed that the websites of its Ministry of Defence and the military 'received an average of over 80,000 cyber attacks from overseas each month from January to March' (Xinhua News Agency 2012). An official Chinese report said that 85 websites of public institutions and companies had been targeted, with attacks on 39 of these originating from US sites (Xinhua News Agency 2013a). While it has long been accepted that military espionage through the cyber system has been underway on both sides of the US–China divide, the revelations about the US National Security Agency (NSA) activities show that those activities have been far more widespread (*Economist* 2013). It appears evident that the major vulnerabilities of cyberspace have included, but have not been limited to, the military fields. Publicly, China responded relatively moderately, however, to the NSA revelations, seeing them simply as staining Washington's overseas image.

Certainly there appear to have been some military use in other contexts of what the Chinese call the informatization of war: Russia is said to have attacked Estonia's cyber networks in a political dispute, and those of Georgia by neutralizing its communication and guidance systems when Russia invaded that country. The Stuxnet computer virus in the Iranian nuclear computer system that famously disabled part of Iran's uranium enrichment processes is widely seen as a military-type attack; it also illustrated, incidentally, the inability to limit its effects just to the targeted country. Moreover, many countries either have, or are developing, cyber weaponry capacity.

Much hacking effort has consisted of the theft of a wide range of national military and other security data and information, industrial espionage, criminal data theft, such as credit card and bank account details, and campaigns against particular issues, select groups or national policies. It would be convenient to be able to separate non-military from military issues, or national from private sector issues, but that is not simple. For China, as for Russia and their Shanghai Cooperation Organisation (SCO) partners, what constitutes an attack on the security of their respective regimes through cyber networks – such as support for a 'colour revolution' or simply attempts to increase interest in human rights in regions such as Tibet and Xinjiang – is not normally seen as a national or military threat in the West. The Chinese military, like that of the US, is concerned about the theft of its military data and intelligence, but the larger losses mostly reflect economic motivations in the industrial sector – intellectual property, blueprints and strategies. These may, of course, include theft of designs in the military–industrial sector.

A characteristic of cyber security is that defence against cyber attacks is difficult. An attacker is in a better position than a defender, in part because the cyber network system was developed to facilitate ease of access at a time when cyber security was not considered a significant issue, and in part because of its technical complexity. The problem is accentuated by the difficulty of identifying the attacker. Attackers can hack into computers in another country and use those computers to launch the attack. Moreover, it is not clear to what extent attacks come from governments, and what from individuals or groups of individuals unconnected with governments. Western analysts, and not only those in the US, attribute responsibility to Chinese sources for most of the attacks on the US and other Western countries at this time. It is not known to what extent Chinese governmental agencies are involved, and Chinese government spokespersons always deny any government involvement. The US view, however, is that, even if not sanctioned by government, China's government should be more active in preventing cyber attacks.

While there are no hard and fast boundaries between categories of cyber insecurity, it is convenient to distinguish four broad classes of cyber attacks: attacks by 'hactivists' for political purposes and by individuals simply demonstrating their skills; attacks by criminals or groups of criminals against credit card companies, banks, financial institutions and the like; industrial espionage to steal data or details of strategies or to destroy digital assets; and attacks motivated by the prospect of strategic or national security advantage. In the media, until the NSA revelations, most have been linked with China, both as attacked and attacker. Chinese 'hactivists' are believed to have attacked the systems of Japanese political institutions, notably the Diet building's computer systems. Domestically, Chinese financial institutions have been attacked, presumably mostly by domestic criminals. Industrial espionage has been targeted on US, Japanese and other advanced countries to gain industrial secrets, allegedly to advance China's objective of an innovation economy.

Although concerns exist about the use of the cyber network by terrorists, strategic cyber security issues normally involve governments more directly than the other categories, although nationalist 'patriotic hackers' are often encouraged by governments. There are periodic disputes between China and the US that involve their governments, such as the complaint by Google that email passwords of senior US government officials and of Chinese dissidents had been stolen by hackers located in China, which China officially denied; more such incidents can be expected from time to time.

In the strategic field, China feels particularly vulnerable because of the considerable advantage held by the US, hence the considerable motives for cyber espionage. Although Chinese and other non-US firms are becoming involved internationally, US companies dominate the hardware and software industries, the network domain naming corporation is beholden to the US government, and nine of the auxiliary root servers are located in the US. Chinese observers also note that the US Cyber Command was established to pursue offensive operations (Segal 2011).

The PLA has been developing competencies in cyber warfare and the exploitation of computer networks. Yet, despite what has been described as threat inflation in Washington (Shachtman and Singer 2011), for a variety of reasons the likelihood of a cyber war outside a major conflict would seem small. Both China and the US, however, are developing and stockpiling weapons – electronic pulses, worms and viruses – for a cyber war should the need arise, but as Goldsmith (2010) also argues, capabilities and contingency plans taken alone, without a plausible scenario, do not constitute a serious threat. In China's thinking, in the event of a major conflict, cyber warfare would be central; in future wars, the combat would be between platforms, but the key to victory will be the information technology systems integrating them (You Ji 2008: 83). As You argued, 'IT upgrading . . . is regarded [by the PLA] as necessary for its survival in future wars'.

The prime future war concern for the PLA today is conflict with the US over Taiwan. The PLA wants to establish dominance of the information flow in any future cross-strait conflict as an asymmetrical response to the US conventional weapon superiority in such a conflict and as a deterrent to US involvement. Whether as a deterrent or an actual downgrading of US communication, guidance and intelligence systems, this could lead to an escalation of the conflict – conceivably to infrastructures, such as power, transport and communication systems, on the US and Chinese mainlands. The US has overall weapon dominance, however, including in cyber technology. There are no natural barriers between military and non-military uses of cyber networks and potentially, if the PLA looked to be losing in a conflict, it could shift China's response out of the military area to cyber networks; ultimately a US counter-response to this could shift further to the conventional weapon or even nuclear arena. That seems improbable, however, and it would be a decision that either government's leaders would hesitate rationally to take except *in extremis*.

That, however, assumes a strong civilian control that recognizes the need for restraint and the benefits from controlling escalation.[8] In China's case, much of the related discussion, however, reflects an assumption of greater coherence and deliberation in Chinese policy making than actually exists. This is particularly so in the cyber networking arena, where it is a relatively new policy issue and bureaucratic coordination has yet to materialize. China's recognition of its international interdependence and the role that cyber networks play in it were reflected in its commitments to international cooperation in its related white paper (State Council Information Office 2010). In the Obama–Hu Jintao discussions early in 2011, it was accepted that greater cooperation was needed in the cyber security field. Liu Xiaoming, China's ambassador to Britain, said that 'the Chinese government has been an active player in international cooperation in cybersecurity' and has signed an agreement with ASEAN and the SCO members (Liu 2011). Certainly, Chinese organizations are active in the UN-mandated Internet Governance Forum and China's state network information centre, China Internet Network Information Center, is a signatory to the Internet Society's Internet Code of Conduct.

Yet cooperation will not be easy. Two reasons follow from the earlier discussion: the practical problems of cyber defence are not easy to overcome, and China's policy making on these issues is by no means coordinated. With respect to the latter, earlier chapters have noted the fragmented nature of China's policy making and governance. This is no less so for cyber policy. The standard Chinese policy-coordinating instrument is a leading small group. In the cyber networking arena, the State Information Leading Group under Premier Wen Jiabao was the major group, but not much is known about its deliberations or its continuation under Li Keqiang. For civilian interests in cyber networks, there is a National Network and Information and Security Coordination Small Group previously under then Vice-Premier Li Keqiang (Goodrich 2012). Despite these ostensibly coordinating processes, no central focal point appears to exist to deal with the large number of bureaucratic gaps or overlaps.

When Chinese officials say that in the cyber field Chinese 'institutions and the legal system are incomplete' (Li Yuxiao 2012: 4), they are reflecting a third reason, as also noted earlier, that the concerns of China differ from those of Western nations. Western countries want freedom for information about human rights and democracy to spread. China sees this as creating dissent that will weaken public support for the government, and undermine domestic stability and potentially the regime. In September 2011, China, Russia and two Central Asian states submitted a draft International Code of Conduct for Information Security to the UN. While the code recognizes the global nature of solutions to problems that the Internet throws up, and the need for the security of the communication networks that the Internet provides, it is clearly designed to protect China and its co-proposers from the vulnerability they see arising from flows of information that originate in the West, and that can undermine stability and the authority of the ruling regimes.

This does not mean that no gains can be made from engagement with China on cyber issues. On some issues there is room for agreement, as a collaborative report on spam found (Rauscher and Zhou 2011). When both sides can agree on various issues, such as technical questions or criminal offences, more progress is possible because both sides gain. When the political issues are under discussion, however, engagement will be more difficult.

CONVENTIONAL WEAPONS

When we turn to conventional weapons, we need to look at the issues within the broader framework of the bilateral relationship. The problems of mutual distrust in the bilateral relationship are long-standing and have been reiterated by leading scholars on both sides (Cui 2012: 17; Lieberthal and Wang 2012). This mutual distrust has increased tensions in the relationship but, except in the Taiwan Strait, the relationship has not yet become solely competitive. China's military modernization, however, is continuing.

China continues to see its military modernization within its foreign policy principle of 'peaceful development'. Chinese analysts often point to Dai Bingguo's (2010) presentation to a forum in Beijing discussing China's white paper on its peaceful development as setting out a clear statement of China's foreign policy objectives, to which its military contributes. This white paper does not answer every question about China's intentions; in any case, given the mistrust that exists, any stated intention that may be in the white paper would probably not be believed. Moreover, it would not be hard to point to breaches by China of its peaceful development principles; but then, breaches also occur frequently in the declaratory statements of other countries' foreign policy intentions.

The rationale behind the growth of China's military is twofold: it is partly to meet its own objectives, and partly to respond to the expanded, military activities (mainly those of the US) in its region. However, in both cases, China's military modernization will have an impact on conventional military interactions. It will impact in particular on the privileges assumed by the US in its traditional dominance in the Asia-Pacific. Future problems of competitiveness are likely depending on the extent to which the US insists on maintaining those traditional privileges. Such competitiveness could disturb the allies and friends that the US is seeking to reassure since, as noted earlier, those allies and friends do not want to have to choose between the two great powers.

China's military modernization and its ambition for an expanded navy need not pose a threat. The reasons for China's naval expansion have included a range of military operations other than war. These fit with China's desire to polish its soft power credentials in line with its new security concept, and to enhance its image as a great power that includes the provision of disaster relief and other humanitarian activities, and that protects Chinese citizens abroad, as in Libya. China also points to its peacekeeping activities as a public good contribution. The stated functions of the PLA Navy include protecting the sea lanes that are so essential for China's energy and economic security concerns, which reflects Hu Jintao's injunction to 'think strategically about the Malacca Strait Dilemma,'[9] and conducting anti-piracy operations off Somalia and the Gulf of Aden.

As discussed in chapter 4, problems have arisen, however, in the South and East China Seas with provocations from one side leading to responses from the other side, which are not helped by outside intervention. Problems arising from the different interpretations regarding the Law of the Sea and military transit in or over China's exclusive economic zone in the Yellow Sea were also discussed in chapter 4. While the US argues its concerns about freedom of the seas, there is presently little evidence that China threatens freedom in the South and East China Seas, as its commercial and economic security self-interest lies in uninterrupted sea lanes, which would therefore make such threats improbable. In the Taiwan Strait, where there is much emphasis on China's modernization programme and where competition with the US already exists, different considerations hold. A major Chinese effort is being made to enhance its naval and air force anti-access and area denial capabilities in the Taiwan cross-strait context.

China's military modernization and expansion are not related solely to the Taiwan Strait. It is difficult to know what China's intentions behind this growth are, hence the quest for greater Chinese transparency, however imprecise the term. In drawing conclusions about military capabilities and intentions, analysts commonly begin with military expenditure. China's official 2012 military budget was US$106 billion; the US Department of Defense's proposed 2012 base budget was some US$553 billion (US Department of Defense 2011).[10] The official Chinese defence expenditure understates China's actual defence expenditure, as it does not include many equipment purchases; estimates of actual expenditure can be as much as 50 per cent more than the official level. This is not, as often suggested, simply due to China's lack of transparency; most countries do not include all defence-related expenditure items in their official budget figures. In the US, for example, nuclear programmes, veterans' affairs and military satellites are some defence-related items that are funded from budgets other than those of the Department of Defense.

Considerable attention is also paid to annual growth rates. Although military spending was low in Deng Xiaoping's priorities, China's military spending has since grown rapidly, averaging over double digit rates in the last two decades, with over 11 per cent growth in 2012. While these rates of growth are high, they are no higher than the growth in China's central government's total outlays, and defence spending now represents some 2 per cent of China's gross domestic product (GDP). (As a proportion of GDP, US official defence outlays constitute over twice the proportion in China.) Whilst China is not moving slowly in its military modernization, it is also not proceeding at a pace that would suggest urgency.

Various projections have been made about future levels of China's military expenditure, which commonly assume a continuation of past rates of expenditure growth and consequently demonstrate a 'closing of the gap' with the US. It is not clear, however, that China's military expenditure will continue to grow at similar rates; internal circumstances may intervene. In a slower growing Chinese economy, with reduced government revenues and growing welfare expenditures, Beijing may have priorities other than its military.

The relationship between the two countries' actual expenditures, however, may not be an accurate way to compare relative strengths because of the difference in the effectiveness and functions of Chinese and US defence spending. The gap between the two, however, is in any case large enough to indicate an overwhelming US military supremacy, and hence to explain China's sense of vulnerability, whatever comfort they may get from proposed US military budget reductions over time. That vulnerability is felt particularly in the naval arena and in the seas around the east coast of China, which account for the Taiwan issue and China's east coast economic heartland. This somewhat explains the effort that has gone into developing China's sea denial capabilities.

China is aware of the concerns that its military modernization stirs in regional countries, although it also argues that those fears are exaggerated deliberately by the US. China's media and many commentators have seen the reassertion of US claims of leadership in the region and the associated 'pivot' or rebalancing outlined by President Obama in 2011 as shifting the engagement/rivalry balance in the China–US relationship towards rivalry although, as noted earlier, China's government has apparently accepted it as inevitable, and its response has been restrained (Zhu Feng 2013).

In the event of a conflict over Taiwan, access and area denial in the Taiwan Strait is a major focus of China's naval modernization. It will also provide China with a greater defence capability for its ocean borders, from where it has frequently been attacked over the last two centuries. Analysts accept that currently, China will not be able to invade Taiwan should it judge that to be necessary (see, for example, Bush and O'Hanlon 2007: appendix); but it can coerce Taiwan and make it difficult for the US to help Taiwan. China, in turn, recognizes that the US is working to ensure that it can maintain that access to Taiwan. In regard to current circumstances across the Strait, those issues have dropped lower on the China–US agenda, reducing the longer-run chance of conflict. If future conflict is to be avoided, however, the US, China and Taiwan will need to continue diplomatic, rather than military, efforts that could sustain cross-strait stability in the future.

It might be argued that, with more relaxed cross-strait relations, the PLA might seek missions further afield. In the longer term, if China pursues acquisition of further aircraft carriers, this may eventuate (Li and Weuve 2011: 211). Yet China's military still has limited capacity to operate in the oceans beyond the first island chain. While China would wish to have a capacity to counter any blockade of its sea lanes, whether at choke points or along the lanes themselves (such as through the Indian Ocean), such capabilities are a long way off. The need would only arise in a conflict situation which puts greater pressure on the need for effective Chinese diplomacy (You 2008: 98–9). Despite dou-ble-digit annual budget growth rates, 'China is expected to continue to lag significantly behind overall US conventional military capabilities in most critical areas, especially with regard to power projection beyond its immediate periphery' (Swaine 2011a: 173). Moreover, despite imaginative media conceptions of a 'string of pearls' consisting of a series of Chinese bases in the South China Sea and Indian Ocean, China already faces problems from a lack of bases from which to provide services and provisions for its vessels that participate in its anti-piracy operations. While the question of bases has been discussed in China's media, any suggestion of building overseas bases would be against a firmly expressed current policy to the contrary. While that could change, there would probably be strong domestic and inter-national opposition to any Chinese establishment of overseas military bases, to which China's leaders would be sensitive.

At the beginning of this chapter, we asked to what extent China would respond to various vulnerabilities in the military field. In the nuclear arena, China is satisfied with an assured retaliation capability in a defensive non-warfighting mode. It would also see China's no first-use of nuclear weapons as a positive soft power contribution. In the field of space weaponry, China appears to be developing its capabilities in an attempt to match the US capability as it affects the Taiwan Strait; that China is seeking a space-related arms control agreement would suggest that it is aiming to contain the US rather than trying to match or surpass the US. In the cyber field, China is aiming to have sufficient capabilities in order to counter and to surpass the US military capability in a Taiwan conflict context, but not to match or surpass overall US capabilities. In the conventional field, although it may want to close the gap with the US, it acknowledges that would be a slow process, hence the shift of emphasis to asymmetric cyber (informatization) war planning.

For the purposes of China's foreign policy, the question is: what does this tell us about what might happen as China's conventional and non-conventional weapon capability expands? While China may eventually reduce the gap in conventional capabilities, this is likely to be a long-term process. While at some stage China could become expansionist, as some analysts have argued, we do not know whether this will happen; a lot will depend upon international developments and pressures. Some US and Chinese analysts look to history for lessons, but the answers they glean are greatly different. Great powers in the past have tended to fight each other (except the US and Britain in the twentieth century). Some analysts in the US see this pattern as likely to be repeated (Mearsheimer 2010), backed up by arguments that China has used violence in a number of disputes, notably with India and Vietnam, although expansionism has not been a motivation. There are, however, other views of China's history.

Fravel (2008: 2, 319) has argued that China's practice in past territorial disputes has been to settle most of the disputes via compromise, and to neutralize many of those remaining. It also abandoned large irredentist claims to territory once occupied by a previous (Qing) regime. In recent years, although China may have become more assertive, that behaviour, as we argued earlier, is more complex than often posited. China's military modernization will certainly be a challenge in the Asia-Pacific region and possibly globally, but there is little evidence of a major change in China's foreign policy approach, and we still need to ask what would motivate a change to expansionist and aggressive Chinese policies. Holslag (2010: 70) argues that China's strategy is basically defensive of its sovereignty and its economic infrastructure along the coast; its tactics in such a defence, however, are often provocative, as are those of the US. That is concerning. Nevertheless, China's leaders are cautious given China's continued vulnerability in hard power capabilities, the PLA's limited experience, the lack of domestic technological strength, China's need for a peaceful environment and economic development, and perhaps, above all, the desire for survival of the regime. This suggests that China's foreign policy approach will continue to be one of crisis aversion with its neighbours and especially the US.

This chapter has necessarily concentrated on China's military relations with the US. In chapters 6 and 7, we range more widely. Chapter 6 deals with China's economic relations, and expands on some of the economic security issues touched upon briefly in this chapter. Chapter 7 deals with China's relations with its neighbourhood, Central Asia and Europe.

6 | Economic Foreign Policy ⎯⎯⎯⎯⎯

In chapters 4 and 5, we examined how China's vulnerabilities affect and largely constrain its foreign policies. In this chapter, we consider a more complex situation. As well as meeting prosperity goals, it is customary to view economic power in terms of what it means for the expansion of military capabilities, and in China's case these have grown significantly. While China is cautious and defensive in its military and strategic foreign policy, its growing economic power has allowed it to be active in its economic foreign policy. Since its regionally lauded willingness to refrain from devaluing its currency during the 1997–8 Asian financial crisis and its associated activities, China has frequently claimed that its policies in this area have shown it to be a responsible great power.

China's economic growth has greatly increased its international power and influence to the point where it is looked upon to provide global leadership. At the same time, however, it is vulnerable in its overall interdependence with the international economy, but also in its particular reliance on international sources of energy and raw materials. In this chapter, we will concentrate on several influences on China's economic foreign policy: China's apprehensions about the stability of the global economic system; its concern with international institutions and their related rules and practices, looking particularly at the Group of Twenty (G20), the International Monetary Fund (IMF) and the World Trade Organization (WTO); its bilateral relations with the US on trade imbalances and exchange rate issues; and its 'going out' policies. We then look at China's use of its economic power to influence, bribe and coerce; effectively for what purposes beyond the pursuit of prosperity.

Many experts, including those in the IMF (admittedly on a purchasing power parity basis), foresee that at some time in the current decade, or soon thereafter, China will become the world's largest economy. Should this happen, that development will carry more symbolic than practical importance, because many constraining factors will remain. If it does not overtake the US, however, this is likely to be because of domestic economic or political events that are potentially more significant for China's foreign policies than China's emergence as the number one global economic power.

China will have reached that primary position by opening up its economy to the world, and by taking advantage of the markets and technologies of Western countries, mostly in association with a flood of foreign investment into China. In China's rhetoric and practice, economic development remains a dominant priority. China's economic growth has already greatly reshaped the direction and impact of China's foreign policy. Helped by its large stimulus package, China became a global growth centre after the global financial crisis of 2007–8. This strengthened its links with those regional economies that supply raw materials and inputs for China's assembly and processing industries.

Adoption of market systems, and integration with the international market economy and with international economic institutions, played a major role in shaping China's reform and opening up. Although China understands this and wants to preserve the positive aspects of the existing system, since the global financial crisis it has argued that reforms of the international economic system are needed to reflect changes that have occurred since the existing system, including the major institutions, was established. The three main areas where China has sought reforms are in global economic governance, global economic institutions and the international monetary system (Huang et al. 2011: 41; Ren 2012).

China has sought institutional improvements in global economic governance, and has supported the G20 (of which China is a member) rather than the Group of Seven/Eight (G7/8) (of which China is not a member). China's influence has become important in G20 summits which have emerged as the significant grouping in global economic management. Established in 1999 following the Asian financial crisis, the G20 became a 'leaders-of-government'-based forum in 2008 after the emergence of the global financial crisis. There was some interest among commentators in the US and China in a Group of Two (G2) arrangement, but this was not supported by China (Xinhua News Agency 2009). In practice, however, an implicit G2 centrality does seem inevitable within the G20, a development with which China is likely to be more comfortable. The G20's emphasis on financial issues is a reflection of its origins, the global debt crises, and financial imbalances; it is also a reflection, however, of China's influence and interests.

While China's bilateral relationship with the IMF is constructive, and it is increasingly compliant with the IMF's rules and norms, China has developed a special interest in reforming what it sees as an unbalanced and unstable international financial system (Wang Yong 2011) that is dominated and unsuccessfully managed by the US and Europe. China needs secure investments for its large surpluses, which have been adversely affected by the fall of the dollar and the euro, leading to domestic criticism in China (Yu 2011).

In the first G20 leaders' meeting in 2008, China argued for 'a new international financial order that is fair, just, inclusive and orderly' to recognize changes that have taken place in the existing system, and for balanced, incremental, gradual and results-oriented reform (Hu Jintao 2008) or, as Jiang Yang (2011) argued, China tries to have a louder voice without appearing revisionist. China considered that a number of changes were crucial: first, there needed to be a comprehensive response to the US sub-prime crisis, which had called into question the effectiveness of financial regulation and the international reserve system, with consequential adverse effects on the stability of the dollar-based international system. Second, there was a need to respond to the rise of emerging economies, which includes China, and to the special problems facing the developing countries in the global financial crisis.

Consequently, China has been pressing for reforms in the Bretton Woods institutions (notably the IMF) to devote more attention to developing countries, and to give them a bigger role, with shareholdings matching countries' relative weight in the global economy. This has been accepted in principle by the G20. China has been a member of the IMF and World Bank since 1980, and reform of the IMF in particular has become a target of China since the late 1990s. Progress in these reforms has been helped by the rise of the group of emerging countries, the BRICS (Brazil, Russia, India, China and South Africa), who are members of the G20. The BRICS now meet before G20 meetings, with China increasingly playing a leading role within this group.

Changes that have been accepted in the G20 include increased voting power for the emerging countries, including China, although implementation has been delayed by the US. Full implementation of these reforms will include the European Union (EU) relinquishing two seats on the IMF governing board. Both the World Bank and the IMF have moved to put in place personnel reforms that better reflect a balance of country-based representation at senior levels. China has also been active in Asian regional financial developments, which we discuss in chapter 7.

CURRENCY AND EXCHANGE RATES

China's longer-term aims for reform are more substantial. While it views as unfair the advantage that the US gains from the use of the dollar as a reserve currency, it is also concerned at the instability of an international monetary system that is based on a single currency (the dollar), and that is subject to national management (Cheung et al. 2011). Currently, 'quantitative easing' practices have exercised the minds of China's financial specialists, given the effects on the value of the dollar. Hence China's interest, expressed by the Governor of the People's Bank of China, Zhou Xiaochuan (2009), in other forms of international reserve currencies, such as IMF statutory reserve deposits, as a super-sovereign reserve currency, and greater use of China's renminbi (RMB). While in their present form statutory reserve deposits are not a currency, except for transactions between governments and international institutions, there is increased international use of the RMB, and the Chinese government is trying to make it more of an international currency. Reasons put forward for China's interest in this include advantages for China in sharing the currency exposure of its international trade and investments, reducing transaction costs, increasing its financial influence in Asia, and its prestige value.

The Chinese government's measures to support the internationalization of the RMB include currency swap agreements with other central banks, trade settlement arrangements, particularly with Hong Kong, and some easing of capital controls. The growing use of the RMB for trade and investment transactions, although still small, is being helped by government measures; the possibility of it becoming a reserve currency, however, does not seem imminent given that the pre-conditions for a reserve currency, such as a fully open capital account, do not exist.

The value of the RMB has been a major, politically disputed, foreign policy issue between China and the US, and it is usually linked in the US with China's large export surpluses in its trade with the US. China's foreign policy in this respect has consisted of defending itself against attacks by the US whereby the US sees an undervalued RMB as an unfair trading policy that causes high levels of unemployment in the

US manufacturing sector. Consequently, China has been under intense US pressure to revalue the RMB in order to increase China's imports of US products and slow the export flow.

There is considerable uncertainty attached to calculations of misalignments of the RMB depending on the method, data and time period used in the calculation, as well as which exchange rate is chosen. Consequently, many different estimates exist, and not all showed the RMB to be undervalued. China severed the dollar link in mid-2005 to permit the exchange rate to appreciate, but under pressure from exporters of high-labour-content products, notably textiles, re-established the link in the crisis period in 2008. As the situation improved, it severed it again in 2010. From mid-2005 to almost the end of 2011, when political hostility over China's currency was strong in the US, Cheung et al. (2011) estimate that the fundamental equilibrium exchange rate, which takes into account macroeconomic factors, had appreciated by 30 per cent.[1] This has helped in global or US–China rebalancing; the effects have not been quite as expected, however, since further factors come into play.

While attention tends to centre on China's currency, exchange rates are only one among many factors that account for imbalances in US–China trade. Broader macroeconomic factors, including the consumption gap in China and the savings gap in the US, are the main reasons for trade imbalances between the two countries, and these are not susceptible to change simply through changes in exchange rates.

Despite appreciation of the RMB, China's trade surplus with the US continued in 2012. As would be expected, US exports to China continued to rise; Chinese exports, however, remained strong. One problem is that the trade statistics used to demonstrate China's surplus are misleading. More generally, trade statistics do not allow for effects of globalization, one consequence of which is that exported items are commonly no longer wholly produced in the country of export. Given global production networks and associated assembly processes, conventional trade statistics inflate bilateral trade deficits in countries such as China that import substantial inputs for their export industries,[2] as the extreme example of the Apple iPhone illustrates.[3] Much of China's exports to the US consists of products of Asian and European suppliers, and to that extent the Chinese component of the surplus with the US is exaggerated. Moreover, if China's exports became uncompetitive through exchange rate appreciation, many of China's export industries would likely shift to regional or other low-cost countries to meet the continuing US demand. This would lower China's surplus with the US, but it could also lower economic activity in China, reducing rather than increasing imports from the US and thus leaving the US's problems largely unresolved.

With the gradual appreciation of the RMB resuming from 2010 onwards, the IMF noted that the RMB's undervaluation was moderate (Davis 2012). It was widely accepted by 2012 that any remaining undervaluation of the RMB was modest (Cline and Williamson 2012; Cline 2013). The Chinese government has resumed its slow easing of controls on the RMB, and the RMB is expected to be allowed to continue to appreciate for domestic fiscal and monetary policy reasons, but will probably do so slowly given the conflicting interests of the central bank in improved macroeconomic management, and of the Ministry of Commerce for stability (He 2010). Much of the US diplomatic heat should have diminished, but the continued US trade deficit with China and high unemployment in US manufacturing means that it will continue for some time.

THE WORLD TRADE ORGANIZATION

Although China continues to accept the rules of the existing international economic order, it has not been as active in the trade institutions, including in influencing rules development, as it has been in the monetary field. Although its move to join the WTO (previously the General

Agreement on Tariffs and Trade [GATT]) was mooted in the early 1980s, and began formally in 1986, the process of admission was long and slow; China was finally admitted in December 2001. Chinese analysts believe that they paid a high price for membership of the WTO and for some it was another unequal treaty; certainly it involved commitments that 'went far beyond those required of any other new entrant' (Blustein 2011: 7). On the other hand, China's economic and export trade growth has been so rapid since it joined the WTO that this has led some countries to question the wisdom of China's admittance and to criticize China's participation. Despite increased elite questioning within China, however, Chinese leaders seem to accept that the process of integrating with the WTO and the international system should be maintained (*Beijing Review* 2011).

From China's perspective, joining the WTO was important for its international status, for eliminating discriminatory barriers to its exports, and for supporting domestic economic reform efforts. The latter included extending and consolidating substantial trade liberalization that had taken place preparatory to WTO accession through, among other things, trade liberalization within the Asia-Pacific Economic Cooperation process in the 1990s.

GATT was originally designed to help prevent countries going to war again, by solving international trade and other international economic problems on a technical rather than a political basis, thus removing political barriers to the operation of the market system. This has not been totally successful as the great powers are unwilling to leave economic interchange simply to the market; it has, however, considerably constrained the economic role of the state and its political influence on trade. China's economic power has grown mostly because it has reduced the state's political influence. The answer, therefore, to whether it will remain committed to its participation in the existing trade system and its associated market principles appears on balance affirmative.

There are, however, negative aspects that include issues of intellectual property and lack of national treatment in certain industry sectors that discriminate against foreign investors, and an apparent growing political influence on trade. Arguably, a move back towards 'state capitalism' and an increased role for the state is evident (Lee 2012). This is in part due to China's 2009 economic stimulus package being directed especially to state-owned enterprises (SOEs), together with a desire for 'national champions'. China's chief WTO negotiator, Long Yongtu, reportedly worries that China may be moving 'further and further away from the spirit of the WTO' (cited in China Track blog 2011). Thus, for example, Hu Jintao emphasized the importance of advancing the WTO Doha Round of trade negotiations; but, despite also saying that the G20 should 'continue to oppose protectionism in all forms' (Reuters 2012), China is one of the top ten states that has imposed protectionist measures since the global financial crisis (Evenett 2012).

There are also positive signals. Given the WTO's role in managing the international trading system and the priority that trade and other economic issues play in China's foreign policy, China's decade-long experience in the WTO can be seen as a test of China's compliance with the international system. Over its more than half a century of existence, the GATT/WTO has built up an immense range of rules, regulations, principles (notably non-discrimination and transparency) and practices that impact upon the commercial activity in China's economy, and these are now substantially reflected in China's laws and regulations.

The WTO's main functions are to reduce trade barriers through trade negotiations and to settle international trade disputes. In the decade since China's accession to the WTO, the only comprehensive trade negotiation that China could be involved in was the Doha Development Agenda (DDA), which involved a round of trade negotiations that has made little progress. Despite Hu Jintao's comments, noted earlier, about the importance of the Doha Round progress, China believes it has limited scope for contributing further to reductions in trade barriers in this negotiation. It had only just finished meeting its industrial tariff reduction commitments associated with its accession, which now average a relatively low 10 per cent, and, unlike other participants, China had no 'water' in its tariff.[4]

China was blamed publicly, however, for undermining the DDA by blocking consensus, and US officials accused China of bad faith for reneging on a previous agreement at a 2008 ministerial meeting (*Washington Post* 2008). Whilst it appears that China was unable or unwilling to contribute to a hoped-for compromise arrangement, it did not cause the breakdown nor go back on any agreement made. Blustein's (2008) critical examination of the negotiations suggests the blame lay elsewhere, notably with India, and to a certain degree, the US. Scott and Wilkinson (2011: 14) argue that in the Doha negotiations, 'the available evidence, based on analysis of negotiating texts and on interviews with negotiators, suggests that China has consistently played a broadly concessional and positive role' (see also Gau 2012: 69–70). Because of the relatively short period since China's accession and despite its steep learning curve, China clearly has not yet finessed its international media management.

The other major field of WTO activity is in dispute settlement processes. Despite expectations that China's membership would lead to an increase in bilateral trade disputes being brought to the WTO, this has not happened. There have been many anti-dumping or countervailing duties imposed, mainly by the US and Europe, on China's exports, but most have not become formal WTO disputes. Since 2002, China has been a respondent to 27 cases and a complainant in 9 cases. As Thomas (2011: 483) observes, even with a total trade comparable with the US and the EU, China has significantly fewer cases – either as a respondent or a complainant – than either. So far, China also seems to have accepted most decisions in cases that have gone against it.

For the first few years of its membership, China, in a learning mode, brought few disputes to the WTO. Until 2006, the US and others were also restrained in bringing disputes to the WTO against China; at that time China preferred to resolve disputes through non-adversarial, diplomatic exchanges at the bilateral level and it often conceded relatively easily. In the meantime, China participated as a third party in many cases, largely to learn how the effectively Western WTO litigation proceeded. From 2007, US political changes led to a number of cases being brought against China and China responded with its own claims against the US. The US in particular tended 'to target Chinese industrial policy and challenge the dominance of state-owned enterprises (SOEs) in the Chinese economy' based on China's continuing support for them (Zeng 2013: 35); countervailing and anti-dumping duties, however, have been the main source of China's WTO claims. Both countries, Zeng suggests, tend to select politically salient issues for WTO adjudication. Although multilateralizing trade disputes has probably eased bilateral trade tensions, more assertiveness on either side might be expected.

Over half of China's claims arise from anti-dumping duties applied to its exports; since China is a designated non-market economy, this allows somewhat arbitrary anti-dumping procedures to be utilized. This provision of the accession agreement is scheduled to be lifted in 2015; in the meantime, China has put considerable diplomatic effort into being recognized as a market economy by individual trading partners, but with limited success.

'GOING OUT'

The reforms that accompanied China's entry into the WTO included Beijing's interest in Chinese companies investing overseas. Although China had accepted such investments gradually in the 1990s, as it moved towards joining the WTO, it set out its 'going out' policy formally in the Tenth Five Year Plan in 2000. This led to substantial Chinese outward direct investment (ODI), from less than US$3 billion before 2005 to over $60 billion in 2010 and 2011 (Hanemann and Rosen 2012: 10). China's Twelfth Five Year Plan calls for 'speeding up the implementation of the "Go Out" strategy' (People's Republic of China Government 2011: chapter 52, section 2).

The largest single element of China's overseas investments is held in US Treasury bonds and other mostly official or semi-official financial assets that make up its international reserves of over US$3 trillion. We discussed earlier in this chapter China's concerns about the security of the value of these reserves, but there have also been US concerns that China could threaten to withdraw its US Treasury bond holdings of over US$1 trillion as a bargaining or coercive instrument. Such concerns, however, have limited substance, since a consequent fall in the value of the dollar would damage China and its dollar-denominated assets; moreover, China has few alternatives in which to place its reserves securely.

The more controversial element of China's 'going out' strategy is its development financing which embraces China's official development assistance (ODA), other official finance flows, mainly commercial loans and credits, and ODI including equity holdings.[5] Energy resources remain an important stimulus for China's 'going out' policy. Speaking at the Fifth Plenum of the Central Committee of the Communist Party of China in October 2000, Jiang Zemin said '[f]rom a strategic perspective, China should "go out", actively explore and develop resources abroad through various means, and develop petroleum resources' (cited in Kong 2010: 46). While expressing particular concern about oil, on which China was becoming increasingly import-dependent, Jiang also expressed worries about China's growing demands for food and other resources. At that meeting, the Central Committee adopted the 'going out' strategy, but extended it across the range of China's competitive sectors.

The search for energy security has been a major motivation, particularly when prices are high. When oil prices reached record levels in 2008, energy security was seen as central to China's diplomacy. In the same year, security in mineral resource supplies, such as iron ore, copper and nickel, also became important on the foreign policy agenda.

China's investments in resources and related infrastructures, largely in Africa, would have helped ease the upward pressure on oil prices. Resources security remains important, but in China's overseas development financing, energy and mineral resources do not make up the majority of the total; they constitute about one-quarter of outward foreign direct investment (Clegg and Voss 2012). Other motives behind China's 'going out' include gaining competitive technological, financial and managerial experience, developing international competitive companies, especially establishing Chinese 'brand names', expanding Chinese export markets and seeking commercial profits. Domestic macroeconomic management favours 'going out', while political influence is also an important factor, even if more directly linked to aid.

China's ODA falls mainly into three types: grants, interest free loans and concessional loans. While at times it can be a useful springboard to investment, China's aid is relatively small: from 1950 to 2006, China provided foreign aid worth US$37 billion, of which 22 per cent went to Africa (State Council Information Office 2011a). China's ODA is a small part of China's financial involvement in Africa, which largely comes under the definition of 'other official financial flows'; these largely consist of export credits, guarantees for supplier finance and commercial loans, often with concessional interest rates although falling short of the Organisation for Economic Co-operation and Development (OECD) criteria to be classified as ODA. In 2008, China's ODA to Africa was not greatly over US$1 billion, less than any other major donor, although its ODA has since been increasing (Brautigam 2009: chapter 6; 2012). Unless it has relations with Taiwan, each country in Africa receives some of China's relatively small aid budget, normally not provided in cash, in order to reinforce China's political and diplomatic relationships, and Chinese authorities accept that most of the interest-free loans will never be repaid.

Precise information on China's official overseas funding is limited for various reasons, but China is a major provider of development finance to Africa. Yet despite fears that China's financial efforts in Africa are swamping other development finance providers, Brautigam's estimates indicate that China was behind the US, France and Germany as a funding source in 2007. China's energy investment in Africa, in particular, attracts a great deal of international attention. Nevertheless, resource projects 'do not provide a full explanation for the form and trajectory of China's Africa policy' (Alden and Large 2011: 25); Africa plays an important role in China's foreign policy approach, in part because there is a large bloc of support for China in international forums that emanates from within the 54 countries of Africa. On their frequent visits to Africa, China's leaders draw on its history of involvement as an anti-colonial advocate and on its early aid projects before and even during the Cultural Revolution.

Questions arise with respect to China's 'going out' strategy: why do overseas countries accept or welcome Chinese investments? Why are Chinese enterprises stimulated to 'go out'? Much of China's ODI is, in practice, directed to developed countries which are increasingly open to foreign investment. This normally has few foreign policy implications, although nationalism and security concerns have arisen from time to time in the US – for example, a hostile US political response to a takeover offer for a small US oil company by the China National Offshore Oil Corporation led to it withdrawing its bid – and the related political sensitivities in both countries remain high, leading to caution on China's part. National security concerns have arisen in other countries as well as the US over the efforts of Huawei, a large Chinese, non-state-owned communications company, to invest in them, but there have been fewer barriers in Europe. There are also more general concerns about how far SOEs are ultimately instruments of the Chinese government.

In developing countries that often already carry high debt loads, demand for investment capital is usually strong and foreign capital is relatively scarce; investment is welcome, particularly if it comes with concessional terms and no policy conditionality or political links. Even so, given the past mixed record of much inward investment and China's ideological past, China had to overcome concerns about its approach to governance, and environmental and social standards. At times it also faced competition from Taiwan. On the other hand, as a developing country that shared a history of at least quasi-colonialism, achieved successful economic development, and had a rhetoric that offered mutual benefit and equal political standing, China had credibility.

Chinese enterprises, including those that invest in resource projects, invest overseas for a number of reasons, but mainly for profits. National SOEs are also subject to persuasion or pressure from the central authorities; provincial SOEs are pressured to expand by their provincial leaders when expansion or other limits have been reached locally. Concessional credits and subsidies to assist Chinese enterprises to establish overseas are also used as incentives, and in the last decade, China's government has established a number of overseas industrial and trade zones for the same purpose.

The main mechanisms through which the government implements its 'going out' objectives are the two banks that are designed to support government policies – the Export Import Bank, set up in the early 1990s, and the China Development Bank, which lends on commercial terms and has increasingly moved into financing outward investments. The approval of the National Development and Reform Commission, the Ministry of Commerce, and the State Administration of Foreign Exchange are needed for large projects.

Increased funding for Africa comes via the Forum on China–Africa Cooperation (FOCAC). The Forum was established in 2000 when it held its first heads of government summit in Beijing. The fifth ministerial meeting of FOCAC was held in Beijing in 2012, where further promises of Chinese development aid and financial assistance were made. While major deals are generally concluded bilaterally, the multilateral meeting context is valuable for China in reinforcing its Africa links, and for African countries in politically reinforcing a pan-Africa impulse.[6]

Sudan provides an early example where investment by a state-owned Chinese oil company occurred before the 'going out' policy was formalized, and it became an example for other Chinese companies and oil-rich countries. Linked to these investments are projects aimed at improving the physical infrastructure in transport, power supply, port facilities and telecommunications (Alden 2007: 13). Chinese ODI is often described as 'oil for infrastructure'; this reflects both the positive lessons from the importance that China gives to infrastructure in its own development, and an important method of securing its loans overseas.

China's 'going out' practices reflect the lessons it learned when it received aid from Western countries, particularly Japan. Consequently, the methods it employs include an emphasis on infrastructure, provision of commercial loans to countries that are in a sound financial state, and linking its limited aid with concessional loans to countries that tie repayments to resources. China's development cooperation funding commonly constitutes a form of barter. Under the Angolan model, large loans or credits are provided, funded wholly or in part by China at competitive rates, but rather than those loans or credits being paid directly to the borrowing country, a Chinese company would undertake the infrastructure project, tied to Chinese inputs of machinery, equipment and materials, and implemented by Chinese contractors with mostly Chinese labour. In exchange, China gains concessions in natural resource projects either as an equity holding or as a right to produce. Repayment of the loan is linked to oil, to other resources or simply to a country's major export item, such as cocoa in Ghana.

As we have already noted, there are many other areas of Chinese activity unconnected to resources. For example, in Africa, they range from agricultural research, to textiles, medicines, forest products, and engineering and construction (including of prestige buildings such as the headquarters of the African Union). Not all involve national SOEs – provincial SOEs and small to medium enterprises are also important – and there is an extensive range of Chinese retail traders across Africa in particular. China's interests in the Arctic are partly linked to resources, notably in Greenland, but it has also become an observer in the Arctic Council because of an opening up (due to global warming) of the transport channels for its exports to Europe.

China's activities in overseas development cooperation, especially in Africa, have generated extensive criticisms, some valid, and some not. The rapid expansion of China's investment in oil, in particular, led to many media and political claims that in its search for energy security, China was seeking to 'lock up' global energy supplies to the detriment of other, particularly US, consumers. Perhaps some in the Chinese system might have hoped that such 'locking up' was possible. Yet not only is locking up difficult to achieve, but it would have had a limited impact on the global energy market. Obtaining oil from a locked-up supply source would have reduced China's demands on the open market for an equivalent amount of oil. The overall net market effect would be little different. Moreover, most of China's oil from its overseas investment or agreements is sold on the global market for various reasons – for example, transport costs and unsuitable grades or qualities of oil. The 'going out' process may not deliver China's security objectives, but in the event of a crisis, it no doubt gives leaders some comfort to be 'within' rather than 'outside' the international energy system.

In the past, China criticized the West for its economic neo-colonialism and its exploitation of developing country oil and other mineral resources. Ironically, China is now being accused of the same thing. When visiting Zambia in 2011, US Secretary of State Hillary Clinton referred to a possible return to the continent of 'neo-colonialism', a comment which was assumed to be directed at China. Such assertions are often, but not always, based on misperceptions that China's outward investments are mainly direct investments in resources, and that China's exploitation is similar to that of past colonial powers. Western countries that have been donors to Africa argue that Chinese lending to these countries equates to Chinese freeloading on the debt relief that the traditional donors have provided; yet China has also provided some US$10 billion in debt relief. It is also argued that corruption is enhanced, democracy is impaired and debt tolerance is weakened by China's financial practices.

While there is no complete answer to these criticisms, the Angolan model reduces, without eliminating, the scope for corruption, and China's loans often impact positively on debt ratios through the exports and growth they stimulate (Reisen and Ndoye 2008: 37). Other well-known criticisms relate to the provision of military aid to Burma, Ethiopia, Sudan and Zimbabwe, and diplomatic support to Sudan and Zimbabwe despite their poor human rights records, which thereby damages China's international reputation. In the cases of Sudan and Zimbabwe, China has gradually changed somewhat – it helped shape a compromise on a peacekeeping force in Sudan through diplomacy and financial contributions to the cost of that peacekeeping force, and through persuading acceptance by a reluctant Sudan (Lee et al. 2012); and it supported African pressure for a 'national unity' government in Zimbabwe.

China is not a member of the OECD and thus is not bound by the rules and norms that the OECD has developed regarding aid and development finance. There is interest, however, in whether China's policies are becoming consistent with those rules and norms. China is a latecomer to the outward investment and development world, and the rules and norms of those practices have changed in recent decades. Non-interference in the domestic politics of the grants and concessional loans beneficiaries can no longer be without criticism, nor can a disregard of environmental and social concerns continue as it did for foreign investors in China when China first opened up. Practices among the OECD countries have changed in principle and to a large extent in practice. In response to growing complaints, the Chinese government has established guidelines for the behaviour of its companies overseas, including following local labour and environmental standards and regulations. The national SOEs are more likely to heed these injunctions; provincial SOEs may be less likely to do so. Private companies, over which the Chinese government has even less control, may be more likely to behave as they do in China. Overall, China's 'going out' policies, despite their obvious successes and recognition of their contribution to African development, will pose increasing challenges for China's foreign policies.

While energy resources feature centrally in discussion of resource security, fish are also important in a security context, as we saw in chapter 4. As the largest or second largest producer of marine catch, however, China's leaders are also concerned about China's overall access to fishery resources. A recent study of China's fishery industry policies makes the point that China is encouraging distant water fishing because of the security dimension of Asian fishery territories. The conclusions of the study are that China participates in several international ocean resource-related institutions and 'largely accepts international norms and rules governing the ocean, but faces challenges in its capacity to meet commitments to such norms and rules' (Mallory 2013: 99). The author also notes, however, that China observes and imitates developed country practices, even when those practices are unsustainable.

THE USE OF ECONOMIC POWER

We noted in chapter 3 that countries pursue foreign policies by means of threats, bribes and persuasion. China is a relatively weak military power and a strong economic power. It is not surprising that, even if its Marxist heritage did not tell it so, it realized relatively early that its economic strength gave it advantages in utilizing any one of those three foreign policy instruments. How far it exercises that capacity is an important interest of this study. China also sees its economic relationships as an important source of soft power, even though most Western scholars do not see it as such. While China has moved towards being a market economy, it still has considerable influence on trade and investment flows as a tool of foreign policy that it can use to influence outcomes. That China is a major economic power might suggest that it can use that power, rather than military power, to achieve its strategic objectives.

Most countries use economic power in each of the three diplomatic instruments. Sanctions under the United Nations are a legitimate form of coercion, many countries have aid programmes that commonly have political objectives, and the promise of markets or resource supplies are often persuasive influences. Great powers often use economic diplomacy to achieve their political objectives. Famously, President Dwight Eisenhower brought oil supply and financial pressure on Britain, in particular, to force the withdrawal of British, French and Israeli forces from their Suez Canal adventure in 1956; among other examples, the US has mandated unilateral sanctions on Iran over its oil exports. The record of success of such use is mixed. China has certain advantages in its domestic economic controls, but given its global interdependence, it is also vulnerable to economic retaliation. Particular fears have been expressed, however, that China's use of economic power threatens Western values (Wu 2009; Glaser 2012).

A major economic power like China does not always have to be explicit in its coercion. A country that is economically dependent upon China tends to be sensitive to China's interests without China needing to make its wishes explicit. Thus, given Cambodia's dependence on China's aid, the Cambodian chair's actions at the Association of Southeast Asian Nations (ASEAN) 2012 Summit, which favoured China's view over that of many of the other ASEAN members and led to a failure to agree to a final communiqué, may have needed little more than a hint from China or from a Chinese representative seeking to please the leadership.

There have, however, been a number of explicit examples of China's use of economic coercion, most notably with respect to countries selling arms to Taiwan and to foreign leaders meeting with the Dalai Lama. Underlying China's responses are its concerns for its territorial unity; in the past, powerful forces and interests have been more overtly threatening to that unity. While to a degree unity depends on China's domestic enforcement of its control or, in the case of Taiwan, its policies towards potential control, it is sensitive to international opinion and actions that directly or indirectly affect Taiwan, Tibet and, to a lesser extent, Xinjiang.

Two major examples of economic coercion relate to European sales of major items of military equipment to Taiwan, which China viewed as threatening or potentially undermining its territorial unity. In 1981, the Netherlands government authorized the sale of two submarines to Taiwan. In response, China expelled the Dutch ambassador, downgraded the relationship, and suspended diplomatic relations for three years. In 1992, French sales of military aircraft to Taiwan resulted in the closure of its consulate in Guangzhou, which was important to French commercial activities. The German military industry was also keen to sell arms to Taiwan, but given the previous examples, this was ruled out by successive leaders for fear of economic reprisals.

In Chinese eyes, the Dalai Lama poses a threat to China's territorial integrity and therefore so do his meetings with foreign leaders. This remains China's position despite general acceptance, at least by the major powers, that China has sovereignty over Tibet. While the Dalai Lama travelled widely throughout the world as a religious leader, and Chinese opposition to his contacts was interpreted in the West as an attack on freedom of religion, China was viewing the Dalai Lama as the leader of a government in exile; hence China's negative responses to meetings between the Dalai Lama and Western leaders, and the significant consequences that followed. While at times China's threats do not amount to much, often these threats are not empty. Fuchs and Klann (2010) have estimated that over the period 2002 to 2009, China's responses to leaders' meetings with the Dalai Lama led on average to a significant reduction in export sales in the following year, although that reduction did not last into the second year after the meeting.

Arms sales to Taiwan and the Dalai Lama case are seen by China as defensive or deterrent uses of economic weapons. Others are less simply defensive. From discussions with well-connected Chinese scholars following Australian leaders' criticisms of the killings around Tiananmen Square in 1989, it is understood that the State Council was asked to examine the possibility of placing an embargo on Australian supplies to China of iron ore and coal. The finding, however, was that such an embargo would disrupt the Baoshan steelworks operations, given their requirement for specific grades and qualities of iron ore and coal that Australia in particular provided.

Australia had apparently been targeted not only for its outspoken criticisms but because it had limited means of retaliation, unlike the similarly critical US. This pattern is not uncommon. Salmon exports from Norway to China were reduced substantially following the Nobel Prize Committee's award of the 2010 Peace Prize to Liu Xiaobo, a Chinese dissident.[7] Following disputed claims by the Philippines in the South China Sea, Chinese quarantine officials allegedly found pests in Filipino banana shipments intended for China, and imports were blocked and inspections of other fruit were slowed. This is not an uncommon tactic in international disputes; if officially sanctioned, it is deniable, and if it is simply a bureaucratic decision, it may be tolerated for a time at more senior levels while convenient to do so. This was an argument made about customs barriers put on exports of rare earths to Japan in response to Japan's arrest of a Chinese fishing captain in 2010 in the Senkaku/Diaoyu Islands as discussed in chapter 5. In this case, whether authorized by China's leaders or not, the long-term effects for China are not likely to be beneficial, as China's move has stimulated Japanese and others' activity to find alternative sources of rare earths. Zeng (2013) points to the possibility of retaliatory responses in WTO dispute settlement cases between the US and China in an attempt to influence the settlement outcomes, although it seems that this has had limited success. Threats of retaliatory responses were also made to the EU over a trade dispute regarding solar products (Khor 2013).

Wu (2009) argues that, even with globalization, China's ability to control foreign capital within its own territory provides it with a capacity to impose political values on foreign investors from the developed countries that compete for business opportunities in China.[8] Thus, although Western engagement with China has influenced China to adopt many Western norms, as we have seen in its involvement with the international economic system, there may have been an influence in the other direction on Western norms and values because of Western industry's dependence on China's economy. It is also evident that China is willing to use its economic power when its interests are affected, or when it has its own political and strategic objectives. In regard to larger countries, it will proceed cautiously, but in regard to its core interests, it will use its economic power, even if this comes at a cost. In regard to smaller countries that have less ability to counter China's actions, it will proceed more freely.

In chapter 7, we examine China's policies towards its neighbourhood and related institutions, and towards Asian regional trade, financial developments, trade agreements and financial reforms, as well as political and strategic policies, in a broader examination of China's foreign policies towards its neighbours.

7 | China, Its Neighbours and Beyond _____

'For China, it's all about America' headlined a Michael Auslin (2012) article, drawing attention to China's lack of other close relationships. Yet, four major powers – the US, Russia, India and Japan – together with North and South Korea and members of the Association of Southeast Asian Nations (ASEAN), interact with China, and China's neighbourhood reflects a dynamic interplay of geopolitical influences, ambitions and tensions. With extensive land borders and often disputed sea borders, China is party and at times central to many of those influences and tensions. Chinese relationships with its neighbours are not all directly about the US, nor are China's efforts to sustain national unity, but they are often concerned with countering US activities or at times furthering China's influence with the US.

China's strategic analysts commonly see US relationships with countries in China's neighbourhood as aimed at bolstering US competition with China to maintain its regional dominance. This has been reinforced by the US 'pivot', a strategic rebalancing towards Asia that involves expanding, among other things, the US's military footprint in Asia. Given the discussion in chapters 4 and 8, we limit attention here to how the pivot relates to issues of regional economic order and related institutions. We have discussed most of China's global and wide-ranging interests in resources and markets with countries beyond the region in previous chapters. In this chapter, we limit coverage beyond the region to China's relations with Europe.

China's neighbourhood has extensive boundaries; it is best defined here in terms of China's economic or security interdependencies, thereby embracing Russia, Central Asia, East Asia and South Asia. Without being exhaustive, we look at China's bilateral relations with the major powers in its neighbourhood or periphery. Before doing so, however, we consider how China's engagement with its neighbourhood took on a new shape after the end of the Cold War. Given its need for a peaceful international environment for its economic development, a good neighbour policy has been a priority for China's foreign policy (Chen 1993; Chung 2009) since the Fourteenth National Party Congress in 1992. In the 1990s (as in the 1960s), it resolved by negotiation disputes over almost all its land borders, including those with Russia; in doing so, as Fravel (2008) has noted, China settled for less than half the outstanding claims that it had maintained historically. Border disputes with India remain, but they have largely stabilized. As we saw in chapter 4, however, disputes remain over various maritime borders, notably in the South and East China Seas.

China's changed approach to its neighbourhood was caused partly by the cold diplomatic environment in which it found itself after the 1989 Tiananmen Square killings, and partly by a need to fill the vacuum left by the dissolution of the Soviet Union in 1991. Although, as noted previously, one response of China's foreign policy was to look forward to global multipolarity, at the end of the Cold War, this was not forthcoming. While China looked for bilateral strategic partnerships in its neighbourhood, it also embraced multilateralism. China had absorbed lessons from its initially tentative involvement in the 1980s with regional institutions, such as the Pacific Economic Cooperation Council, and with other track two mechanisms. These gave it confidence to participate in official multilateral meetings such as the Asia-Pacific Economic Cooperation (APEC) gathering in 1991, and the ASEAN Regional Forum (ARF) in 1994, even though its initial participation was primarily intended to defend its interests, including those in regard to Taiwan. These experiences helped China accept the idea of multilateralism as important in its approach to ASEAN, and multilateralism was endorsed as one element of China's foreign policy in 1997.[1]

ASEAN

Although China had already developed bilateral relationships with some ASEAN members prior to the change, the links were generally weak. During much of the Cold War, Vietnam and Cambodia had posed regional problems for China, and the smaller ASEAN members leaned towards the West and against China. ASEAN, however, was less willing than Western countries to isolate China after the 1989 Tiananmen upheaval, and reached out to China (Shambaugh 2005: 26). In 1991 China's foreign minister, Qian Qichen, was invited to ASEAN's annual ministerial meeting, and cooperative relations developed leading to China gaining dialogue partner status with ASEAN in 1996. In 2001, China formally proposed a China–ASEAN Free Trade Agreement (CAFTA) which was accepted by ASEAN and came into operation in 2010. The agreement provided favourable terms for ASEAN, including an early lowering of some tariffs and beneficial treatment for exports of poorer ASEAN members to China.

China's regional policy included participation in institutions such as APEC and the ARF, and in shaping international cooperation processes in ASEAN+3 (China, Japan and South Korea).[2] China became active in regional financial cooperation in 1997 during the Asian financial crisis. Japan proposed an Asian monetary fund that would provide financial support to countries affected by the crisis. This idea was not supported by the International Monetary Fund (IMF), the US, nor China. China, however, recognized that there were financial capacity limitations in the IMF and gaps in available regional financial mechanisms. In 2000, Japan proposed the Chiang Mai Initiative (CMI), which was envisaged to monitor capital movements and establish a set of bilateral currency swap arrangements among the ASEAN+3 members. In contrast to its attitude to the Asian monetary fund, China strongly supported the idea of a CMI (Jiang 2012). The reasons for this support included wide regional resentment of the IMF and the US for their weak responses to the Asian financial crisis, and recognition of regional pressure to act regionally. Since the CMI did not compete with the IMF, the IMF and the US were more relaxed about it. There had also been prior consultation between Japanese and Chinese officials. The emergence of the CMI at an early ASEAN+3 meeting tended to institutionalize the relationship initially around the CMI.

Although recognized as perhaps the first specific act of regional economic cooperation, the CMI was limited and symbolic rather than substantive, as illustrated in 2008 when the CMI was unable to respond effectively to the regional consequences of the global financial crisis. Following this, ASEAN+3 agreed to multilateralize the bilateral swap arrangements, and the CMI Multilateral (CMIM), a self-managed reserve pooling arrangement with enlarged funds available, was established. China, Japan and South Korea account for most of the funds committed. Questions remain, however, about how effective the new arrangements are and, given its close links with the IMF, whether it is truly regional (Hill and Menon 2012). Nevertheless, the CMIM has helped develop a sense of region that has strengthened ASEAN+3 to the point where it could potentially be a major regional economic institution.

China's ASEAN policy has two dimensions. First, China wants to ensure that ASEAN does not bandwagon with the US against China. Thus China built upon the favourable view of itself and its cooperative measures during the Asian financial crisis, which included providing financial support to Thailand and Indonesia, and its regional monetary policy activism. Moreover, China was concerned that its entry into the World Trade Organization (WTO) in 2001 might disadvantage

ASEAN members and drive them closer to the US. Trade between ASEAN and China has increased substantially, however, helped by CAFTA; in two-way trade terms, China is now ASEAN's second largest trading partner, exceeded only by trade amongst the ten ASEAN members themselves.[3] ASEAN's fear of China's growing strength had been countered by China's peaceful rise/development rhetoric early in the twenty-first century, and by the symbolism of it signing the ASEAN Treaty of Amity and Cooperation in 2003.

ASEAN has also held concerns about Chinese activities in the Spratly Islands in the South China Sea, notably on Mischief Reef in 1995 in the face of Filipino sovereignty claims. Since 2010, concerns over islands in the South and East China Seas have returned, undermining China's peaceful rise rhetoric. As noted in chapter 4, ASEAN's concerns in the South China Sea were not necessarily a result of China's unilateral actions; China's actions were largely triggered by responses to a UN Convention on the Law of the Sea deadline for establishing claims. Yet China's relations with ASEAN as a consensus-based institution have been affected given that at its July 2012 ASEAN ministerial meeting, for the first time in its history, ASEAN could not reach agreement on a communiqué over references to the disputes, arguably because of China's influence over the Cambodian chair.

The second dimension of China's ASEAN policy relates to ASEAN's role in regional multilateral institutions. Regional cooperation and economic integration have been important objectives for Southeast Asian countries. Two distinct cooperation philosophies and geopolitical drives are apparent: an open formulation of the Western oriented countries linked to the US and Japan in groups such as APEC; and a closed, Asian-only group of East and Northeast Asian countries, including China, as in ASEAN+3. ASEAN has effectively managed both forms of integration with considerable overlap of memberships: China is a member of APEC and the US is in the East Asia Summit

(EAS), but differences remain. The ASEAN way of decision making through dialogue, consensus and non-interference in the internal affairs of other countries suits China's preferences, but China did not move to exclude Australia, India and New Zealand from membership of the EAS nor, later, the US and Russia. In their competition for leadership in Asia, however, both China and Japan find it convenient to view ASEAN as the organizational centre of the region.

In the 1970s and 1990s there were debates about whether China, as a global power, had a regional policy; in particular, some, such as Zhang and Tang (2005) argued that China had regional rather than global interests. Part of the difference here lies in the emphasis on multilateral rather than bilateral links. China's earlier preferences for bilateral relationships needed to change if it wanted to develop relations with ASEAN; this was similarly so with the Shanghai Cooperation Organisation (SCO). Given the rapid changes in China's domestic and international environment, by the 1990s it had both regional and global interests. It also had a regional policy with a greater acceptance of multilateralism; this implied supporting and shaping efforts for an Asian regional community and an emerging regional order.

THE UNITED STATES/TRANS-PACIFIC PARTNERSHIP

In 1990, Malaysia proposed the establishment of the East Asian Economic Group, a regional grouping that would include the then six ASEAN members together with China, Japan and South Korea. Strongly opposed by the US, with Japan declining membership, it survived with little effect as the East Asia Economic Caucus (EAEC) until 1996 when ASEM, including Japan, restored the EAEC concept. The US was more receptive, and indicated that it would not oppose EAEC 'so long as it did not split the Pacific Rim down the middle' (Stubbs 2002: 443).

It has been argued that US President Barack Obama's 2011 announcement of the rebalancing of US policy towards Asia, or the 'pivot', has the potential to do just that. An important economic component of the pivot is the Trans-Pacific Strategic Economic Partnership Agreement, now known as the Trans-Pacific Partnership (TPP) Agreement. In 2005, Brunei, Chile, Singapore and New Zealand sought to establish a free trade zone that would be open to membership by others. The US joined in 2008 and substantially expanded the TPP Agreement's scope and direction including what Secretary of State Hillary Clinton (2011) noted was adding 'values' to economic issues. Although the TPP Agreement was intended to deal with behind-the-borders regulatory and other barriers to trade, the US focus, as well as being on state-owned enterprises, is on property rights, and labour and environmental law, which are not priority issues for improving market efficiency but potentially benefit US economic interests. The TPP Agreement is not just an economic agreement; the US agenda is powerfully driven by foreign policy and geopolitical considerations (Armstrong 2011; Capling and Ravenhill 2013). As envisaged by the US, the TPP Agreement would be another discriminatory, rather than an open, agreement; and the standards required for labour, environment and intellectual property could not be met by a number of developing countries in the region including China, India, Indonesia and probably Vietnam, which would effectively split the region down the middle.

Officially, China has responded mildly to developments in the TPP Agreement negotiations. A Ministry of Foreign Affairs (MFA) spokesperson said that China has followed progress on the TPP Agreement negotiations and is ready to maintain communication with relevant members (cited in Swaine 2012c). China's senior trade negotiator Long Yongtu said that China was taking an active interest in the TPP and was preparing to engage on it with the US (Fu Jing 2013). It is probable that Beijing doubts the likely effectiveness of the negotiations given the existence of other trade agreements including CAFTA, and other economic integration processes being negotiated, such as the Regional Comprehensive Economic Partnership (RCEP), an ASEAN initiative supported by China and Japan.[4] Many Chinese commentators are more critical of the US motives behind its membership of the TPP Agreement, which they see as political rather than economic in intent.[5] While it reinforces Chinese beliefs that the US wants to contain China and hold back its economic development, there is also scepticism about the ultimate outcome; MFA vice foreign minister Fu Ying doubted whether containment of China was feasible in a globalizing world (see interview in Yoon 2012).

NORTH KOREA

China's most complex, regional relationship with North Korea is substantially, but not wholly, about the US. North Korea's behaviour has been both provocative and unpredictable since its establishment in 1948, and most particularly from 1950 when North Korea invaded South Korea, and China sided with North Korea, incurring heavy casualties. An armistice between North Korea and the US-led UN Command was agreed in 1953, but no peace agreement has ever been signed. There have been long periods of international concern, initially about North Korea's handling of plutonium from its small nuclear power plants, and then about moves to achieve a nuclear weapon capability which, at least as a nuclear device, it has achieved. This has resulted in confrontation between the US and North Korea since the early 1990s, with China becoming increasingly involved.

Considerable efforts were made over nearly 20 years to reconcile North Korea's security and power needs with the international community's desire for a non-proliferation compliant, peaceful, nuclear power regime in Pyongyang. These efforts were linked for a number of years to a further exercise in multilateralism, the Six Party Talks (involving China, Japan, Russia, North Korea, South Korea and the US) hosted by China.

Many Western commentators argue that North Korea's foreign policy is 'far from reality', but others, and many Chinese analysts, argue that North Korea's security concerns are indeed real.[6] China's foreign policy towards North Korea is now increasingly criticized within China as being both self-defeating and unhelpful to regional stability. The US, Japan and South Korea have at various times expressed annoyance and frustration at China's apparent lack of concern about North Korea's nuclear proliferation and its unwillingness to pressure North Korea to move towards denuclearization of the Korean peninsula.

China's concerns with North Korea differ from those of the US. While the US sees Pyongyang's nuclear activities as security threats, China views them as a nuclear proliferation problem arising from North Korea's concerns over US threats to its security. Despite, or perhaps because of, this difference, important opportunities were missed on both sides and the Six Party Talks ended in failure, leaving deep scars in both the US and North Korea. Efforts continue to revive the talks, with China keen to maintain a central role. That North Korea has enshrined in its constitution its nuclear weapon status and apparently in 2013 even disavowed the long-standing ceasefire will probably make any further talks more difficult.

China's leaders reportedly remain anxious about US strategic intentions towards China and have a strong security interest in a relationship with the North Korean regime (Shen 2006, 2013; You 2011). This may have been accentuated by the announcement of the US pivot strategy (Sun 2012), but the leadership may also have in mind the possibility of future conflict with the US over Taiwan, or over regime collapse in North Korea. Consequently, China wants to prevent other powers, notably a US and US-allied South Korea playing a dominant role in Pyongyang in the event of regime collapse. The existing North Korean regime is an essential buffer for China against that happening, and has a higher priority than denuclearization.

China is uncomfortable with its policy towards North Korea, especially given that North Korea's provocative policies have not abated following the succession of Kim Jong-un after the death of his father Kim Jong-il in 2011. North Korea's nuclear programme and hostility towards South Korea are against China's interests, create regional instability, and provide reasons or excuses for the US to expand its missile defences in Northeast Asia, which adversely affects China's nuclear deterrent. A US announcement of further deployment of missile interceptors, including in Asia, supports China's fears. China's support of North Korea is extensively debated internally, with some arguing that it is against China's national interest. China strongly disagrees with North Korea's nuclear weapons programme activities; after North Korea's third nuclear test in 2013, China supported a UN Security Council Resolution that imposed more sanctions. Moreover, Chinese officials felt that Pyongyang's hostility towards South Korea, which was reflected in the sinking of the *Cheonan*, a South Korean warship,[7] and the shelling of Yeonpyeong island in 2010, could lead to war on the peninsula, provoking US intervention (You 2011).

China has supported North Korea with substantial economic aid. Little remains of the former 'lips and teeth' relationship, however, except perhaps in parts of the military. North Korea, on the other hand, appears to believe that being China's buffer means that there is less need to succumb to China's pressure, whether on nuclear or missile issues or on economic reform.

The two countries signed the Sino-North Korea Mutual Aid and Cooperation Friendship Treaty in 1961. During the 1990s, the treaty's mutual assistance provisions were downplayed because relations cooled with Pyongyang after China recognized South Korea in

1992, and because China feared North Korea could provoke a conflict on the peninsula. China has been ambiguous about its obligations under the treaty, and reserves the right to choose under what circumstances it would aid North Korea (Choo 2008: 369–70). Yet in 2011, both parties celebrated the fiftieth anniversary of the treaty's signing. According to Qin Jize and Wang Chenyan (2011), the treaty is still important for stability on the Korean peninsula; the report cites Huang Youfu, a Chinese Korean expert who, while downplaying the importance of its mutual assistance articles, argues that the US should not overlook the treaty when deciding its strategy towards North Korea.

SOUTH KOREA

Developments within China's strategic cooperative partnership with South Korea are substantially influenced by its policy towards North Korea. China's interest in maintaining the existence of the North Korean regime would seem at odds with the presumed South Korean aim of reunification, in due course, under South Korea's influence. Yet China was sensitive to the closer links between Seoul and Washington in the bilateral alliance under South Korea's Lee Myong-bak government. South Korean President Park Geun-hye has been a little warmer to China with her northern trustpolitik policy, although China knows that the US has also encouraged closer links between Seoul and Tokyo in order to strengthen the US regional position. This has been hindered by Japan's dispute with South Korea over its claim to the Dokdo Islands that are also claimed and occupied by South Korea.

South Korea is China's third largest investor and third largest trading partner, and Beijing and Seoul are looking to increase those trade and investment links. Despite the growing economic ties, however, there are political problems, such as disputes over fisheries, histories, territory (the Socotra Rocks) and, more recently, the lack of a Chinese response to the sinking of the *Cheonan*.

Moves have been made to increase multilateral cooperation. Since 2008, however, a trilateral dialogue has been established among China, Japan and South Korea, separate from ASEAN+3, to discuss North Korea and other regional relations issues, the global economy and disaster relief. A Trilateral Cooperation Secretariat was established in 2011 to coordinate these annual dialogues, and discussions continue; the fifth leaders' meeting was held in 2012.

VIETNAM

An important, but at times contentious, part of China's neighbourhood has been Vietnam. Long, often unfriendly, historical interactions, together with recent history, have created considerable mutual distrust. Although communist North Vietnam was strongly supported by China in the early years of the Vietnam War, relations soured as North Vietnam moved closer to the Soviet Union. As Vietnam shifted its allegiance, Chinese leaders believed that the Soviets wanted to use Vietnam as a hostile base from which to encircle China. The Vietnamese invasion of Cambodia, an ally of China, in 1978 triggered the Chinese invasion of Vietnam in 1979. With the dissolution of the Soviet Union and Vietnamese withdrawal from Cambodia, relations were restored in 1991. Although disputes over land borders and territorial waters in the Gulf of Tonkin have been settled peacefully, disputes over the Paracel Islands (which China occupies), and the Spratly Islands (which both claim), have become serious. Despite these tensions, economic exchanges have expanded with China becoming Vietnam's major trading partner. Vietnam has accepted closer, but still limited, defence relations with the US, as a way to reduce its dependence on China but without fully allying with the US, a development that is not welcomed by China (Thayer 2012).

SHANGHAI COOPERATION ORGANISATION

Deng Yong (2011: 181) has argued that, while multilateralism normally dilutes sovereignty, within Asian institutions multilateralism has strengthened the Chinese government's control within its borders. Southeast Asia's debates about Asian values deflected criticisms of China's record on human rights, and the SCO (which consists of China, Kazakhstan, Kyrgyzstan, Russia, Tajikistan and Uzbekistan), has enhanced political security for its members, including China. Following the dissolution of the Soviet Union and independence of the Central Asian republics, previously problematic and at times disputed borders with the Soviet Union and the Central Asian states have been settled peacefully, and confidence-building measures have been developed on border deployments of armed forces. From this experience, China launched the Shanghai Five in 1996 that became the SCO in 2001, a formal organization with annual ministerial meetings and periodic, usually biennial, military exercises primarily concerned with counter-terrorism, and with Afghanistan, India, Iran, Mongolia and Pakistan as observers.

Western analysts often see the SCO as aimed at limiting US influence in Central Asia. Suspicion remains of US objectives in Central Asia, including towards China, following the US obtaining bases in several Central Asian states after 11 September 2001. Interest continues, therefore, in balancing US influence in the region, although China's relatively low-key approach towards the US reflects its recognition that Russia would be more vocal diplomatically on the issue. In practice, however, China and other SCO members give higher priority to regime stability. China is concerned at ethnic nationalism in its Central Asian borderlands with the associated potential for separatist movements, especially as it affects its Uighur population in Xinjiang. It shares its concerns in Central Asia with other SCO members, and SCO priorities have shifted to combating terrorism, religious extremism, separatism and arms and drug trafficking. China's efforts to strengthen the SCO's collective security functions and its support for domestic stability reflects concerns about its interests in the region.

China also has a particular interest in Central Asian energy supplies, the security of those supplies, and their transportation through pipeline connections. Hence its interest in the stability of governments which it sees as at risk from domestic transitions through democratic processes, 'colour revolutions' and human rights activities.

RUSSIA

The SCO has enabled China to expand its influence in Central Asia, and Russia remains watchful of China's activities in Russia's traditional sphere of influence. Irritated at the internal Russian politics of the East Siberia–Pacific Ocean pipeline, China has developed oil and gas pipelines with Kazakhstan and Turkmenistan (not a member of the SCO) that avoids the pipeline network centred on Russia. Yet there is only limited rivalry between Russia and China within the SCO over the Central Asian states. Partly this is because Russia's primary interest is security, whereas China's primary focus is economic, and China has been careful not to impinge on Russia's security interests. Differences do exist, however. China has proposed that the SCO become an economic free trade area, an idea not supported by Russia, as it expects that China would dominate such an arrangement. Given its principles of territorial integrity and national sovereignty, China also opposed Russia's war with Georgia, refused to recognize Abkhazia and South Ossetia as independent states, and ensured that the SCO did not support Russia.[8]

The SCO has helped China develop a relationship with Russia that has historically reflected a lack of trust, and is still well described as 'an axis of convenience' (Lo 2008). Its strategic partnership, however, provides a good basis for the relationship, given that Russia supports much that is of key interest to China: firm support for the UN, sovereignty and non-interference, particularly in relation to human rights and democracy, a multipolar world, a stable Central Asia, and opposition to the militarization of space. That their positions converge on many international issues is often seen as a challenge to the US. As already noted, however, differences remain. Russia is concerned about potential Chinese influence in Central Asia and Chinese migration into Russia. Although China has relied on Russia for arms and military technology, it understands that Russia's military has concerns about sales of advanced military technologies to China; China often experiences difficulties in purchasing the latest advanced military items and notes that Russia's military cooperation with China, although extensive, falls behind that of Russia's military cooperation with India. Among other things, this may reflect the continuing lack of a China–Russia alliance relationship. However, despite revised thinking about alliances (including one with Russia) among influential Chinese analysts such as Yan Xuetong (2011: 142–3), this will not change soon (see also Zhang Feng 2012: 132–3). Ultimately, there are fears in Russia about a China threat that are not matched by Chinese fears of a Russian threat. In the future, therefore, the partnership is likely to be characterized by differences as much as by convergences.

INDIA/PAKISTAN

In India, according to Pakistan's ruling elite, the arch rival is Pakistan. But India's arch rival is China (Thakur 2010). Analysts in India are more inclined to fear China than their counterparts in China are to fear India; the possibility of future conflict, however, is not absent from some Chinese military analysts' writings. Both are major economic and growing military powers. India, like China, aspires to be accepted as a great power.

Since the establishment of the People's Republic of China (PRC), the bilateral relationship has seen dramatic shifts from a close relationship in its first decade, until the Dalai Lama was granted refuge in India following China's invasion of Tibet in 1959, and the brief China–India war of 1962. China's defeat of India's military still colours India's attitude towards China, although there has been some easing of relations. The relationship remains mixed; while currently stable, it lacks warmth, depth and texture (although there is growing trade ballast).

Since the early 1990s, the economies of India and China have grown rapidly, but China's earlier start, generally faster growth and its associated military modernization worries India's strategic analysts. Moreover, 'Chinese awareness of economic and social changes in India came very slowly' (Huang 2005: 212), perhaps not coincidentally as did that of the US and Europe in the mid-2000s. Trade has grown rapidly, however, in the last decade: two-way trade has grown from US$3 billion in 2000 to US$74 billion in 2011 and is expected to reach US$100 billion by 2015 (Saxena 2012). Efforts have also been made by China in recent years to improve political relations with India and to offset perceptions of a China threat. This has been helped by close cooperation with India on a number of international issues in multilateral forums. On many international issues, the two countries hold common views: a shared belief in the importance of sovereignty and non-intervention, concerns to balance US power, common views as developing countries about the Western dominance of the global economic order, and opposition to the militarization of space. These have been reflected in presenting common positions at the UN, WTO and G20, and participating as observers in other multilateral forums including in the SCO (India) and in the South Asian Association for Regional Cooperation (China). These common views also reflect the development of the Brazil, Russia, India, China and South Africa (BRICS) grouping, where China's MFA spokesperson referred to the close contact and communication on major international and regional issues in China–India relations but, as Raman (2011: 342) noted, made no mention of bilateral relations. It is basically in their bilateral relations that problems remain and points of friction exist, even if multilateral meetings ease somewhat the underlying mistrust.

The relationship has been periodically tense, commonly associated with China's close relationship to, and support of, Pakistan. Beijing's relations with Pakistan will remain a contentious issue in Chinese–Indian relations. China's long-held foreign policy interest in Pakistan was as a strategic counter to India, but that may have become less central to China than its concern that Pakistan may collapse or become more radical and support Islamic fundamentalism and independence movements in Xinjiang (Yuan 2007). China's neutrality in the 1999 Kargil conflict between India and Pakistan reflected a concern to avoid involvement in a potential nuclear conflict. Other issues include China's strong response to India's 1998 nuclear weapons tests, which was not helped by a prompt nuclear test response by Pakistan that India saw as possible only as a consequence of assistance that China had already given Pakistan, and its non-acceptance of India's nuclear status after 1998; India's sensitivities regarding Jammu and Kashmir, and the related territorial dispute over the Aksai Chin area; the Tibetan presence in India; China's water diversion from the Tibetan plateau affecting particularly the flow to the Brahmaputra river; competition for influence in Myanmar, Nepal and, to a degree, Afghanistan, although both are concerned about Taliban extremism; and India's desire for a permanent seat on the UN Security Council, for which China has expressed at best only vague support.

India's growing links with the US, and its civil nuclear cooperation and growing military ties, are also issues among some Chinese, notably the People's Liberation Army (PLA) commentators, but others appear less concerned.[9] The US has pressed the role of India as a counterbalance to China in Asia but, given India's aim to maintain strategic autonomy, as Pant (2011) indicates, 'it is not entirely clear that India is ready to play that kind of role'. The China–India border issue has been a subject of continuing dispute and often tension but, although broad principles by which a compromise could be reached were agreed in 2005, China appears not to be hurrying to resolve the issues. Fravel (cited in Fried 2011) speculated that China may be content with the status quo in which it occupies part of the Aksai Chin plateau. Chinese pronouncements at times, however, refer to China's claim on Arunachal Pradesh, calling it southern Tibet, protesting officially when Indian ministers visit and at visits of the Dalai Lama, and blocking an Indian application for an Asian Development Bank loan to Arunachal Pradesh. China seems unlikely, however, to push the issue further. Despite the limited progress made in decades of formal discussions on the border, a step forward was to settle more or less the line of actual control and to set up a mechanism in 2012 to deal with incursions along the line of actual control, seemingly inevitable given its imprecise demarcation.

A concern for China is India's naval development and its potential impact on China's sea lanes in the Indian Ocean. China's need for resource supplies, notably but not limited to oil, are being met largely through the sea lanes from the Middle East and Africa, which cross the Indian Ocean. India's naval build-up and claims of Indian Ocean dominance and a 'go East' policy linking with ASEAN but extending into the Pacific, added to reports of naval exercises with the US and Japan, have excited various Chinese strategic analysts (Fravel and Liebman 2011). For their part, Indian naval and other commentators have expressed concerns about China's increased activities in the Indian Ocean, including constructing ports in Pakistan and Sri Lanka and a special economic zone in Mauritius, seeing them as possible forerunners of a long line of military bases for which at present there is no evidence but much Indian and US speculation on a so-called 'string of pearls' (see Swaine 2011a: 198, note 285 on this myth). The long-held reluctance of China to establish overseas military bases, however, was reaffirmed by China's Defence Minister Liang Guanglie in September 2012 (*The Hindu* 2012), while acknowledging the need for logistical supply for its naval vessels in piracy escort patrols around the Horn of Africa. Liang Guanglie's visit reflects a Chinese effort to improve the PLA's ties with India's military. This is just a step, but presumably a necessary one, towards greater stability and trust in China's foreign policy towards India which, with the response by India, will shape importantly the future regional and global order.

MYANMAR

China's influence in Myanmar has been a long-standing source of competition, although not a major point of contention, with India. The takeover by Myanmar's military in 1988 left it isolated internationally and dependent upon China (with India) for economic and military aid. China's economic interests in Myanmar are now substantial. China's outlet through Myanmar to the sea and the existence of land-based access to the Bay of Bengal for its energy and other trade are important interests for China. It also supported Myanmar on human rights issues in the UN.

Since taking office in 2011, President Thein Sein's reformist government wants to expand its international relationships while welcoming its reduced dependence upon China. The influence of China, which has supported the reforms, will likely remain, albeit diminished (*Global Times* 2012). It continues to invest in Myanmar resource and infrastructure projects, despite the cancellation of a major dam project by the reform government, and expects benefits from more stable borders including improved control of the drug traffic crossing the Myanmar–China border. Given the US interest in relations with Myanmar, however, China may be more concerned about competition with the US than with India.

JAPAN

Despite the importance of multilateralism in China's neighbourhood, an institutional gap remains in Northeast Asia. Hopes that the Chinese-hosted Six Party Talks would develop into a Northeast Asian multilateral security organization have been disappointed. Existing multilateral groupings are scenes of competition between China and Japan for leadership of the region. For China, ASEAN+3 is the preferred group that brings the three major Northeast Asian powers together without a US presence. Japan is concerned at China's dominance in ASEAN+3 and worked for an outward-oriented EAS, its wider membership including the US, India and Australia.

The China–Japan bilateral relationship has been difficult and sensitive since China's defeat in the 1894–5 war with Japan. For much of the period since then, China's experience of Japan has been one of confrontation and violence, associated at times with xenophobic impulses. With the end of the Pacific War and the PRC's rise, the relationship has reflected not just the response to history but different perceptions of the history of their interactions. In its early years, the PRC's policy towards Japan, sending Japanese prisoners of war home, and forgoing reparations was, in China's view, a forward-looking leniency, despite bitter memories of the Japanese occupation, with a positive approach to Japanese business reflecting the economic needs of the two countries. For China this was helped by Japan's US-drafted 'peace' constitution and Japan's concentration on economic development, a concentration maintained for several decades. China's links with Japan developed more rapidly subsequent to the opening of diplomatic relations in 1972. Although Japan was by then becoming important to US economic and security policy in Asia, Japan shared China's concerns over the Soviet Union.

While for much of the post-Second World War period, Japan looked to be part of the regional and global economic order, China was concerned with the security order, initially with the Soviet Union and then the Western international security order. Ultimately, China moved to participate in the Western international economic order; Japan sought to be a political and military power, due in part to its desire to become a 'normal' nation and in part responding to perceptions of a security threat with China's economic and military development. China had initially mixed feelings towards the US–Japan treaty, but hoped it would prevent resurgent Japanese militarism; now it is not so sure. Despite Japan's periodic efforts at greater autonomy within its alliance, and an ambivalent view of China, China has seen Japan as increasingly part of the US-led security order, moving gradually from a relationship with the US that simply gave it a nuclear umbrella to one that envisaged building up its military and becoming a central plank of the US position in East Asia directed, in China's view, particularly against itself and to interference in the Taiwan issue. Unless Japan were to be involved with the US in a conflict over Taiwan, there is little evidence of an intention on the part of China to threaten Japan; military conflict over their territorial disputes appears a low probability despite an apparent increase in Japanese nationalism.

China's bilateral relations with Japan have been characteristically unstable, although both sides have tried periodically to improve bilateral relations. Given the sustained negativity of Chinese views of the Japanese (despite enjoyment of their technology), shifts in policies, nationalist outbursts or leadership changes in Japan can disturb the relationship; since the 1980s, the publication of Japanese school textbooks that downplay Japan's occupation of China has been a continuing irritant.

According to Ye Zicheng (2011: 151), a majority of Chinese think 'Japan's attitude towards its past aggression is the biggest obstacle to Sino-Japanese relations'; this was evident in the 1995 demonstrations in China responding to Japan's desire to achieve permanent membership of the UN Security Council. Although this view is commonly dismissed in the West as due to governmental influence, a Rand report noted that Japan's problem in the region is its 'tardiness in coming to terms with its record of colonialism in the 20th century' (Khalilzad et al. 2001: 5).

Despite periodic political outbursts at Japanese provocations, whether over textbooks, the Nanking massacre, official visits to the Yasukuni Shrine, participation in regional security (read Taiwan) under the new alliance defence guidelines, and participation in the US missile defence system, China has generally kept such differences distinct from economic relationships which ran their course largely unaffected. China's economic links with Japan, starting with considerable Japanese aid, as well as trade, investment and technology, made a large contribution to China's growth. Moreover, Japan moved to discourage Western economic sanctions against China after the Tiananmen incident. The economic links, moreover, remain of central importance today.

Since the early 1990s, tensions have frequently re-occurred, mainly over the territorial claims each makes to the islands named Senkakus in Japan and Diaoyu in China, but since 2010 have remained high.[10] As we saw in chapter 4, no solution to these complex issues is evident without a political compromise, presumably involving a return to a form of the status quo ante.

Tensions also emerged as China's navy has expanded its activities in breaking out of the constraints of the first island chain into the Pacific Ocean, which requires passage through relatively narrow straits within the Japanese archipelago, notably the Miyako Straits. These are international waters but Japan is asking for prior notice of passage by Chinese military vessels. Although this appears analogous to China's requests to the US in the Yellow Sea, China has not accepted the Japanese request.

China believes that Japan is taking a harder line towards China and accentuating disputes, including over territory. As with the case of the Chinese fishing vessel captain in 2010, earlier implicit or explicit agreements not to accentuate problems were disregarded or perhaps inadvertently overlooked by Japan's Democratic Party of Japan government and by the Liberal Democratic Party government which took office in 2012. China's policy towards Japan appears also to have changed, with economic links being affected in ways not previously characteristic: as with rare earths but in reverse, customs officials in 2012 reportedly slowed handling of Japanese imports into China; Chinese nationalists also took action against Japanese properties in China, whether encouraged by Chinese authorities as many media reports argue, or perhaps also managed by the authorities to minimize as far as possible domestic instability, or possibly both. In either case, this is potentially costly to China, as it is to Japan. Japan is China's major trading partner; two-way trade in 2011 was US$345 billion but dropped to around US$334 billion in 2012. Japan's exports to China usually represent around 20 per cent of Japan's total exports. Japanese companies have considerable investments in China; while some appear to be withdrawing investments, Japanese provisional data indicate a further increase in Japanese foreign direct investment in 2012. Given that economic prosperity is also central to China's interests, its government's legitimacy and stability, continued tensions would seem contrary to both their interests.

THE EUROPEAN UNION

We started this chapter noting the importance of the US in shaping China's foreign policy, particularly in its neighbourhood. We also noted how China, to offset its isolation in the 1990s, embraced multilateralism in order to develop relationships with an institutionalized Southeast Asia in the form of ASEAN. In the 2000s, China extended its search for relationships beyond its neighbourhood to Europe. While links with Europe were not new, particularly in the economic field,

2004 saw the declaration of a comprehensive strategic partnership with the EU that reflected various common interests, including developing multilateralism and constraining American hegemonic behaviour (Shambaugh 2004; Xiang 2004); it also seemed to fit China's wish for a multipolar world (Gaenssmantel 2010).

The Chinese diplomatic emphasis on Europe was not sustained for long. While Europe is China's largest export market, just ahead of the US, a variety of problems in trade, such as protection against imports of Chinese textiles and shoes, the EU's unwillingness to provide China with 'market economy status' or to lift the arms embargo left over from the EU's Tiananmen sanctions, were important irritants; political issues including the Darfur crisis and leaders' meetings with the Dalai Lama were also a factor. Arguably more important was the recognition by China that the EU was not able to make a significant difference to the shape of the global order because of its lack of a unified foreign policy. Relations were consequently downgraded by China from the middle of the 2000s until the onset of the global financial crisis when there seemed to be advantage to be gained bilaterally from China's economic leverage. Debt-laden European countries encouraged China to invest both in bonds and through foreign direct investments in local enterprises. Bond purchases were commonly linked to investment opportunities in the country concerned. China's foreign direct investment in the EU had picked up substantially during the 2000s. While China is said to be 'buying up Europe', the EU's concern is the inability of the EU countries to come together as a unit to manage China's investment (Godement et al. 2011); even so, the economic footprint and impact of Chinese investment remains currently small (Clegg and Voss 2012: 10).

China's approach to foreign policy in its neighbourhood has moved in the last two decades from a defensive search for friends to a clearer stance as an emerging power. In looking to avoid its international isolation following the Tiananmen Square upheaval and the dissolution of the Soviet Union, it found comfort in its neighbourhood in multi-lateral groupings, notably ASEAN and then the SCO, moving gradually from suspicion of such regional groupings to finding them useful for presenting China's position and defending its interests.

Although it now has global influence and an increasing global reach, China has been and largely remains a regional power. Yet in the region it is now doing what emerging powers tend to do – changing the institutional framework to fit more clearly with its interests, increasing its ability to control the international environment, particularly on its periphery, and being more active in doing so.

Yet, for the last quarter century, China has put considerable effort into developing peaceful relationships with its neighbours, whether through its new security concept or China's peaceful rise/development approach, to ensure a peaceful international environment it needed for its economic development. It also sought to avoid the security dilemma that greater hard power assertiveness would be likely to stimulate. For much of the 2000s, its policy had considerable success. China accepts that this success has been put in question by the South and East China Sea disputes and China's responses to them although, not without some justification, it argues that external factors are largely to blame. It has appointed a special representative to handle relations with Asia, although concentrating initially on Myanmar, while foreign minister Wang Yi has worked to improve relations with ASEAN.

We examine domestic influences on China's foreign policy and draw together some of the threads from this and earlier chapters in chapter 8.

8 | Foreign Policy in Transition ──────

What would China's foreign policy look like if, or when, as Martin Jacques (2012) argues, China rules the world? We do not know and we cannot speculate here as prospective foreign policies are contingent on uncertain future international and domestic developments. In any case, should there come a time, however improbable, when China rules the world (some influential people within China's elite circles, like Lui Mingfu, have such an aim),[1] it will be a long way in the future. In the next decade, China will be under the direction of the leadership selected in 2012, headed by Xi Jinping.

Within its aim of a peaceful international environment, the principal directions of the Hu Jintao foreign policy have been to maintain stable relations with the US, which China accepts as essential for national revitalization; to manage constructively the regional problem areas that could lead to major conflict with the US, in particular Taiwan and North Korea, or threaten the unity of the Chinese state, notably Xinjiang and Tibet; and to develop further its involvement in multilateral systems, with a greater focus on general issues, rather than bilateral relationships. The limited references to foreign policy in Hu Jintao's report to the 18th Party Congress included (although outlined in a section on ecological progress) the need for China to become a maritime power to safeguard China's maritime rights and interests. While not the first time this has been stated, it is perhaps the most significant addition to China's official foreign policy approach. The report also stated, in familiar terms, the continuing military modernization including nuclear deterrence and cyber capabilities, Taiwan, and peace and development. As well as continuing Hu Jintao's more patient approach to Taiwan, the report did not appear to foreshadow much change elsewhere, including with respect to the ongoing sovereignty disputes (Hu Jintao 2012).

President Xi Jinping, who, as Vice-President, would have been substantially involved in the preparation of the report, has not indicated any plans for basic changes to China's foreign policy. While his speeches have emphasized some of Lui's 'China dream' rhetoric which could portend a firmer foreign policy position, Xi Jinping's government proposes a new type of great power relationship 'looking for cooperation and win–win relations with Washington as central in hardline thorny issues' (Zhu Feng 2013; see also Yang Jiechi 2013).

DOMESTIC INFLUENCES ON FOREIGN POLICY

In previous chapters, we examined China's insecurities and vulnerabilities in the international sphere. In this chapter, we look at the domestic vulnerabilities that are relevant to China's leaders in their foreign policy decision making. These two aspects overlap.

China's authoritarianism and the tendency of authoritarian regimes to be more militarily assertive, together with the speed of China's emergence as a major power, have been important influences on those arguing the 'China threat' thesis. The thesis is usually accompanied by assumptions that China's rapid economic development will continue, that its military capabilities will grow to challenge others in the region if not the world, and that its political and economic influence will expand substantially. Such assumptions may hold; China's recent economic performance has been exceptional, as has its ability to cope with problems as they have arisen. In this chapter, however, we examine challenges in both economic and political fields that question the assumption of continued rapid development and influence.

We then consider how domestic factors may affect China's foreign policy. Chinese leaders remain sensitive to their many domestic challenges, recognizing that failure to deal effectively with them would lead to domestic disorder. Although external interference of the kind that the People's Republic of China (PRC) experienced in its recent historical past is now less feasible, China's concern is that domestic unrest may be used by unfriendly external interests to destabilize China and undermine its progress in building material strength. Its political system has been a major source of stability but, despite a relatively smooth transfer of power in 2012 to the fifth generation of leaders, problems have emerged. For various reasons, therefore, Chinese leaders are still preoccupied with domestic challenges, as reflected in the Party's Document 9, a conservative attack on constitutionalism and its supporters who favour political reform. Foreign policy will be a high priority for China's leaders only to the extent that external events force it to be so.

In examining these aspects of China's foreign policy, some indicators of China's practices and intentions that may offer some guidance in contemplating future developments in China's foreign policy are discussed later in this chapter; in particular, we discuss how much continuity there has been in China's foreign policy, its use of coercion, including force, to achieve its ends, whether its stated ambition to be a responsible great power rules out territorial expansion, and how far it will adhere to the international system as it is, or seek to change it. Since China accepts the need for a constructive and stable relationship with the US, we then discuss the possible consequences for US–China relations. A final question is how far can China be seen to be part of the international system and the international community?

It has been common in studies of foreign policies to distinguish domestic influences on foreign policy from international influences and imperatives. This reflected a time when foreign policies were set at the national government level and were dealt with at a government-to-government level more or less rationally and coherently. That time has changed. When discussing the most important determinants of China's foreign policy, some analysts privilege the influence of Chinese culture, tradition, leadership, ideology, politics and economic development; others emphasize developments in the international environment to which China has to respond. Another group of scholars believes that the two are inevitably linked (Hao 2005). This seems increasingly to be the case.

Globalization and the Internet now link domestic and external factors. China has become dependent on the international system and linkages across borders are now substantial. These linkages have made a major contribution to China's development; there are, however, many negative consequences that constrain China's policy. Given the extent of the domestic–international linkages, coherence and consistency in the various elements of foreign policy are difficult to maintain. This applies to China even more than it does to many other countries, given the complexity of China's domestic power relations.

THE ECONOMY

Should China's economy slow significantly, it will affect China's domestic stability and development. While there are debates among economists on the reliability and possible overestimation of China's growth rate figures (see, for example, Scissors 2012; Orlik 2013), the economy remains the central instrument of China's success and, along with national unification progress (Taiwan) and periodic doses of nationalism, the major legitimating factor of the Chinese Communist Party's leadership. Although initially the global financial crisis led to a fall in China's exports and investment inflows, the consequences for China of the crisis have been much less than for other major economies, as China benefited, despite major problems of inflation, from its large economic stimulus package. China's economy has remained a support for the regional and global economies, while continuing to provide its leaders with the wealth and strength that give China its international power and influence.

Many Chinese economists, however, doubt whether China's economic success can continue at the same rate as in the past; some argue that the economy is more fragile than commonly thought, and emphasize the need for reform. There are concerns about the economy at two levels. First, there is considerable agreement that further economic reform is needed and that the existing economic model needs to be adjusted in order to fit the changed circumstances of China's economy (including in World Bank and Development Research Center of the State Council 2013); China's premier, Li Keqiang, has said that China's development is all about economic reform. Many economists want to move from investment and export-based growth, despite the importance of exports in providing employment, to consumption-based growth, and to increase productivity by not just catching up with the West but autonomously innovating. There are also argued to be growing systemic risks to the Chinese financial system from the statist policies of the Chinese authorities (Walter and Howie 2013).

The continuing debate between nativists and the modernists, discussed in chapter 1,[2] reflects long-term continuity among the influences on China's foreign policy. Economic reform is opposed by various groups, including special interest groups who benefit from existing economic policies, and nativists, who believe that high growth rates have caused high levels of income inequality and potential social instability.

A second concern is that China's stimulus response to the global financial crisis was heavily weighted towards the state-owned enterprises (SOEs), which provided them with considerably more influence. The reformers argue that this influence reduces economic competitiveness. While mostly accepting that continued economic growth means moving up the technology scale, nativists in China see this as best achieved through the SOEs, which implies more support for a greater role for the state. They will have welcomed Hu Jintao's strong support for the SOEs when he argued for the consolidation and development of public ownership (see Hu Jintao 2012). It is argued that the increasing importance of the SOEs makes the formation of foreign policy less predictable, since the SOEs represent interests that often oppose further market-opening reform measures, despite an official policy that is more attuned to reform-friendly policies.

Any significant downturn in the economy will have an important impact on the legitimacy of the Party and its leadership and on China's stability. China's leaders fear that domestic unrest will provide opportunities for external interference. In the face of increasing evidence of large-scale corruption, significant income inequality and widespread environmental degradation, public tolerance seems to be diminishing and there is increased anger and hostility. In 2010, 180,000 'mass incidents' occurred and it is believed that these numbers are increasing.[3]

Most of these issues do not impinge directly on China's foreign policy, although a slowing economy will affect China's regional influence and the China–US balance. The impact, however, is often indirect: either increased domestic instability could reduce the regime's legitimacy and prompt China to overreact in regional and international disputes, as Göbel and Ong (2012) suggest; or breaches could occur, for example, of quality standards of export products, such as food and medicines, or of arms control regulations or agreements accepted internationally by China. Rising domestic discontent or frustrated expectations of improvement could also explain a lower priority given to foreign policy by the leadership. As is true of other countries, domestic interests and values influence China's involvement in the international system, and its willingness and ability to comply with international rules and norms.

While a more utilitarian than ideological aspect of soft power, China's economic policy or 'model' is extensively debated within and outside China. A link between authoritarian politics and market economics, often termed the Beijing Consensus, has been a major feature of China's success, and is attractive to many developing countries, although until the global financial crisis, China had not pushed this aspect in its foreign policy rhetoric, arguing its particularity to China. It seems to have gained strength, however, among national leaders as an example for developing countries as Wang Jisi has argued (Lieberthal and Wang 2012).

Even when it eventually becomes the largest economy, China is unlikely to replace the US as the pre-eminent political state for a long time.[4] It will, however, have greater influence than other major powers and will be number two globally. Its international influence comes largely from its economic strength – it is a major importer and exporter, a major host to foreign direct investment, a foreign investor in a wide range of developing countries in Asia, Africa and Latin America, and a major global creditor. It affects the global order because, although it has joined the existing international order, it is not fully satisfied with that order; nor, of course, are many other countries such as Japan and the other BRICS (Brazil, Russia, India and South Africa). Yet the international political structure is likely to be multipolar with power more widely distributed; other countries, including Brazil, India, Indonesia, Turkey and Vietnam, will have greater influence than they do today, while the European Union, Japan and Russia will remain major players.

In many emerging countries, populations are growing whereas China's population is likely eventually to decline. Moreover, the ageing of China's population presents China with a significant problem. Not only are population numbers expected to peak at around 2030 and then decline, but this will be accompanied by a declining workforce and a rising dependency of aged people with effects on economic growth and growing demands on government finances for pension and health insurance commitments (Peter Ghilchik in Anderson 2006; see also Frazier 2013).

MARKETS AND RESOURCES

China's need for markets and access to technology are shaping its foreign policy approach to developed countries, the US in particular. It is also heavily dependent on global markets for energy and raw materials (on which its economic growth depends) which has led to substantial Chinese involvement in developing countries. Its efforts to remedy its serious water constraints by tapping the Tibetan Plateau run-off, however, have created tensions with its Indo-China neighbours as well as others in South Asia that will increase as China's further plans materialize (Pomeranz 2013).

China's foreign policies have been influenced most notably by its dependence on international sources for raw materials (energy and minerals), and its dependence on vulnerable sea lanes. Hu Jintao expressed frequently his concern about the Malacca 'dilemma' – China depends heavily on shipping through the Malacca Strait, but cannot defend its shipping from interdiction by others. The foreign policy response to this problem included building up a naval capacity and seeking alternative energy resource transport avenues, such as overland pipelines through Myanmar and Central Asia.

China's need for food is also becoming more important and is of great concern to China's elites. A rising population, increased incomes, urbanization and changing diets based increasingly on livestock products has led to a dramatic growth in food demand. China has maintained a high degree of food self-sufficiency so far but, as Morton (2012: 23) has argued, taking 'a longer-term perspective, China is increasingly food insecure. China faces enormous challenges in maintaining food self-sufficiency given increasing problems of deteriorating arable land, falling rainfall levels, declining water tables and water shortages, and the hollowing out of farm labour supply without offsetting mechanization.

Chinese companies, including SOEs, are investing abroad in farmland for food production. This has led to claims of Chinese land grabbing and neo-colonialism, particularly in Africa; precautionary reactions are evident by various governments where such overseas investments are being made or proposed. The arguments are generally no more valid, although more politically sensitive, than those about 'locking up' oil supplies as discussed in chapter 6, and Chinese investment is still small. In any case, China's interest appears to be more to enlarge food supply generally, and provide profit to the companies involved, rather than to increase food supplies specifically for China.

Reflecting more specific concerns about food for Chinese consumption is the Chinese interest in sourcing its food supplies from the seas (Zhang Hongzhou 2012) as reflected in China's Twelfth Five Year Plan. Hu Jintao's interest in China as a maritime state could be widely interpreted, within as well as outside China, as referring to China's blue water naval capacity and extending China's power projection capability, but it could also reflect its interest in accessing fishery resources (including in disputed and distant waters) to increase China's food supplies.

For various reasons, therefore, China faces substantial challenges which explains the leadership's emphasis on domestic issues at the expense of foreign policy. These challenges also throw up the question about China's continued wealth and power development at the same rapid pace of recent decades. Should economic growth slow, there is also reason to question how far China's military capabilities will grow to challenge others in the region, if not the world.

CONSISTENCY OF FOREIGN POLICY

As a possible guide to figuring out China's future foreign policy, we can look at the consistency of China's foreign policy after the establishment of the PRC in 1949. Certain consistencies exist in all foreign policies, particularly the emphasis on security, and that is also the case for China. Given its history of invasion and international humiliation, China puts especial weight on sovereignty and non-interference in its internal affairs and, with some minor qualifications, that has remained largely unchanged.[5]

Yet, in defending and pursuing its interests, China's broad foreign policy approach has changed over time – from Mao Zedong's Marxist–Leninist revolutionary policy to its alliance (leaning to the left) with the Soviet Union, then a slow movement towards integration with the international system as it replaced Taiwan in the United Nations and became a permanent member of the Security Council, then a slow waning of China's revolutionary fervour, followed by a cautious socialization within the international system. A short period of 'independence' ensued, followed by a limited quasi-alliance with the US; in the meantime, China was increasingly integrating with the international system and sought a peaceful international environment. In the 2000s, China emphasized peaceful rise/development, a good neighbour policy, its new security concept and a harmonious world. Despite all these changes, Wang Jisi (2011: 68) judged China's foreign policies since 1980 to be remarkably consistent and well-coordinated with China's domestic priorities, his meaning being that meeting international challenges did not undermine domestic reforms. There is a question about whether the increased assertiveness in the seas around China, which is interpreted widely as China's greater use of military and political strength, reflects a considered, well-thought through change of policy or, as is more likely, whether it is largely a reaction to events including the US–China competition that we discuss below.

Much of China's foreign policy is linked to domestic affairs through its defence of the periphery – ethnically different areas in the cases of Tibet and Xinjiang, originally acquired for border security purposes to protect the core Han population against external influences. Defence of the periphery also includes Taiwan which, from China's perspective, is an integral component of the China that 'stood up' in 1949. Yet while China's broad principles remain consistent, policy implementation differs as China's policies towards Taiwan illustrate. Most recently, while Jiang Zemin urgently wanted to reunify Taiwan with China, Hu Jintao took a more patient position (Chen 2012). In part, this was in response to a less assertive US position. How Xi Jinping and his colleagues address the Taiwan issue in the future will be critical for regional and global stability, but will also partly depend on the US approach.

USE OF FORCE

Most large countries, including Britain, France, Russia and the US, have been accustomed to the use of force, as has China in the past, and the use of force is usually described as defensive, as it sometimes is. Historically, China has shown a willingness to use violence over territory to secure its current borders and to regain homeland areas. Taiwan remains a potential case today. As the PRC, China has been involved in military conflict on four occasions: with Korea, India and Vietnam (twice).[6] Smaller militarized conflicts have included Russia and Vietnam. In a comparative study of China's use of force, Gilboy and Heginbotham (2012) found that in the period 1949–80, the PRC had slightly more militarized conflicts than India, whereas in the period 1980–2001, China and India were equal. In both cases, the incidence of violence has declined compared with the earlier period. Since the Deng Xiaoping reforms, the only intentional use of violence by China was to teach Vietnam (and the Soviets) a 'lesson' over Vietnam's invasion of Cambodia in 1979.

China has not traditionally been territorially expansionist and occasional netizens' stirrings of irredentism have not been supported by
China's leaders. Nor is violence an effective means of securing economic resources in China's region or elsewhere (Harris 2005). Fravel
(2008: 9) concluded that fears that China might pursue broad territorial changes or fight frequently over its territorial claims are overstated.
Nor is there evidence that China is a threat to freedom of the seas,
except to military transit within China's exclusive economic zone.

CHALLENGING THE US

Various transitions will affect China's foreign policies. While periodic
changes in leadership in China, the US, Japan and South Korea have
an impact on China's foreign policies, as indeed do changes in influential policy advisers in China and the US, the transition associated with
the emergence of China and its presumed challenge to the US is more
critical.

China's volatile relationship with the US, characterized as a 'superficial friendship' (Yan 2010), has fluctuated substantially because of US
policy shifts and Chinese attitude shifts. The ready mobilization of
underlying US nationalist sentiments at election times, and the sensitivity of China's nationalists to international events that appear to
challenge China's status, as Shirk (2007) illustrated, demonstrate how
attitudes can easily change or be changed.

When we discuss the 'China threat' in the US–China context, we
need to distinguish between threats at the state-to-state level and
threats of localized clashes between the US and China. There is little
evidence that China poses a threat to the US at the global level, despite
hawkish views in the US that see security competition with China as
a zero-sum process. A common basis for the 'China threat' belief – the
German challenge to Britain which led to the First World War – does
not offer a close parallel because of the relatively dominant strength of

the US. Moreover, even were such analogies useful, it is not clear what a China threat would mean to the US, rather than just to its allies. Regional competition, however, is a different issue as we discuss later.

From China's perspective, China needs to respond to US policies towards it, but the US shares with China the problem of compartmentalized policies. For the US, this reflects unresolved issues about the balance between engagement and hedging (or containment), which is due to the range of hawkish and liberal opinions in the US and the shifts from time to time in who has foreign policy influence. Thus, while Secretary of State Hillary Clinton's March 2012 speech that dealt with the bilateral relationship on the fortieth anniversary of President Richard Nixon's visit to China talked of seeking a mutually acceptable balance between cooperation and competition (Clinton 2012), President Barack Obama's November 2011 speech to the Australian parliament, outlining the rebalancing to Asia, while seeking cooperation with China, was somewhat stridently concerned with countering China's challenge and made no concession to the Chinese regime; regimes other than democracies fail because they 'ignore the ultimate source of power and legitimacy – the will of the people' (Obama 2011). This speech was seen by various Chinese analysts as reflecting a more assertive US intent to maintain its dominance by containment.

In the growing competition between China and the US, two differences are important – China's concerns are domestic and the US concerns are international – but both can be seen as defensive. In Wang Jisi's view, 'Beijing protects its leadership in China, while Washington defends its leadership in the world' (Wang Jisi in Kato 2012). A linked factor is that there are different strategic objectives within the US that shape the US position to which China has to respond. The US does not have territorial claims on China, nor does China threaten US territory, other than in retaliation for a US attack. According to one ex-senior US official, however, 'the ultimate aim of the American strategy is to hasten a revolution, albeit a peaceful one, that will sweep away China's one-party authoritarian state and leave a liberal democracy in its place' (Friedberg 2011: 184). The US and others in the West have an array of policies promoting democracy and human rights; they underpin the West's engagement with China, but there are limits to what can be done to 'hasten a revolution' of this kind. Nevertheless, it may be understandable that trust is lacking at the state-to-state and elite levels, and that China's leaders and strategic analysts tend to see regime change as a US objective.

China's leaders are pushing back against this pressure. Since the US is the principal external threat to their interests and regime, they want to reduce US influence in the region; according to Friedberg (2011) they want to displace ultimately the US as the predominant East Asian power, although China accepts that at best that is a long-term ambition. Nevertheless, given its history of sea-based, foreign invasions and interventions, it is not surprising that China has a continued sense of vulnerability in regard to its long coastline.

We have pointed to China's difficulty in speaking with one voice on foreign policy issues. When then vice foreign minister Cui Tiankai wrote about China's official view of the bilateral US–China relationship, he cited Hu Jintao and Xi Jinping as referring to the need for a new type of major power relationship, one that would be reassuring to the Chinese and American peoples (Cui and Pang 2012). It was not clear, however, how to achieve that new type of relationship. One consistent policy element, however, is that the drive for a stable US relationship continued as a basic principle of China's foreign policy under Hu Jintao (despite what Chinese leaders saw as periodic outbursts of hostility from the West) with care taken to avoid challenging US interests, such as, for example, in its dealings with radical countries such as Venezuela in the US 'near abroad'.

That principle is unlikely to change under Xi Jinping. China is less willing, however, to accept US actions that it judges to be against its interests, such as, for instance, with US arms deals to Taiwan, in part because of the likely pressure from China's citizens and netizens to respond more firmly to what is seen as increasing US assertiveness and weak Chinese responses. Moreover, as China's global interests expand, it may be more difficult to avoid policy clashes with the US.

Maintaining that stable relationship is also likely to be more difficult in the future if the US fears that its status as the dominant power in the region is uncertain and conditional. It is true that the two countries have common interests, although less so than when they both were concerned about the Soviet Union; but they are also competitive. Despite the argument that without a framework the relationship will suffer from diplomatic drift (Wang 2009), and despite steps towards a strategic partnership under the Bill Clinton administration or suggestions of seeking mutual reassurance in the early Obama period, no attempt firmly to establish such a framework is evident. Although the Zoellick stakeholder framework met a need at the time, it has been seen by some Chinese analysts as, in practice, another way of tying China to the US leadership.

THE PIVOT

Even before Obama's pivot, as Lowell Dittmer (2009: 337) saw it, to 'many Chinese strategic thinkers, the PRC is now confronted with the problem of a "nervous hegemon"' attempting 'to maintain superiority against a rising tide of inevitably rising contenders'. According to many Chinese analysts, US efforts to maintain superiority and to hold back China's growth is underpinned by the containment policy of the US, exemplified by the pivot. China sees underlying hostility by the US as the US default mode. While the US contends that it is not containing China (and it is doubtful that such a comprehensive policy is in place given the continuing extent of US engagement), one can see why

China's strategic analysts, if not the government, should think that a US containment policy has been in place for some time.

Under President Clinton and in the early stages of the George W. Bush administration in particular, the US reinforced its military forces in Asia, strengthened relations with existing allies in Asia, and developed partnerships with India, Indonesia and Vietnam (Manyin et al. 2012). The events of 11 September 2001 led to a US extension of its Central Asian involvement that seemed to encircle China further. US administrations have strengthened the base in Guam with a substantial build-up of military assets and infrastructure that potentially could threaten China's shipping, intensified its military relationship with and support for Japan, and extended military cooperation further with allies and friends in the region.

While the US 'pivot' or rebalancing of its approach to Asia is therefore to a degree a revival of policies of previous US administrations, the Obama administration's pivot extends its diplomatic and defence links further with other Asian allies and gives it greater emphasis. For some years, US economic involvement in Asia has been growing less than that of China. China's exports to Asia now match those of the US. The apparent aim of the Trans-Pacific Partnership – to encourage more US economic involvement with allies and friends in Asia at the expense of China – is unlikely to change that, as regional countries, while welcoming a US presence, will still see their economic futures tied substantially to China.

The pivot has been the subject of considerable debate in the US and in China. Ross (2012) is critical of the pivot, arguing that it is unnecessary and counterproductive, and that recent developments reflect China's relative weakness rather than an assertion of strength. A somewhat formulaic response to the Ross argument suggested that rather than seeing the pivot as directed at China, it was 'an acknowledgment of the changing geopolitical realities of the twenty-first century – not simply a response to China' (Brimley and Ratner 2013: 177). Chinese commentators blame the pivot for the worsening of US–China relations. Chinese scholars are split, however, between whether the pivot is a strategic adjustment for the long term, or was a tactical adjustment linked to the 2012 US presidential election (Yan and Qi 2012). A further irritant is the US administration's claims that the Air–Sea Battle concept is not directed against China when it is widely accepted by senior figures in Washington as being just that (see O'Rourke 2013: 53; Welch 2012; and detailed critique in White 2012: 76–7).

We argued in chapter 5 that China's military capability is often overstated, that China accepts that it could not match the US Navy globally, and to do so would take many decades. There is little evidence that is China's present intention. Erickson and Collins (2012) argue that China's developing naval strength is a mix of two capabilities: over and above domestic defence and homeland security, a 'high end' capability is being developed rapidly to focus almost entirely on contested areas close to home; and 'low end' capabilities are being pursued for low-intensity peacetime missions in order to extend political influence, and to protect vital economic interests and its citizens working overseas, as it did in the case of Libya in 2011. Erickson and Collins conclude that China's shipbuilding program is designed to replace ageing vessels and modernize the fleet, rather than developing blue water power projection. China's intentions, however, could change over time; like the US, China has a military–industrial complex that is interested in more sales as a result of naval expansion. Such a change, however, would be evident, despite claims of a lack of transparency, and would take decades to implement. Moreover, White (2012: 73–5) distinguishes between sea 'denial', which is achievable for China in closely located waters, and sea 'control'. China can 'deny' the US the exercise of sea 'control' in the western Pacific; the US, and other countries such as Japan and India, however, have the advantage in sea 'denial' elsewhere, preventing China from projecting naval power in Asia or beyond, including for defence of sea lanes in the event of conflict.

The evidence of China's strength suggests substantial gaps if global military assertion and expansion is the intention. The regional context, however, is different. It would be surprising if China did not want more say in regional developments. China did not react well to the South China or East China Seas sovereignty problems, and its foreign policy objective of assuring its regional neighbours of its peaceful, non-threatening, intentions has taken a knock; however, that is not solely China's fault. China is not without arguments to defend some of its sovereignty claims and they cannot simply be dismissed in favour of arguments of a Western ally simply because they are those of an ally.

It is now difficult, however, to separate the South China and East China Sea issues from the pivot. Territorial disputes have intensified, perhaps, as Lieberthal (2013) suggests, linked to the pivot and the enhanced security commitments to US friends and allies. The US has inserted itself into the complex sovereignty issues and has possibly become part of the problem, rather than taking a global leadership role and dealing with the problem. As Buszynski (2012) has argued, these issues have been linked with wider strategic developments relating to China's naval strategy and a US forward presence in the area. He notes the danger for US–China rivalry in the western Pacific now that they have become a focal point.

More immediately worrying than the China 'threat' is the potential for inadvertent clashes at the local level. Overall, despite its rapid economic and military growth, China remains an insecure power. As Ross (2012) has argued, Beijing's tough diplomacy does not reflect confidence in its might, but stems from a deep sense of insecurity. At the same time, the US is hesitant about its potential loss of dominance in the region and is increasingly assertive in its involvement in the disputes. In a context in which the US is uncertain and China's leaders are preoccupied domestically, mistakes can easily be made. Both are competing in the region and are sensitive to domestic pressures, and either could overreact to any local incident.

CHINA AND INTERNATIONAL ORDER

Finally, we are interested in factors that affect China's contribution to the international order. Although China did not contribute to framing that order, it has put considerable effort into demonstrating that it is a responsible great power and that it has been a substantial rule-taker in the economic field and elsewhere. Domestic politics, interests and values influence how countries relate to the international system, and provide significant constraints on adherence to political and civil rights norms in China. However, starting from a relatively low level of consistency in compliance with the normative framework of a global order, China has, over the reform period, moved to a higher level of behavioural consistency (Foot and Walter 2011: 274–5). In most areas now, perhaps it could be said to comply as well as many other countries; it is a member of around 300 international organizations, and Chinese organizations are members of between 2,000 and 3,000 international organizations. Given its considerable economic interdependence with the rest of the world, and its involvement in the UN Security Council and other major institutions, it is hard to deny that China is highly integrated within the international system. A substantial belief in the West, however, is that China has long-term objectives that are not compatible with the Western system or its underlying values and beliefs.

Yet China shows little sign of wanting to move away from the existing international system or to change substantially the global order. This does not mean, however, that China wants to preserve the existing international system (Breslin 2010). Present indications are that, as with the human rights example cited in chapter 3, it will work within the system to pursue its interests, such as a more equitable economic system. Ye Zicheng (2011: 260) argued that China's fundamental notion is to uphold the international system with international law at its core and on this foundation to carry out transformation and improvement. He acknowledges that such changes may not always be readily welcomed in the West.

China has already indicated its interest in changes in the international financial system. Some small steps have been made by the IMF and World Bank towards accommodating those wishes, but the influence of the US Congress continues to dominate; among other things, it is unlikely that the US will relinquish its IMF veto power. More generally, China wants developing countries to have a greater involvement, and wants more equality among states in power and wealth, partly to reduce the influence of the West, notably the US. As Cui Liru (2012: 17) put it, 'a search is on for a stable and effective structure of the international system that fits reality'.[7]

On the other hand, China has shown some reluctance to be involved greatly in the provision of international public goods, arguing that it does not have the resources or ability to do so in the way the West thinks it should. It does, however, provide some public goods – it is a member of the Nuclear Non-Proliferation Treaty and the Comprehensive Test Ban Treaty, it is an important manpower contributor to UN peacekeeping activities, and it contributes to global maritime efforts off the coast of Somalia to protect against piracy, although, safeguarding its sovereignty and independence, it cooperates substantially rather than coordinates with Western navies (Chan et al. 2012: 170). Its efforts in the Six Party Talks that dealt with North Korea's nuclear activities were regarded as a public good contribution, but China's inability to constrain Pyongyang has put that in question. In the environmental field, despite differences with developed countries over responsibility for carbon emissions, it has taken significant steps to limit its emissions, although these will presumably reduce growth of emissions rather than an overall reduction of emissions. China's reluctance to lead internationally, except in limited areas where its interests are affected, is also due to an incremental conservatism that Foot and Walter

(2011: 300) suggest shows a reluctance to mount a major challenge to the existing global order.

VALUES

The question of values poses more complex issues. We have referred extensively in this study to China's participation in the international system. We have limited the use of the term 'international community', commonly used by the West and China to mean mutual acceptance and a sharing of values. It is a vague symbolic concept that reflects those in the world that will join together, at any time, to face a particular task. Who defines membership of the international community is unclear and it partly depends on the issues involved. However, usually it is defined by the powers with influence (the US and its allies and friends) or by those that created the rules and institutions in the first place (the US and Europe) (Gowers 2002). As a term it is used to legitimize actions – such as by the US in its invasion of Iraq on behalf of the international community, or by China as it seeks to keep Taiwan isolated. Yet it is not evident that China is accepted fully in the international community or that China sees itself as a full member of the international community: 'both sides have fallen far short of accepting each other and identifying with each other' (Wang Hongying 2010: 209). Nor is that likely to change soon.

Among the West's reasons for this state of affairs is ideology: for the West, China is a communist state, and the state plays an extensive role in the life of the people. From China's perspective, it relates to values. The West criticizes China's policies such as the 'one-child' policy or China's control of the Internet. Yet Wang Hongying (2010) argues that US surveys (such as those conducted by the Pew Research Center) indicate that these policies are supported by the majority of Chinese people and are consistent with Chinese values. Western criticisms are therefore criticisms of Chinese values, which are not necessarily linked to any particular system of government. While Chinese values are changing because of a growing interest in the rights of the individual and democratic rights, major change is likely to be slow. To the extent that the Pew Research Center survey results hold, value differences provide a major constraint on US–China relations, absent a return to the more pluralistic view of the international community that acknowledges differences in political systems and domestic value systems, and pursues mutually acceptable rules regarding global order accordingly. This is important if we accept that global order, in terms of financial issues and climate change, depends on both the US and China. China's response to being seen as an outsider, and not being treated as an equal or given the respect it feels it merits, may change its willingness to be bound by the rules and norms of the international system.

In the meantime, although mutual suspicion remains, it is not clear in China's foreign policies that it is presently contesting in principle the US determination to maintain its global leadership and military predominance, as stated in its strategic guidance of January 2012 (US Department of Defense 2012). China's global objectives, at this stage at least, appear more limited; defending the regime and its claim to Taiwan are central. Regionally, China's foreign policies reflect the objective of limiting US strategic options, defending its borders, and maintaining international stability; it also wants Washington to provide more space for a rising China. Given the nature and extent of its domestic problems and its international interdependencies, international tensions over relatively marginal islands are not something that China wants. It cannot, however, simply move away from its position on sovereignty. What is needed is not more military, the usual US solution to problems as Stanley Hoffmann famously said, but political leadership, diplomatic negotiation, bargaining and compromise on all sides.

Notes

PREFACE

1 Michael Howard, 'Ideology and international relations', reproduced in Michael Howard, *The Lessons of History*, New Haven, CT: Yale University Press, 1991, p. 150, emphasis in original.

CHAPTER 1: CONTINUITY AND CHANGE IN CHINA'S FOREIGN POLICIES

1 More detail of this strategy, formulated by John Foster Dulles, US Secretary of State in the early 1950s, and its current significance can be found in Barmé (2010).

2 This is a broad brush distinction. For a more nuanced discussion of the various schools of thought, see Shambaugh (2011).

3 Lui Zhemin, then Legal Advisor to the Chinese Ministry of Foreign Affairs, cited in Shan (2008: 69).

4 This is reminiscent of Stanley Hoffmann's argument that American and European views on how to deal with international problems differed: the US approach tended to assume all problems had solutions and the solution was often a military one, whereas Europeans did not see all problems as having solutions nor preferred a military approach. See, for example, Hoffmann (1968: chapter 6).

5 Zhou's Four Modernizations were for reforms in agriculture, industry, national defence, and science and technology.

6 For example, after a formal meeting in 1985 concluded, the author was asked to explain the theory of comparative advantage to a Chinese

vice-premier (comparative advantage is a technical economic term, basic to international trade theory). Confidence in the explanation was helped by the fact that the concept was developed from work by David Ricardo, an English economist well known in China for providing the basis of Marx's labour theory of value.

CHAPTER 2: FOREIGN POLICY DECISION MAKING

1 The following analysis draws particularly on Lu Ning (2000, 2011), Cabestan (2009), Jakobson and Knox (2010), Miller (2008, 2011), and Kiselycznyk and Saunders (2010).

2 The communiqué of the November meeting of the Third Plenary Session (Plenum) of the 18th Party Central Committee stated that China would set up a state security committee. Although the domestic aspects of state security appear its major focus, some Chinese analysts saw this as covering related foreign policy aspects (Cui 2013).

3 In 1993, the US government claimed that the *Yinhe* was carrying chemicals for Iran's weapons programme. The US Navy stopped the vessel in international waters, and the ship was later searched by a joint Saudi-US team after the Chinese government reluctantly agreed to the search. The search found no chemicals. The MFA was criticized for allowing the search to take place.

4 In 1997, the NPC passed the National Defence Law and a number of related laws that provide for administration of the military according to law, and which led to a limited increase in the state's jurisdictional control of the military.

5 See, for example, Xinhua News Agency (2011); Chase (2012). The senior officer referred to in the title of the Xinhua News Agency article was the Director of the PLA General Political Department, and a member of the CMC.

6 Subsequently dismissed, reportedly on corruption charges (Xinhua News Agency 2013b).

CHAPTER 3: CHINA, THE WORLD AND THE INTERNATIONAL SYSTEM

1 As Chen and Wang (2011) illustrate, Deng's original statement has evolved to include a further injunction emphasized by Jiang Zemin, while still drawing on Deng's words adding 'do something useful'. The full translation they give of what evolved into the 24 character principle is: 'observe calmly, secure our position, cope with affairs calmly, never seek leadership, hide brightness and cherish obscurity, get some things done' (Chen and Wang 2011: 198).

2 A useful introduction to these issues is Morton (2011) and the response of Brown (2011).

3 From the Treaty of Westphalia of 1648, which was linked to the end of the Central European Thirty Years' War and the Spanish-Dutch Eighty Years' War. For a detailed discussion of the concept of sovereignty, see Krasner (1999). The norm of non-intervention, however, was only added in the nineteenth century.

4 Legal sovereignty – involving international legitimacy and recognition – is best seen as distinct from Westphalian territorial sovereignty and the non-intervention norm (Krasner 1999: 3–4). Although embracing Westphalian sovereignty, China was denied legal sovereignty from 1949 to the early 1970s; China denies legal sovereignty to Taiwan which effectively has Westphalian sovereignty.

5 The official Chinese paper on UN reform includes this provision (Ministry of Foreign Affairs 2005).

6 Kim (1999: 45–6) argued that this reflected a change from a system-reforming orientation of its UN approach to a system-maintaining approach.

7 The Five Principles are: mutual respect for the territorial integrity and sovereignty of other states, mutual non-aggression, mutual non-interference in the internal affairs of other states, equality and mutual benefit, and peaceful co-existence.

8 Although the UN resolution stated that Kosovo should remain within Serbia, the West supported its unilateral declaration of

independence, which for China had implications in regard to Taiwan and Tibet.

9 See particularly the comments of Li Shaoxian, Vice-President of China Institutes of Contemporary Relations, in *Global Times* (2011).

10 The G4 nations put forward a joint bid for Security Council expansion in a UN General Assembly closed meeting on 27 January 2012.

11 Jacobson and Oksenberg (1990) detail China's joining the Bretton Woods institutions.

12 In his essay *On Liberty*, J.S. Mill saw the determination of the balance between individuals' responsibilities to the community and their rights as individuals as one of the most difficult and complicated questions in the art of government. For the more recent debate on the overlap between economic and political rights, see Kent (1993: chapter 2).

13 Some counter to this process may be underway as reflected in the Party's reaction to the debate on 'constitutionalism'. See Bandurski (2013) and Buckley (2013).

CHAPTER 4: INSECURITY AND VULNERABILITY

1 An official denial would not be expected, and it would be highly provocative to China's vocal nationalist public and to some in the military. In any case, Dai Bingguo's second core interest concerned with protection of sovereignty could be read to mean this.

2 Both sides claim that the other fired first.

3 In 2005, China, with Vietnam and the Philippines, agreed on a joint energy resource development project in the South China Sea. The Philippines unilaterally withdrew in 2008.

4 Storey (2011: 8) argues this was a pointed challenge to China's nine dashed line map that is the basis of its claims. In practice, China does not claim all the waters within the nine dashed line, but merely all the land features.

5 See, for example, Agence France-Presse (2010) citing Philippine Foreign Secretary Alberto Romulo. For Clinton's remarks, see Clinton (2010).

6 Austin (1998) concludes that, based on precedents in past judgements of the International Court of Justice, China has as good a claim to some Spratly Islands as any other claimant.

7 This was a conclusion Austin and the present author came to in a study of the China–Japan relationship (Austin and Harris 2001). As Hoffman (2012) notes, this was also true in the case of China–Philippines trade, until China raised quarantine barriers against Philippine bananas in May 2012.

8 Vietnam and China agreed in October 2011 on principles for dealing with bilateral maritime disputes.

9 For example, in 2013, Japan claimed that 'something like fire-control radar' was aimed at a Japanese warship (BBC News Asia 2013). This was a potentially dangerous act.

10 An extended critical discussion of the Japanese arguments can be found in McCormack (2013).

11 Wang Jisi is Dean of the School of International Studies at Beijing University and a member of the Foreign Policy Advisory Committee of the MFA; he was also Director of the Institute of Strategic Studies at the Central Party School of the CCP from 2002 to 2009.

12 Should Taiwan's Democratic Progressive Party win the next presidential election, it appears unlikely to support the '1992 consensus'.

13 Provincial party leader and governor, Bo Xilai, was dismissed.

CHAPTER 5: MILITARY THREATS AND RESPONSES

1 The CD is currently deadlocked. The US is pressing for action on a fissile material cut-off treaty, which is an important non-proliferation measure, but other members want concurrent action on other measures which they regard as equally important. One of those measures is a treaty on weapons in space being pressed by China, although China has de-linked the fissile material cut-off treaty and the space treaty.

2 Notably, the establishment of the Department of Arms Control in the Ministry of Foreign Affairs in 1997.

3 The Wassenaar Arrangement is the successor to the Coordinating Committee for Multilateral Export Controls, which oversaw export controls to communist countries during the Cold War.

4 Precise numbers in both cases are unknown but are relatively small. There are also definitional problems over terms such as arsenal (warheads, delivery vehicles and so on).

5 For illustrations of past overestimations and projections of China's nuclear weapon numbers, see Lewis (2007) on intelligence estimates, and Kristensen (2011) on both academic and intelligence estimates.

6 See the comment of Major General Zhu Chenghu in *Taipei Times* (2012).

7 Data from the Union of Concerned Scientists database.

8 The broad issue of the desirability and feasibility of mutual restraint in the cyber security field is discussed at length in Gompert and Saunders (2011: chapter 6).

9 Up to 65 per cent of China's oil imports from the Middle East and Africa pass through the Malacca Strait, which China sees as vulnerable to pirates, terrorism and blockades by the US and India.

10 Or US$670.8 billion if Overseas Contingency Operations are added.

CHAPTER 6: ECONOMIC FOREIGN POLICY

1 *The Economist* (2010) concluded that the real effective exchange rate, a measure of the RMB relative to the weighted average of a basket of currencies of China's major trading partners adjusted for inflation, had appreciated by 50 per cent from mid-2005 to the end of 2011; the real effective exchange rate affects trade balances or imbalances, rather than the nominal bilateral exchange rate.

2 One estimate puts China's processed exports at over 50 per cent of total exports (Yu and Tian 2012); Benedetto (2012), however, cites analyses that suggest an overall average Chinese component of total exports of 60 per cent.

3 China's contribution to the iPhone is a little under 4 per cent of the total export value, inputs for which come largely from Germany, Japan, South Korea and the US (Xing and Detert 2010).

4 Most countries' tariffs are less than the levels they are bound to or have committed not to increase in the WTO, the difference commonly referred to as 'water'. Thus for most countries, bound rates could be cut in bargaining without difficulty.

5 In the case of equities, at least a 10 per cent holding.

6 China has established other similar forums with the Arab states and the Pacific Islands, but these have lower profiles than FOCAC.

7 Norway could have retaliated by blocking China's request for observer status on the Arctic Council, but it chose not to do so; and its other trade appears unaffected.

8 Wu cites the examples of Yahoo and the Chinese jailing of a journalist, Shi Tao, as Chinese pressure on foreign companies to adhere to Chinese law, even if doing so conflicts with Western values. Such pressure has subsequently affected Apple.

CHAPTER 7: CHINA, ITS NEIGHBOURS AND BEYOND

1 See Jiang Zemin's Report to the Fifteenth Party Congress of the Communist Party of China, Beijing, September 1997.

2 ASEAN+3, which came into being in 1997, originated in the 1996 coordinating meetings around the Asia–Europe meetings (ASEMs) that included Northeast Asian powers.

3 China–ASEAN two-way trade grew from US$38 billion in 2001 to US$362 billion in 2011 (*China Daily*, 20 April 2012).

4 RCEP, an open agreement, is seen to be a compromise between overlapping agreements being developed – notably one among the members of ASEAN+3 (termed the East Asia Free Trade Area), and one among the ASEAN plus six members of the EAS (in this case termed the Comprehensive Economic Partnership in East Asia).

5 Cai Penghong (2011: 13), Director of the APEC Research Center, Shanghai Academy of Social Sciences, states that it 'seems that U.S. [sic] is using the TPP as a tool as a part of its Asia Pacific Strategy to contain China'. See also Wang (2013).

6 Sigal (1998: 20) noted that North Korea had been the target of at least seven nuclear threats from the US since 1945. Since then, President George W. Bush listed North Korea in his 'axis of evil' speech and implied threats to the country within the 'all options are on the table' mantra.

7 China did not join the South Korean (international) investigation of the sinking and questions some of the evidence provided by South Korea.

8 Jakobson et al. (2011: 10) argue that, consequently, Russia is seeking to strengthen its links with Central Asia in areas other than through the SCO.

9 Krishnan (2010) cites a cross-section of Chinese analysts who do not see a problem, among them Shen Dingli of Fudan, Pie Yianying, a former Chinese ambassador to India, Ma Jiali, from the China Institutes of Contemporary International Relations, and Sun Shihai at the Chinese Academy of Social Sciences.

10 Taiwan also claims sovereignty over the islands.

CHAPTER 8: FOREIGN POLICY IN TRANSITION

1 Senior Colonel Lui Mingfu is a professor at the National Defense University. See Hughes (2010) for a discussion of Lui's 2010 book, *China Dream: The Great Power Thinking and Strategic Positioning of China in the Post-American Age.*

2 This is a broad brush distinction. As noted in chapter 1, a more nuanced discussion of the various schools of thought is available in Shambaugh (2011).

3 Although these figures are often seen as a threat to the regime, they are often not directed against the central authorities (apart from those in Tibet and Xinjiang), but mostly concern local injustices.

4 US strength includes its leadership capabilities, experience and willingness to lead, the extent and scope of its international involvement, and its material strength. Beckley (2011/12) makes a careful case against US 'declinism'.

5 The US similarly emphasizes sovereignty, no doubt partly due to gaining its independence historically from a colonial master.

6 The situation with Tibet could also be included as a military conflict, depending on whether one sees this as an invasion of an independent country, or as a restoration of order in a breakaway administration.

7 Cui Liru is President of China's Institutes of Contemporary International Relations.

References

Acronym Institute (2002) Russia and China introduce draft treaty on space weapons. *Disarmament Diplomacy* 66, September, available at: www.acronym.org.uk/dd/dd66/66nr07.htm

Agence France-Presse (2010) Manila says US not needed in South China Sea row, 9 August.

Air Force Space Command (2003) *Strategic Master Plan FY06 and Beyond.* US Department of Defense, Washington, DC.

Alden, Chris (2007) *China in Africa.* Zed Books and David Philip, London and Cape Town.

Alden, Chris and Large, Daniel (2011) China's exceptionalism and the challenges of delivering difference in Africa. *Journal of Contemporary China* 20(68), 21–38.

Anderson, Jonathan (2006) *How To Think About China.* UBS Investment Research, January, available at: s3.amazonaws.com/zanran_storage/www.ceibs.edu/ContentPages/52742413.pdf

Armstrong, Shiro (2011) Australia and the future of the Trans-Pacific Partnership Agreement. EABER Working Paper No. 71. East Asian Bureau of Economic Research, Crawford School, Australian National University, Canberra.

Auslin, Michael (2012) For China, it's all about America. *The Diplomat*, 6 July.

Austin, Greg (1998) *China's Ocean Frontier: International Law, Military Force and National Development.* Allen & Unwin, St Leonards, NSW.

Austin, Greg and Gady, Franz-Stefan (2012) *Cyber Detente between the United States and China: Shaping the Agenda.* East–West Institute, New York.

Austin, Greg and Harris, Stuart (2001) *Japan and Greater China: Political Economy and Military Power in the Asian Century.* Hurst, London.

Bandurski, David (2013) China's constitutional debate. China Media Project, Hong Kong University, Hong Kong, 14 August.

Barmé, Geremie (2010) The harmonious evolution of information in China. *The China Beat*, 29 January.

BBC News Asia (2013) Japan protest over China ship's radar action, 3 February.

Beckley, Michael (2011/12) China's century? Why America's edge will endure. *International Security* 36(3), 41–78.

Beckman, Robert (2012a) The China–Philippines dispute in the South China Sea: Does Beijing have a legitimate claim? RSIS Commentary 036. S. Rajaratnam School of International Studies, Singapore, 7 March.

Beckman, Robert (2012b) Geopolitics, international law and the South China Sea. Paper to the Trilateral Commission Plenary Meeting, Tokyo, 21–22 April.

Beijing Review (2011) China commemorates 10th anniversary of WTO entry, 12 December.

Benedetto, John (2012) Implications and interpretations of value-added trade balances. *Journal of International Commerce and Economics* 4(2), 1–15.

Blustein, Paul (2008) The nine-day misadventure of the most favored nations: How the WTO's Doha Round negotiations went awry in July 2008. Brookings, Washington, DC, 5 December.

Blustein, Paul (2011) China's impact on the Doha Round. In: Meléndez-Ortiz, Ricardo, Bellmann, Christophe and Cheng, Shuaihua (eds) *A Decade in the WTO: Implications for China and Global Trade Governance*. International Centre for Trade and Sustainable Development, Geneva, December, 7–10.

Bobrow, Davis, Chan, Steve and Kringen, John (1979) *Understanding Foreign Policy Decisions: The China Case*. The Free Press, New York.

Brautigam, Deborah (2009) *The Dragon's Gift: The Real Story of China in Africa*. Oxford University Press, New York.

Brautigam, Deborah (2012) Chinese development aid in Africa: What, where, why, and how much? In: Golley, Jane and Song, Ligang (eds) *Rising China: Global Challenges and Opportunities*. ANU E Press, Canberra, pp. 203–22.

Breslin, Shaun (2010) China's emerging global role: Dissatisfied responsible great power. *Politics* 30(S1), 52–62.

Brimley, Shawn and Ratner, Ely (2013) Smart shift: A response to 'the problem with the pivot'. *Foreign Affairs* 92(1), 177–81.

Brown, Kerry (2011) China's normative challenge. ASPI Strategic Policy Forum, 22 June, available at: www.aspi.org.au/research/spf.aspx?tid=14

Buckley, Chris (2013) China takes aim at Western ideas. *New York Times*, 19 August.

Bull, Hedley (1977) *The Anarchical Society: A Study of Order in World Politics*. Macmillan, London.

Bush, Richard and O'Hanlon, Michael (2007) *A War Like No Other: The Truth about China's Challenge to America*. Wiley, Hoboken, NJ.

Buszynski, Leszek (2012) The South China Sea: Oil, maritime claims, and US–China strategic rivalry. *Washington Quarterly* 35(2), 139–56.

Cabestan, Jean-Pierre (2009) China's foreign- and security-policy decision-making processes under Hu Jintao. *Journal of Current Chinese Affairs* 38(3), 63–97.

Cai Penghong (2011) The Trans-Pacific Partnership: A Chinese perspective. Presentation to the 20th PECC General Meeting, Washington, DC, 29 September, available at: www.pecc.org/resources/doc_view/1752-the-trans-pacific-partnership-a-chinese-perspective-ppt.

Capling, Ann and Ravenhill, John (2013) Symposium: Australia–US economic relations and the regional balance of power: Australia, the United States and the Trans-Pacific Partnership: Diverging interests and unintended consequences. *Australian Journal of Political Science* 48(2), 184–96.

Chan, Gerald (2001) Power and responsibility in China's international relations. In: Zhang Yongjin and Austin, Greg (eds) *Power and Responsibility in Chinese Foreign Policy*. Asia Pacific Press, Canberra, pp. 48–68.

Chan, Gerald, Lee, Pak K. and Chan, Lai-Ha (2012) *China Engages Global Governance: A New World Order in the Making?* Routledge, London.

Chase, Michael (2011) Fear and loathing in Beijing? Chinese suspicion of US intentions. *China Brief* 11(18), 30 September.

Chase, Michael (2012) Army day coverage stresses PLA's contributions and party control. *China Brief* 12(16), 17 August.

Chase, Michael and Purser, Benjamin (2012) Pivot and parry: China's response to America's new defense strategy. *China Brief* 12(6), March.

Chen Chien-Kai (2012) Comparing Jiang Zemin's impatience with Hu Jintao's patience regarding the Taiwan issue, 1989–2012. *Journal of Contemporary China* 21(78), 955–72.

Chen Dingding and Wang Jianwei (2011) Lying low no more? China's new thinking on the *Tao Guang Yang Hui* strategy. *China: An International Journal* 9(2), 195–216.

Chen Qimao (1993) New approaches in China's foreign policy: The post-Cold War era. *Asian Survey* 33(3), 237–51.

Chen Shenyan (2011) The space debris problem. *Asian Perspective* 35(4), 537–58.

Chen Zhimin (2009) International responsibility and China's foreign policy. In: Iida, Masafumi (ed.) *China's Shift: Global Strategy of the Rising Power*. National Institute for Defense Studies, Tokyo, pp. 7–28.

Cheung Yin-Wong, Ma, Guonan and McCauley, Robert (2011) Why does China attempt to internationalise the renminbi? In: Golley, Jane and Song, Ligang (eds) *Rising China: Global Challenges and Opportunities*. ANU E Press, Canberra, pp. 45–68.

China Copyright and Media (2012) Hu Jintao's article in Quishi magazine – translated, 4 January, available at: chinacopyrightandmedia.wordpress.com/2012/01/04/hu-jintaos-article-in-qiushi-magazine-translated/

China Daily (2012) Beijing against sanctions on Syria, 2 February.

China Digital Times (2009) Dai Bingguo: The core interests of the People's Republic of China, 7 August, available at: chinadigitaltimes.net/2009/08/dai-bingguo-戴秉国-the-core-interests-of-the-prc/

China Track blog (2011) 10th anniversary conference wrap up, 1 November, available at: chinatrack.typepad.com/blog/2011/11/index.html

Choo Jaewoo (2008) Mirroring North Korea's growing economic dependence on China: Political ramifications. *Asian Survey* 48(2), 343–72.

Christensen, Thomas (1996) Chinese realpolitik. *Foreign Affairs* 75(5), 37–52.

Chu Shulong (2001) China, Asia and issues of sovereignty and intervention. *Pugwash Occasional Papers* 2(1).

Chu Shulong and Guo Yuli (2008) Change: Mainland's Taiwan policy. *China Security* 4(1), 130–6.

Chubb, Andrew (2013) Radar incident obscures Beijing's conciliatory turn toward Japan. *China Brief* 13(4), 15 February.

Chung Chien-peng (2009) The 'good neighbour policy' in the context of China's foreign relations. *China: An International Journal* 7(1), 107–23.

Chung Jongpil (2011) Weibo and 'Iron Curtain 20' in China: Who is winning the cat-and-mouse game? EAI Issue Briefing No. MASI 2011-07, East Asia Institute, Seoul, December, available at: www.eai.or.kr/type/panelView.asp?bytag=p&code=eng_report&idx=10700&page=21

Clegg, Jeremy and Voss, Hinrich (2012) *Chinese Overseas Direct Investment in the European Union*. Europe China Research and Advice Network, London.

Cline, William (2013) Estimates of fundamental equilibrium exchange rates, May 2013. Policy Brief Number PB 13–15, Peterson Institute for International Economics, Washington, DC, May.

Cline, William and Williamson, John (2012) Estimates of fundamental equilibrium exchange rates, May 2012. Policy Brief Number PB 12–14, Peterson Institute for International Economics, Washington, DC, May.

Clinton, Hillary (2010) Remarks at press availability. National Convention Center, Hanoi, 23 July.

Clinton, Hillary (2011) America's Pacific century. Remarks to the East–West Center, Honolulu, 10 November.

Clinton, Hillary (2012) Remarks at the US Institute of Peace Conference, Washington, DC, 7 March.

Collins, Gabe and Erickson, Andrew (2011) Implications of China's military evacuation of citizens from Libya. *China Brief* 11(4), 10 March.

Cui Jia (2013) China to set up state security committee. *China Daily*, 12 November.

Cui Liru (2012) Peaceful rise: China's modernisation trajectory. *International Spectator* 47(2), 14–17.

Cui Tiankai and Pang Hanzhao (2012) China–US relations in China's overall diplomacy in the new era. *China International Strategy Review*, 20 July, available at: www.fmprc.gov.cn/eng/zxxx/t953682.htm

Dai Bingguo (2010) Stick to the path of peaceful development. *China Daily*, 13 December.

Davis, Bob (2012) IMF softens tone on yuan's value. *Wall Street Journal*, 9 June.

Deng Yong (2011) Too big to fit: China's regionalisms and the limits of institution building in East Asia. In: Li Mingjiang and Lee Dongmin (eds) *China and East Asian Strategic Dynamics: The Shaping of a New Regional Order.* Lexington Books, Lanham, MD, pp. 177–95.

Dittmer, Lowell (1995) Chinese informal politics. *The China Journal* 34(July), 1–34.

Dittmer, Lowell (2009) Conclusion. In: Hao Yufan, Wei C.X. George and Dittmer, Lowell (eds) *Challenges to Chinese Foreign Policy: Diplomacy, Globalization, and the Next World Power.* University Press of Kentucky, Lexington, KY, pp. 335–48.

Economist (2010) The yuan-dollar exchange rate: Nominally cheap or really dear? 4 November, available at: www.economist.com/node/17420096

Economist (2013) Look who's listening, 15 June, 21–3.

Erickson, Andrew and Collins, Gabe (2012) China's real blue water navy. *The Diplomat*, 30 August.

Etzioni, Amitai (2011) Point of order: Is China more Westphalian than the West? Changing the rules. *Foreign Affairs* 90(6), 172–5.

Evenett, Simon J. (ed.) (2012) *Débâcle: The 11th GTA Report on Protectionism.* Global Trade Alert Report, Centre for Economic Policy Research, London.

Fewsmith, Joseph and Rosen, Stanley (2001) The domestic context of China's foreign policy: Does 'public opinion' matter? In: Lampton, David (ed.) *The Making of Chinese Foreign and Security Policy in the Era of Reform.* Stanford University Press, Stanford, CA, pp. 151–87.

Foot, Rosemary (2001) Chinese power and the idea of a responsible state. *China Journal* 45(January), 1–19.

Foot, Rosemary and Walter, Andrew (2011) *China, the United States, and Global Order.* Cambridge University Press, Cambridge.

Franckx, Erik (2011) American and Chinese views on navigational rights of warships. *Chinese Journal of International Law* 10(1), 187–206.

Fravel, M. Taylor (2005) Regime insecurity and international cooperation: Explaining China's compromises in territorial disputes. *International Security* 30(2), 46–83.

Fravel, M. Taylor (2008) *Strong Borders, Secure Nation: Cooperation and Conflict in China's Territorial Disputes.* Princeton University Press, Princeton, NJ.

Fravel, M. Taylor (2012) Prepared Statement to Investigating the Chinese Threat, Part I: Military and Economic Aggression. Hearing before the Committee on Foreign Affairs, US House of Representatives, Washington, DC, 28 March.

Fravel, M. Taylor and Liebman, Alexander (2011) Beyond the moat: The PLAN's evolving interests and potential influence. In: Saunders, Phillip, Yung, Christopher, Swaine, Michael and Yang, Andrew Nien-Dzu (eds) *The Chinese Navy: Expanding Capabilities, Evolving Roles.* National Defense University Press, Washington, DC, pp. 41–80.

Fravel, M. Taylor and Medeiros, Evan (2010) China's search for assured retaliation: The evolution of Chinese nuclear strategy and force structure. *International Security* 35(2), 48–87.

Frazier, Mark (2013) What happens when China goes 'gray'? *The Diplomat*, 14 January.

Fried, Erin (2011) China's response to a rising India: An interview with M. Taylor Fravel. National Bureau of Asian Research, October.

Friedberg, Aaron (2011) *A Contest for Supremacy: China, America, and the Struggle for Mastery in Asia.* W.W. Norton, New York.

Fu Jing (2013) China, US 'ready to engage' on TPP talks. *China Daily*, 1 November.

Fuchs, Andreas and Klann, Nils-Hendrik (2010) Paying a visit: The Dalai Lama effect on international trade. Discussion Papers Number 113. Center for European Governance and Economic Development Research, Goettingen, October.

Gaenssmantel, Frank (2010) Chinese diplomacy towards the EU: Grand vision but hard to manage. *Hague Journal of Diplomacy* 5(4), 379–403.

Gallagher, Nancy and Steinbruner, John (2008) *Reconsidering the Rules for Space Security.* American Academy of Arts and Sciences, Washington, DC.

Gau, Henry (2012) China's participation in global trade negotiations. In: Li Mingjiang (ed.) *China Joins Global Governance: Cooperation and Contentions.* Lexington Books, Lanham, MD, pp. 57–74.

Gilboy, George and Heginbotham, Eric (2012) *Chinese and Indian Strategic Behaviour: Growing Power and Alarm.* Cambridge University Press, Cambridge.

Glaser, Bonnie (1993) China's security perceptions: Interests and ambitions. *Asian Survey* 33(3), 252–71.

Glaser, Bonnie (2012) China's coercive economic diplomacy – a new and worrying trend. *PacNet* #46, 23 July.

Global Times (2011) China sticking to non-intervention on Syria, 12 December.

Global Times (2012) China, Myanmar vow to encourage investment, trade, 25 September.

Göbel, Christian and Ong, Lynette H. (2012) *Social Unrest in China*. Europe China Research and Advice Network, London.

Godement, François and Parello-Plesner, Jonas with Richard, Alice (2011) The scramble for Europe. Policy Brief. European Council on Foreign Relations, Paris, July.

Goldsmith, Jack (2010) The new vulnerability. *The New Republic*, 7 June.

Gompert, David and Saunders, Phillip (2011) *The Paradox of Power: Sino-American Strategic Restraint in an Age of Vulnerability*. Center for the Study of Chinese Military Affairs, National Defense University Press, Washington, DC.

Goodrich, Jimmy (2012) Chinese civilian cybersecurity: Stakeholders, strategies, and policy. In: *China and Cybersecurity: Political, Economic, and Strategic Dimensions*. Report from Workshops held at the University of California, San Diego, April, pp. 5–7.

Gowers, Andrew (2002) The power of two. *Foreign Policy* 132(September/October), 32–3.

Gries, Peter Hays (2004) *China's New Nationalism: Pride, Politics, and Diplomacy*. University of California Press, Berkeley, CA.

Gupta, Sourabh (2010) China–Japan trawler incident: Reviewing the dispute over Senkaku/Diaoyu waters. *East Asia Forum*, 6 December.

Gurtov, Mel and Hwang, Byong-Moo (1998) *China's Security: The New Roles of the Military*. Lynne Rienner, Boulder, CO.

Hanemann, Thilo and Rosen, Daniel (2012) *China Invests in Europe: Pattern, Impacts and Policy Implications*. Rhodium Group, New York.

Hao Yufan (2005) Introduction: Influence of societal factors: A case of China's American policy making. In: Hao Yufan and Su Lin (eds) *China's Foreign Policy Making: Societal Force and Chinese American Policy*. Ashgate, Aldershot, pp. 1–17.

Harding, Harry (1984) China's changing roles in the contemporary world. In: Harding, Harry (ed.) *China's Foreign Relations in the 1980s*. Yale University Press, New Haven, CT, pp. 137–223.

Harris, Stuart (2002) Political crises in Northeast Asia: An anatomy of the Taiwan and Korean crises. In: Jain, Purnendra, O'Leary, Greg and Patrikeeff,

Felix (eds) *Crisis and Conflict in Asia: Local, Regional and International Responses.* Nova Science Publishers, New York, pp. 151–69.

Harris, Stuart (2005) China's regional policies: How much hegemony? *Australian Journal of International Affairs* 59(4), 481–92.

Harris, Stuart (2008) Case studies in China's 'new' diplomacy: United States, Latin America, six-party talks, energy security, and regional neighbors. In: Kerr, Pauline, Harris, Stuart and Qin Yaqin (eds) *China's 'New' Diplomacy: Tactical or Fundamental Change?* Palgrave Macmillan, New York, pp. 211–28.

He Xingqiang (2010) The RMB exchange rate: Interest groups in China's economic policymaking. *China Security* 19, 23–36.

Hill, Hal and Menon, Jayant (2012) Asia's new financial safety net: Is the Chiang Mai Initiative designed not to be used? *VoxEU,* 25 July.

Hille, Kathrin (2011) A show of force: Fears are growing over the hold China's well-equipped Army has on foreign policy. *Financial Times,* 29 September.

Hoffman, Samantha (2012) Sino-Philippine tension and trade both rising amid Scarborough standoff. *China Brief* 12(9), 26 April.

Hoffmann, Stanley (1968) *Gulliver's Troubles, or the Setting of American Foreign Policy.* McGraw-Hill, New York.

Holslag, Jonathan (2010) *Trapped Giant: China's Military Rise.* Adelphi Series 50(416).

Hong Nong and Jiang Wenran (2011) Chinese perceptions of US engagement in the South China Sea. *China Brief* 11(12), 1 July.

Howard, Michael (1991) Ideology and international relations. In: Howard, Michael, *The Lessons of History.* Yale University Press, New Haven, CT, pp. 139–51.

Hu Jintao (2008) Tide over difficulties through concerted efforts. Remarks at the Summit on Financial Markets and World Economy, Washington, DC, 15 November, available at: www.fmprc.gov.cn/eng/zxxx/t524323.htm

Hu Jintao (2012) Full text of Hu Jintao's report at 18th Party Congress, 17 November, available at: news.xinhuanet.com/english/special/18cpcnc/2012-11/17/c_131981259.htm

Huang Jinxin (2005) China rethinks India. In: Friedman, Edward and Gilley, Bruce (eds) *Asia's Giants: Comparing China and India.* Palgrave Macmillan, New York, pp. 211–26.

Huang Yiping, Dang Weihua and Wang Jiao (2011) Reform of the international economic system: What does China want? In: Golley, Jane and Song, Ligang (eds) *Rising China: Global Challenges and Opportunities.* ANU E Press, Canberra, pp. 29–44.

Hughes, Christopher (2010) In case you missed it: China dream. *The China Beat*, 5 April.

Hunt, Michael (1996) *The Genesis of Chinese Communist Foreign Policy.* Columbia University Press, New York.

Interfax News Agency (2012) West plotting against our cyber security, says deputy head of Russian FSB, 27 March (BBC translation).

International Crisis Group (2012) Stirring up the South China Sea (I). *Asia Report* 223. International Crisis Group, Beijing/Brussels, 23 April.

Jacobson, Harold and Oksenberg, Michel (1990) *China's Participation in the IMF, the World Bank, and GATT: Toward a Global Economic Order.* University of Michigan Press, Ann Arbor, MI.

Jacques, Martin (2012) *When China Rules the World: The End of the Western World and the Birth of a New Global Order*, 2nd edn. Penguin, London.

Jakobson, Linda and Knox, Dean (2010) New foreign policy actors in China. SIPRI Policy Paper No. 26. Stockholm International Peace Research Institute, Stockholm.

Jakobson, Linda, Holtom, Paul, Know, Dean and Peng Jingchao (2011) China's energy and security relations with Russia: Hopes, frustrations and uncertainties. SIPRI Policy Paper No. 29. Stockholm International Peace Research Institute, Stockholm.

Japan Times (2010) Clinton: Senkakus subject to security pact, 25 September.

Jiang Yang (2011) 'Great power style' in China's economic diplomacy: Filling the shoes of a benign hegemon? *Hague Journal of Diplomacy* 6(1), 63–81.

Jiang Yang (2012) Response and responsibility: China in East Asian financial cooperation. *Pacific Review* 23(5), 603–23.

Johnston, Alastair Iain (2003) Is China a status quo power? *International Security* 27(4), 5–56.

Johnston, Alastair Iain (2008) *Social States: China in International Institutions, 1980–2000.* Princeton University Press, Princeton, NJ.

Kang, David (2007) *China Rising: Peace, Power, and Order in East Asia.* Columbia University Press, New York.

Kato, Yoichi (2012) Interview/Wang Jisi: China deserves more respect as a first-class power. *Asahi Shimbun*, 5 October.

Kent, Ann (1993) *Between Freedom and Subsistence: China and Human Rights.* Oxford University Press, Hong Kong.

Kent, Ann (2007) *Beyond Compliance: China, International Organizations, and Global Security.* Stanford University Press, Stanford, CA.

Kent, Ann (2008) China's changing attitude to the norms of international law and its global impact. In: Kerr, Pauline, Harris, Stuart and Qin Yaqin (eds)

China's 'New' Diplomacy: Tactical or Fundamental Change? Palgrave Macmillan, New York, pp. 55–76.

Khalilzad, Zalmay, Orletsky, David, Pollack, Jonathan, Pollpeter, Kevin, Rabasa, Angel, Shlapak, David, Shulsky, Abram and Tellis, Ashley (2001) *The United States and Asia: Towards a New US Strategy and Force Posture.* Rand, Santa Monica, CA.

Khor, Martin (2013) Solar wars threaten climate fight. *China Daily Asia,* 6 June.

Kim, Samuel (1999) China and the United Nations. In: Economy, Elizabeth and Oksenberg, Michel (eds) *China Joins the World: Progress and Prospects.* Council on Foreign Relations Press, New York, pp. 42–89.

Kiselycznyk, Michael and Saunders, Phillip (2010) Civil–military relations in China: Assessing the PLA's role in elite politics. China Strategic Perspectives 2. Center for Strategic Research, Institute for National Strategic Studies, National Defense University Press, Washington, DC.

Kissinger, Henry (2011) *On China.* Penguin, New York.

Knowlton, Brian (2003) Bush warns Taiwan to keep status quo: China welcomes US stance. *New York Times,* 10 December.

Kong Bo (2010) *China's International Petroleum Policy.* Praeger Security International, Santa Barbara, CA.

Krasner, Stephen (1999) *Sovereignty: Organized Hypocrisy.* Princeton University Press, Princeton, NJ.

Krishnan, Ananth (2010) Behind China's India policy: A growing debate. *The Hindu,* 5 April.

Kristensen, Hans M. (2011) No, China does not have 3,000 nuclear weapons. FAS Strategic Security Blog, 3 December, available at: www.fas.org/blog/ssp/2011/12/chinanukes.php

Kulacki, Gregory and Lewis, Jeffrey (2008) Understanding China's antisatellite test. *Nonproliferation Review* 15(2), 335–47.

Lai, David (2004) Learning from the stones: A *go* approach to mastering China's strategic concept, *shi.* Strategic Studies Institute, US Army War College, Carlisle, May.

Lai Hongyi (2010) *The Domestic Sources of China's Foreign Policy: Regimes, Leadership, Priorities and Process.* Routledge, Abingdon.

Lam, Willy (2011) The rise of the energy faction in Chinese politics. *China Brief* 11(7), 22 April.

Lampton, David (2001) China's foreign and national security policy-making process: Is it changing and does it matter? In: Lampton, David (ed.) *The Making of Chinese Foreign and Security Policy in the Era of Reform, 1978–2000.* Stanford University Press, Stanford, CA, pp. 1–36.

Lee, John (2012) China's corporate Leninism. *The American Interest* 7(5), 36–45.

Lee, Pak, Chan, Gerald and Chan, Lai-Ha (2012) China in Darfur: Humanitarian rule-maker or rule-taker? *Review of International Studies* 38(2), 423–44.

Lewis, Jeffrey (2007) *The Minimum Means of Reprisal: China's Search for Security in the Nuclear Age*. MIT Press, Cambridge, MA.

Li Cheng (2005) One party, two factions: Chinese bipartisanship in the making? Carnegie Institute for International Peace, Washington, DC, November.

Li Cheng (2013) Rule of the princelings. *Cairo Review of Global Affairs*, 10 February.

Li Mingjiang (2012) Chinese debates of South China Sea policy: Implications for future developments. RSIS Working Paper No. 239. S. Rajaratnam School of International Studies, Singapore.

Li Nan and Weuve, Christopher (2011) Chinese aircraft carrier development: The next phase. In: Erickson, Andrew and Goldstein, Lyle (eds) *Chinese Aerospace Power: Evolving Maritime Roles*. Naval Institute Press, Annapolis, MD, pp. 209–24.

Li Yuxiao (2012) Cyberspace security and international cooperation in China. In: *China and Cybersecurity: Political, Economic, and Strategic Dimensions*. Report from Workshops held at the University of California, San Diego, CA, April, pp. 4–7.

Lieberthal, Kenneth (2013) Bringing Beijing back in. Brookings, Washington, DC, 17 January.

Lieberthal, Kenneth and Singer, Peter (2012) *Cybersecurity and US–China Relations*. John L. Thornton China Center at Brookings, Washington, DC, February.

Lieberthal, Kenneth and Wang Jisi (2012) *Addressing US–China Strategic Distrust*. John L. Thornton China Center at Brookings, Washington, DC, March.

Linklater, Andrew (2001) Rationalism. In: Burchill, Scott, Devetak, Richard, Linklater, Andrew, Paterson, Matthew, Reus-Smit, Christian and True, Jacqui, *Theories of International Relations*, 2nd edn. Palgrave, Basingstoke, pp. 103–28.

Liu Xiaoming (2011) China's perspective on cybersecurity. Keynote Speech to the EastWest Institute's Second Worldwide Cybersecurity Summit, London, 2 June.

Lo Bobo (2008) *Axis of Convenience: Moscow, Beijing, and the New Geopolitics*. Chatham House and Brookings Institution Press, London and Washington, DC.

Lo, Chi-Kin (1989) *China's Policy Towards Territorial Disputes: The Case of the South China Sea Islands*. Routledge, London.

Loehr, William and Van Ness, Peter (1989) The cost of self-reliance: The case of China. In: Van Ness, Peter (ed.) Market Reforms in Socialist Societies: Comparing China and Hungary, Lynne Rienner, Boulder, CO, pp. 262–80.

Lu Ning (2000) The Dynamics of Foreign-Policy Decisionmaking in China, 2nd edn. Westview Press, Boulder, CO.

Lu Ning (2011) The central leadership, supraministry coordinating bodies, state council ministries, and party departments. In: Lampton, David (ed.) The Making of Chinese Foreign and Security Policy in the Era of Reform. Stanford University Press, Stanford, CA, pp. 39–60.

Lui Mingfu (2010) China Dream: The Great Power Thinking and Strategic Positioning of China in the Post-American Age. Zhongguo youyi chuban gongsi, Beijing [in Chinese].

Mallory, Tabitha Grace (2013) China's distant water fishing industry: Evolving policies and implications. Marine Policy 38, 99–108.

Mandiant (2013) APT1: Exposing One of China's Cyber Espionage Units. Mandiant, Washington, DC, available at: intelreport.mandiant.com/Mandiant_APT1_Report.pdf

Manicom, James (2011) Why not to sweat about China. The Diplomat, 18 June.

Manicom, James (2013) The state of cooperation in the East China Sea. NBR Analysis Brief, 30 April.

Manyin, Mark, Daggett, Stephen, Dolven, Ben, Lawrence, Susan V., Martin, Michael F., O'Rourke, Ronald and Vaughn, Bruce (2012) Pivot to the Pacific? The Obama administration's 'rebalancing' towards Asia. CRS Report for Congress, 7-5700, Congressional Research Service, Washington, DC, 28 March.

McCormack, Gavan (2013) Much ado over small islands: The Sino-Japanese confrontation over Senkaku/Diaoyu. The Asia-Pacific Journal: Japan Focus 11(21), 1–10.

Mearsheimer, John (2010) Trouble brewing in the 'hood'. Sydney Morning Herald, 3 August.

Medeiros, Evan (2007) Reluctant Restraint: The Evolution of China's Nonproliferation Policies and Practices, 1980–2004. Stanford University Press, Stanford, CA.

Miller, Alice (2008) The CCP Central Committee's leading small groups. China Leadership Monitor 26(Fall), 1–21.

Miller, Alice (2011) The politburo standing committee under Hu Jintao. China Leadership Monitor 35(Summer), 1–9.

Miller, Alice (2013) The new party politburo leadership. China Leadership Monitor 40(Winter), 1–15.

Ministry of Foreign Affairs (2005) Position paper of the People's Republic of China on the United Nations reforms. Ministry of Foreign Affairs of the People's Republic of China, Beijing.

Moore, Gregory (2011) An international relations perspective on the science, politics, and potential of an extraterrestrial Sino-US arms race. *Asian Perspective* 35(4), 643–58.

Morton, Katherine (2011) China and the future of international norms. ASPI Strategic Policy Forum, 22 June, available at: www.aspi.org.au/research/spf .aspx?tid=14

Morton, Katherine (2012) Learning by doing: China's role in the global governance of food security. RCCPB Working Paper 30. Research Center for Chinese Politics and Business, Indiana University, Bloomington, IN, September.

National Institute for Defense Studies (2012) *NIDS China Security Report 2011*. National Institute for Defense Studies, Tokyo.

Northrop Grumman Corporation (2009) *Capability of the People's Republic of China to Conduct Cyber Warfare and Computer Network Exploitation*. Prepared for the US–China Economic and Security Review Commission, Northrop Grumman Corporation, McLean, VA, available at: www.au.af.mil/au/awc/ awcgate/china/uscesc_prc_cyber_capab_16oct2009.pdf

Obama, Barack (2011) Remarks by President Obama to the Australian Parliament. Parliament House, Canberra, 17 November, available at: www .whitehouse.gov/the-press-office/2011/11/17/remarks-president-obama -australian-parliament

Obama, Barack (2013) Remarks by the President in the State of the Union Address. Washington, DC, 12 February, available at: www.whitehouse.gov/ the-press-office/2013/02/12/remarks-president-state-union-address

Orlik, Tom (2013) What the 'unofficial' numbers say about China's economy. ChinaRealTimeReport. *Wall Street Journal*, 22 February.

O'Rourke, Ronald (2013) China's naval modernization: Implications for US Naval capabilities – background and issues for Congress. CRS Report for Congress, 7-5700. Congressional Research Service, Washington, DC, 26 April.

Osborne, Charlie (2013) China's internet population surges to 564 million, 75 percent on mobile. ZDNet, 15 January, available at: www.zdnet.com/ chinas-internet-population-surges-to-564-million-75-percent-on-mobile -7000009813/

Paal, Douglas (2012) Dangerous shoals: US policy in the South China Sea. Carnegie Endowment for International Peace, Washington, DC, 11 August.

Panda, Jagannath (2011) Beijing's perspective on UN Security Council reform: Identity, activism and strategy. *Portuguese Journal of International Affairs* 5(Spring/Summer), 24–36.

Pant, Harsh (2011) India's response to a rising China: Economic and strategic challenges and opportunities. *Policy Q&A*, National Bureau of Asian Research, August.

People's Daily Online (2003) China putting on a brave 'Third Front', 6 December, available at: english.peopledaily.com.cn/200312/06/eng20031206_129810.shtml

People's Republic of China Government (2011) *China's Twelfth Five Year Plan (2011–2015)*. Full English Translation, Delegation of the European Union in China, 11 May, available at: cbi.typepad.com/china_direct/2011/05/page/2/

Pomeranz, Kenneth (2013) Asia's unstable water tower: The politics, economics, and ecology of Himalayan water projects. *Asia Policy* 16(July), 4–10.

Qin Jize and Wang Chenyan (2011) Hu hails friendly ties with DPRK. *China Daily*, 12 July.

Raman, G. Venkat (2011) India in China's foreign policy. *China: An International Journal* 9(2), 342–52.

Rauscher, Karl Frederick and Zhou Yonglin (2011) *China–US Bilateral on Cybersecurity: Fighting Spam to Build Trust*. EastWest Institute and Internet Society of China, New York and Beijing.

Reisen, Helmut and Ndoye, Sokhna (2008) Prudent versus imprudent lending to Africa: From debt relief to emerging lenders. Working Paper No. 268, OECD Development Centre, Paris, February.

Ren, Xiao (2012) A reform minded status quo power? China, the G20, and changes in the international monetary system. RCCPB Working Paper 25, Research Center for Chinese Politics and Business, Indiana University, Bloomington, IN, April.

Reuters (2012) China president urges G20 members to stick together. Beijing, 7 July.

Ross, Robert (2009) China's naval nationalism: Sources, prospects, and the US response. *International Security* 34(2), 46–81.

Ross, Robert (2012) The problem with the pivot: Obama's new Asia policy is unnecessary and counterproductive. *Foreign Affairs* 91(6), 70–82.

Saxena, Shobhan (2012) India, China bilateral trade set to hit $100 billion by 2015. *Times of India*, 22 June.

Scissors, Derek (2012) China's economic data are (still) not credible. Heritage Foundation, 17 January, available at: www.heritage.org/research/reports/2012/01/chinas-economic-data-are-still-not-credible

Scott, James and Wilkinson, Rorden (2011) China and the WTO. RCCPB Working Paper 5, Research Center for Chinese Politics and Business, Indiana University, Bloomington, IN, October.

Segal, Adam (2011) The role of cyber security in US–China relations. *East Asia Forum*, 21 June.

Shachtman, Noah and Singer, Peter W. (2011) The wrong war: The insistence on applying Cold War metaphors to cybersecurity is misplaced and counter-productive. Brookings, Washington, DC, 15 August.

Shambaugh, David (1991) *Beautiful Imperialist: China Perceives America, 1972–1990*. Princeton University Press, Princeton, NJ.

Shambaugh, David (2002) *Modernizing China's Military: Progress, Problems, and Prospects*. University of California Press, Berkeley, CA.

Shambaugh, David (2004) China and Europe: The emerging axis. *Current History* 103(674), 243–8.

Shambaugh, David (2005) Return to the middle kingdom? China and Asia in the early twenty-first century. In: Shambaugh, David (ed.) *Power Shift: China and Asia's New Dynamics*. University of California Press, Berkeley, CA, pp. 23–47.

Shambaugh, David (2011) Coping with a conflicted China. *Washington Quarterly* 34(1), 7–27.

Shan Wenhua (2008) Redefining the Chinese concept of sovereignty. In: Wang Gungwu and Zheng Yongnian (eds) *China and the New International Order*. Routledge, London, pp. 53–80.

Shen Dingli (2005) Nuclear deterrence in the 21st century. *China Security* 1, 10–14.

Shen Dingli (2006) North Korea's strategic significance to China. *China Security* 2, 19–34.

Shen Dingli (2008) China's defensive military strategy: The space question. *Survival* 50(1), 170–6.

Shen Dingli (2011) A Chinese assessment of China's external security environment. *China Brief* 11(5), 25 March.

Shen Dingli (2013) Lips and teeth: It's time for China to get tough with North Korea. *Foreign Policy*, 13 February, available at: www.foreignpolicy.com/articles/2013/02/13/lips_and_teeth_china_north_korea

Shi Yinhong (2012) The returned China with Chinese-ness in history and world politics: A deeper understanding with the intellectual guide from Wang Gungwu. In: Zheng Yongnian (ed.) *China and International Relations: The Chinese View and the Contribution of Wang Gungwu*. Routledge, London, pp. 271–92.

Shih Chih-yu (1993) *China's Just World: The Morality of China's Foreign Policy.* Lynne Rienner, Boulder, CO.

Shirk, Susan (1993) *The Political Logic of Economic Reform in China.* University of California Press, Berkeley, CA.

Shirk, Susan (2007) *China: Fragile Superpower.* Oxford University Press, New York.

Sigal, Leon (1998) *Disarming Strangers: Nuclear Diplomacy with North Korea.* Princeton University Press, Princeton, NJ.

Sisci, Francesco (2011) The scalpel and needle in foreign policy. *Asia Times Online*, 3 November.

Spence, Jonathan (2005) The once and future China. *Foreign Policy*, 146(January/ February), 44–6.

State Council Information Office (1998) *China's National Defense.* Information Office of the State Council of the People's Republic of China, Beijing, July, available at: www.china.org.cn/e-white/5/index.htm

State Council Information Office (2010) The Internet in China, 8 June, available at: www.china.org.cn/government/whitepaper/node_7093508.htm

State Council Information Office (2011a) *China's Foreign Aid.* White Paper, 21 April, available at: news.xinhuanet.com/english2010/china/2011-04/21/ c_13839683.htm

State Council Information Office (2011b) China's National Defense in 2010, available at: english.gov.cn/official/2011-03/31/content_1835499_4 .htm

State Council Information Office (2013) The diversified employment of China's armed forces, 16 April, available at: news.xinhuanet.com/english/china/2013 -04/16/c_132312681.htm

Storey, Ian (2011) Hardening positions over dangerous grounds: Recent developments in the South China Sea dispute. Paper at CSIS Conference on Maritime Security in the South China Sea, Washington, DC, 20–21 June.

Stuart-Fox, Martin (2004) Southeast Asia and China: The role of history and culture in shaping future relations. *Contemporary Southeast Asia* 26(1), 116–39.

Stubbs, Richard (2002) ASEAN plus three: Emerging East Asian regionalism? *Asian Survey* 42(3), 440–55.

Sun Tzu (1963) *The Art of War* (trans. Samuel Griffith). Oxford University Press, London.

Sun Xiangli (2005) China's nuclear strategy. *China Security* 1, 23–7.

Sun Yun (2012) The logic of China's North Korea policy. *PacNet* #39, 21 June.

Swaine, Michael (1998) *The Role of the Chinese Military in National Security Policymaking*. RAND National Defense Research Institute, Santa Monica, CA.

Swaine, Michael (2011a) *America's Challenge: Engaging a Rising China in the Twenty-First Century*. Carnegie Endowment for International Peace, Washington, DC.

Swaine, Michael (2011b) China's assertive behavior. Part one: On 'core interests'. *China Leadership Monitor* 34(Winter), 1–25.

Swaine, Michael (2012a) China's assertive behavior. Part three: The role of the military in foreign policy. *China Leadership Monitor* 36(Winter), 1–17.

Swaine, Michael (2012b) China's assertive behavior. Part four: The role of the military in foreign crises. *China Leadership Monitor* 37(Spring), 1–14.

Swaine, Michael (2012c) Chinese leadership and elite responses to the US Pacific pivot. *Chinese Leadership Monitor* 38(Summer), 1–26.

Swaine, Michael and Fravel, M. Taylor (2011) China's assertive behavior. Part 2: The maritime periphery. *China Leadership Monitor* 35(Summer), 1–29.

Taipei Times (2012) Missile shield may spark PRC nuclear weapons upgrade, 20 July.

Tellis, Ashley (2008) China's military space strategy: An exchange: Response. *Survival* 50(1), 185–98.

Thakur, Ramesh (2010) China and India: Uncertain bedfellows. *Daily Yomiuri*, 7 May.

Thayer, Carlyle (2012) Vietnam looking to play pivotal role with both China and US. *Global Times*, 24 July.

The Hindu (2012) China has no plan for Indian Ocean military bases, 4 September.

Thomas, Kristie (2011) China and the WTO dispute settlement system: From passive observer to active participant? *Global Trade and Customs Journal* 6(10), 481–90.

US Department of Defense (2011) DOD releases fiscal 2012 budget proposal. News Release No. 119-11, 14 February.

US Department of Defense (2012) Sustaining US global leadership: Priorities for 21st century defense, US Department of Defense, Washington, DC, January.

US Department of Energy and US Department of Defense (2008) National security and nuclear weapons in the 21st century, Washington, DC, September.

US Government (2006) Unclassified US national space policy, available at: www.whitehouse.gov/sites/default/files/microsites/ostp/national-space -policy-2006.pdf

US Government (2010) National Space Policy of the United States of America, 28 June, available at: www.whitehouse.gov/sites/default/files/national_space _policy_6-28-10.pdf

US–China Security Review Commission (2002) *Report to Congress of the US–China Security Review Commission.* Washington, DC, July.

Van Ness, Peter (2002) Hegemony, not anarchy: Why China and Japan are not balancing US unipolar power. *International Relations of the Asia-Pacific* 2(1), 131–50.

Walter, Carl and Howie, Fraser (2013) Of China's financial bondage. *Wall Street Journal,* 17 January.

Wang Gungwu (2008) China and the international order: Some historical perspectives. In: Wang Gungwu and Zheng Yongnian (eds) *China and the New International Order.* Routledge, London, pp. 21–31.

Wang Hongying (2010) Understanding the intangible in international relations: The cultural dimension of China's integration with the international community. In: Zheng Yongnian (ed.) *China and International Relations: The Chinese View and the Contribution of Wang Gungwu.* Routledge, London, pp. 203–20.

Wang Jianwei (2009) Building a new conceptual framework for US–China relations. In: Hao Yufan, Wei C.X. George and Dittmer, Lowell (eds) *Challenges to Chinese Foreign Policy: Diplomacy, Globalization, and the Next World Power.* University Press of Kentucky, Lexington, KY, pp. 37–55.

Wang Jisi (2011) China's search for a grand strategy: A rising great power finds its way. *Foreign Affairs* 90(2), 68–79.

Wang Jisi (2012) Understanding strategic distrust: The Chinese side. In: Lieberthal, Kenneth and Wang Jisi, *Addressing US–China Strategic Distrust.* John L. Thornton Center at Brookings, Washington, DC, pp. 7–19.

Wang Yong (2011) China in the G20: A balancer and a responsible contributor. *East Asia Forum,* 31 October.

Wang Yong (2013) The politics of the TPP are plain: Target China. *Global Asia,* 26 March.

Washington Post (2008) China casts dismaying veto on free trade, 1 August.

Welch, Dylan (2012) US blueprint for war with China flawed and could spark nuclear strikes, says expert. *Sydney Morning Herald,* 9 August.

White, Hugh (2012) *The China Choice: Why America Should Share Power.* Black Inc., Melbourne.

World Bank and Development Research Center of the State Council (2013) *China 2030: Building a Modern, Harmonious, and Creative Society.* World Bank, Washington, DC.

Wu Guoguang (2009) A shadow over Western democracies: China's political use of economic power. *China Perspectives* 2, 80–9.

Xia Liping (2004) The new security concept in China's new thinking of international strategy. *International Review* 34(Spring).

Xiang Lanxin (2004) China's Eurasian experiment. *Survival* 46(2), 109–21.

Xing Yuqing and Detert, Neal (2010) How the iPhone widens the United States deficit with the People's Republic of China. ADBI Working Paper 257. Asian Development Bank Institute, Tokyo, December.

Xinhua News Agency (2009) Wen: China disagrees to so-called G2, 18 November, available at: www.china.org.cn/world/obamas_asia_tour/2009-11/18/content_18913266.htm

Xinhua News Agency (2011) No nationalization of military in China: Senior PLA officer. *People's Daily Online (English)*, 21 June.

Xinhua News Agency (2012) China is victim of cyber attacks: Spokesman, 29 March.

Xinhua News Agency (2013a) China threatened by overseas cyber attacks, 10 March.

Xinhua News Agency (2013b) Senior official sacked as CPC vows further anti-corruption drive. *China Daily*, 10 September.

Yan Xuetong (2010) The instability of China–US relations. *Chinese Journal of International Politics* 3(3), 263–92.

Yan Xuetong (2011) *Ancient Chinese Thought, Modern Chinese Power*. Princeton University Press, Princeton, NJ.

Yan Xuetong and Qi Haixia (2012) Football game rather than boxing match: China–US intensifying rivalry does not amount to cold war. *Chinese Journal of International Politics* 5(2), 105–27.

Yang Jiechi (2013) Innovations in diplomatic theory, practice. *China Daily*, 17 August.

Ye Zicheng (2011) *Inside China's Grand Strategy: The Perspective from the People's Republic*. (ed. and trans. Levine, Steven I. and Liu Guoli). University Press of Kentucky, Lexington, KY.

Yoon, Suthichai (2012) Chinese minister: ASEAN can shape power play in E Asia. *The Nation*, 25 June.

You Ji (1995) A test case for China's defence and foreign policies. *Contemporary Southeast Asia* 16(4), 375–403.

You Ji (2008) China's 'new' diplomacy, foreign policy, and defense strategy. In: Kerr, Pauline, Harris, Stuart and Qin Yaqin (eds) *China's 'New' Diplomacy: Tactical or Fundamental Change?* Palgrave Macmillan, New York, pp. 77–106.

You Ji (2011) Dealing with the 'North Korean dilemma': China's strategic choices. RSIS Working Paper No 229, S. Rajaratnam School of International Studies, Singapore, June.

Yu Miaojie and Tian Wei (2012) China's processing trade: A firm-level analysis. In: McKay, Huw and Song, Ligang (eds) *Rebalancing and Sustaining Growth in China*. ANU E Press, Canberra, July, pp. 111–48.

Yu Yongding (2011) Floating the yuan to protect China's forex. *CaixinOnline*, 24 August, available at: english.caixin.com/2011-08-24/100294212.html

Yuan Jing-dong (2007) The dragon and the elephant: Chinese–Indian relations in the 21st century. *Washington Quarterly* 30(3), 131–44.

Yuan Jing-dong (2009) China and the nuclear-free world. In: Hansell, Christina and Potter, William (eds) *Engaging China and Russia on Nuclear Disarmament*. Occasional Paper 15, James Martin Center for Nonproliferation Studies, Monterey Institute of International Studies, Monterey, CA, pp. 25–36.

Zeng Ka (2013) High stakes: United States–China trade disputes under the World Trade Organization. *International Relations of the Asia-Pacific* 13(1), 33–63.

Zha Daojiong (2005) Comment: Can China rise? *Review of International Studies* 31(4), 775–85.

Zhang Feng (2012) China's new thinking on alliances. *Survival* 54(5), 129–48.

Zhang Hongzhou (2012) China's evolving fishing industry: Implications for regional and global maritime security. RSIS Working Paper 246, S. Rajaratnam School of International Studies, Singapore, August.

Zhang Hui (2008) Chinese perspectives on space weapons. In: Podvig, Pavel and Zhang Hui (eds) *Russian and Chinese Responses to US Military Plans in Space*. American Academy of Arts and Sciences, Cambridge, MA, pp. 31–77.

Zhang Qingmin (2008) Continuities and changes in China's negotiating behavior. In: Kerr, Pauline, Harris, Stuart and Qin Yaqin (eds) *China's 'New' Diplomacy: Tactical or Fundamental Change?* Palgrave Macmillan, New York, pp. 153–75.

Zhang Yongjin (1998) *China in International Society Since 1949: Alienation and Beyond*. Macmillan, Basingstoke.

Zhang Yongjin (2008) Anticipating China's future diplomacy: History, theory, and social practice. In: Kerr, Pauline, Harris, Stuart and Qin Yaqin (eds) *China's 'New' Diplomacy: Tactical or Fundamental Change?* Palgrave Macmillan, New York, pp. 131–49.

Zhang Yunling and Tang Shiping (2005) China's regional strategy. In: Shambaugh, David (ed.) *Power Shift: China and Asia's New Dynamics.* University of California Press, Berkeley, CA, pp. 48–68.

Zhao Suisheng (2010) Chinese foreign policy under Hu Jintao: The struggle between low-profile policy and diplomatic activism. *Hague Journal of Diplomacy* 5(4), 357–78.

Zheng Bijian (2005) China's 'peaceful rise' to great-power status. *Foreign Affairs* 84(5), 18–24.

Zheng Yongnian and Tok Sow Keat (2007) 'Harmonious society' and 'harmonious world': China's policy discourse under Hu Jintao. Briefing Series 26, China Policy Institute, University of Nottingham, October.

Zhou Feng (2011) Formation of strategic planning department caters to PLA's new military reform. *China Military Online,* 2 December.

Zhou Xiaochuan (2009) Reform the international monetary system. *BIS Review 41,* Bank for International Settlements, Geneva, 23 March.

Zhu Feng (2013) China and the United States might not be heading for a 'new Cold War'. *ASAN Forum* 1(1).

Zhu Liqun (2008) The domestic sources of China's foreign policy and diplomacy. In: Kerr, Pauline, Harris, Stuart and Qin Yaqin (eds) *China's 'New' Diplomacy: Tactical or Fundamental Change?* Palgrave Macmillan, New York, pp. 109–30.

Zoellick, Robert (2005) Whither China: From membership to responsibility? Remarks to National Committee on US–China Relations. New York, 21 September, available at: www.ncuscr.org/files/2005Gala_RobertZoellick_Whither_China1.pdf

Index ────────────────────────────────

soft power, 21, 50, 58, 72, 94
  economic, 139, 175
  military policy, 114, 118
sovereignty, and non-intervention
  principle, 9, 17, 54–5, 75,
  157, 178, 186
  differences with Western view
  of, 54–5
  Five Principles of Peaceful
  Coexistence, 16, 193n7
  international law, 56
  legal, 193n4
  order through, 66
  qualifications to, 55, 66
  Russia, 158
  Westphalian, 54, 193n4
space policy, 102–4, 105–6, 118, 159
state-owned enterprises (SOEs),
  38–9, 128, 130, 134, 136,
  138, 173–4
state trading corporations, 38–9
strategic partnerships, 11–12, 20,
  52–3, 91, 145
  see also China, bilateral
  agreements
strategic thinking, 11
  strategy, grand, 50, 53
submarines, 102
territorial integrity, 71, 75, 80, 157,
  193n7
terrorism, 86, 109, 156
Three Worlds theory, 15
Tiananmen Square, 4, 31, 48, 68,
  145
  Australian criticism, China's
  response, 141
  PLA's role, 34, 35
  Western sanctions after, 19, 165,
  167
unipolarity, 47–8, 52

US cooperation, continuing need
  for, 51, 169
  see also United States, and China
'victimhood', 9–10, 50–1, 92
water, resources, 160, 176–7
weiqi, 11
worldviews, 5, 8, 46, 47–9
China–ASEAN Free Trade
  Agreement (CAFTA), 146,
  148, 151
China's government
  Central Committee, 27, 29, 34, 72,
  131, 192n2
  Central Military Commission
  (CMC), 29, 34, 35, 36
  China Development Bank, 9, 134
  Finance Department, 28
  International Department, 27–8
  leading small groups (LSGs),
  29–30, 34, 40, 111–12
  Foreign Affairs Leading Small
  Group (FALSG), 28, 30,
  41
  Ministry of Commerce
  (MOFCOM), 28, 30, 38,
  74, 126, 134
  Ministry of Foreign Affairs (MFA),
  28, 30, 32–3, 38, 43–4, 74,
  150
  Ministry of Public Security, 37, 38
  Ministry of State Security, 28
  National Development and Reform
  Commission (NDRC), 28,
  32–3, 40, 134
  National People's Congress (NPC),
  27, 34, 192n4
  People's Liberation Army (PLA),
  27, 29, 33–7, 38, 79, 117
  anti-satellite missile, 103
  cyber warfare, 107, 110–11